# Nonprofits in Policy Advocacy

Sheldon Gen · Amy Conley Wright

# Nonprofits in Policy Advocacy

## Their Strategies and Stories

Sheldon Gen
Public Administration Program
San Francisco State University
San Francisco, CA, USA

Amy Conley Wright
Sydney School of Education
and Social Work
University of Sydney
Sydney, NSW, Australia

ISBN 978-3-030-43695-7      ISBN 978-3-030-43696-4   (eBook)
https://doi.org/10.1007/978-3-030-43696-4

This Palgrave Macmillan imprint is published by the registered company Springer Nature Switzerland AG
The registered company address is: Gewerbestrasse 11, 6330 Cham, Switzerland

*For the hundreds of nonprofit policy advocates who shared their experiences with us, and the thousands of others who work every day to improve our communities and society*

# Foreword

After twelve years as a practicing social worker, in 1978 I walked into a non-profit organization called Coleman[1] Children and Youth *Services* as its second Executive Director. I expected to use my social work skills to develop programs for abused and neglected children that would make the city's child welfare system less institutional, and more focused on home-like settings and family reunification—as was the goal of the Board of Directors. Within three years, I had changed the name of the organization to Coleman *Advocates* for Children and Youth after deciding that advocacy was the activity (not service delivery) that was going to create the changes we aspired to.

At first, I thought I had invented the idea of a nonprofit being a child advocacy organization. Gradually, I found a handful of peers around the country who escaped their professional isolation by attending the annual meeting of the National Association of Child Advocacy to share insights, but mostly get moral support as we felt we had so few colleagues doing the work we were doing. We were so thrilled to have found each other. I was also inspired in these early years by the work of the Children's Defense Fund (CDF). I learned by observing them closely, but always hoped they would explain the reasons they undertook the strategies they used as well as how to implement them. But like most advocacy organizations, CDF was so busy fighting the good fight that taking time to share their analytical framework was out of the question.

For the 26 years I remained at what became known as Coleman Advocates, I identified as an advocate, and Coleman was over time cited as an organization that was inventing a national model for local child advocacy. And amazingly, we were enormously successful in driving policy change for San Francisco's children and youth. During that period, the civic culture of the city changed—making children a priority that no one dare ignore. This was evidenced in the city's budget, priorities of elected officials, structures within government addressing the needs of children, and the passage of numerous child and youth-related ballot measures. Specifically, San Francisco:

- Became the first city in the country to create its own annual funding stream for children—which currently generates over $100 million for services for almost half of the city's children through over 200 community organizations.
- Implemented a locally funded universal preschool program and created thousands of high-quality childcare slots.
- Created one of the most influential Youth Commissions in the country—which advises on all legislation related to young people.
- Created a network of youth development services that included Beacon Centers in middle schools and more youth jobs per population than any city in the country.
- Developed its own universal healthcare system for children, along with creating health centers in all high schools.
- Cut by 2/3 the population of its juvenile hall and developed a national model of alternatives to incarceration.
- Created an afterschool-for-all policy and system that grew to serve 80% of children in need.
- Created a Department of Children, Youth and Their Families to oversee, plan for, and coordinate the large network of children's services.

Most people attributed the advocacy of our organization, along with our non-profit allies, as the major lever and catalyst behind these transformative changes. I was heralded as a leading child advocate in numerous venues and by numerous organizations.

But actually, I always felt I was making it up as I went along—putting one step in front of the other, rather than operating from any clearly planned path. We went from a single focus on abused and neglected children to the broad mission of improving the well-being of all children in San Francisco and addressing a wide variety of issues and needs including health, child welfare, childcare, juvenile justice, city planning, parks, housing, and schools. We evolved from a small group of policy experts to a vibrant, multi-racial community of parents, youth, and their advocates—adding layers of tactics and strategies one at a time as new challenges emerged, and one success only uncovered an additional problem. But we had no roadmap, no guidebook, no outside theoretical framework from which to analyze our evolution.

Occasionally, I would find time to catalogue the various activities we were engaged in, and even help others learn how to implement those activities. As years went by, I found colleagues in the organizing field, like the Midwest Academy, who had developed manuals about most of the tactics we engaged in. We characterized our work as highlighting: policy development, coalition building, training and empowering youth and parents, communication with the public, and negotiating with policymakers and elected officials. But again, we had no way of knowing how these tactics compared with those of other advocacy organizations, nor even a comprehensive map of when these tactics were used to best implement a given overall strategic approach.

Like most advocates, I believe, I worked on instinct and intuition—built on years of experience—but with never time or knowledge or academic background to develop a full-blown framework for how to think of this work. Or to think across issue areas—like environment and civil rights—to find important commonalities.

Then along come Gen and Wright with their new and groundbreaking book filling in the gaps in our ability to understand and evaluate this all-important work of policy advocacy. If I had been able to think in terms of the six strategies that my colleagues all over the country were using, and the tactics that they prioritized as the most beneficial parts of those strategies, I believe my work could have evolved more quickly and with a scope and depth that took years to development.

At this stage of my professional development, I find myself in the role of technical assistance provider, coach, and movement leader. I have founded Funding the Next Generation, an initiative to promote local dedicated funds for children and youth, to share what I have learned with others around the state and the country. I am trying to help folks develop strategies, understand the premise of their work, start at the beginning, and get to some of the ends I was able to achieve in San Francisco. And, more than ever it is important to have a framework and a guide to understanding and ultimately evaluating what works.

So, I say to my academic colleagues: Take the field of nonprofit policy advocacy seriously. Study this book, teach the content (there are lots of good teaching ideas in it), and help move the research forward. There is still so much to understand and know about policy advocacy in nonprofits. And to my fellow nonprofit advocates: Use the insights, frameworks, and stories in this book to help guide your thinking. You really don't have to reinvent it all on your own, and you can do better than learn by anecdote. You will work much more efficiently and effectively if you can learn from the work and thinking of those who have gone before and those who have studied what successful work is based on.

I believe of all the activities we social reformers engage in, policy advocacy is the most important. After my 26 years as the leader at Coleman Advocates, I was asked to direct San Francisco's Department of Children, Youth and Their Families. As much as I wanted to be a changemaker, I know that without the policy advocates from the nonprofit sector, our governmental institutions would be stymied in the status quo.

And make no mistake, our ability to understand, evaluate, and then conduct policy advocacy can be a matter of life and death, whether it is about transforming the lives of young people incarcerated in our ineffective prison systems, finding the political will to address environmental crises, or ensuring we live in a democracy.

San Francisco, USA                                                        Margaret Brodkin
                                                   Founder, Funding the Next Generation
                                        Former director, San Francisco Department
                                              of Children, Youth, and Their Families
                                              Former director, Coleman Advocates
                                                            for Children and Youth

## Note

1. Gertrude Coleman was the name of the original donor to the organization, founded in 1974. The original Board of Directors named the organization after her.

# Preface

## More to Policy Advocacy Than Simple Victory

In 2008, voters in California were in a heated debate about legalizing same-sex marriage. Prior to then, in 2004, San Francisco had briefly begun issuing marriage licenses to same-sex couples, echoing regional surges of support in Vermont and New Jersey (Los Angeles Times Staff 2013), before an injunction stopped them while San Francisco's actions were challenged in court. In May 2008, the California Supreme Court ultimately struck down an earlier state statute that defined marriage as only between a man and a woman, seemingly clearing the way for San Francisco to resume its initiative. But opponents of same-sex marriage anticipated that judicial ruling and drafted Proposition 8, which would establish in the state's *constitution* that marriage is only between heterosexual couples. The battle was the most expensive of any ballot issue in the country that year (Ballotpedia, n.d.), with over $70 million spent by both sides, and the issue attracted a whopping 79.4% of the state's registered voters. In November of that year, the voters passed the proposition, 52% to 48%. Similar ballot initiatives were passed around the same time in Arizona and Florida.

Thousands gathered to protest the outcome, in major cities around California and across the country. Celebrities, gay and straight, made emotional remonstrations about its passage and donated funding to the opposition campaign (People staff 2008). Donations were also made to the opposition campaign by notable corporations. Public anger was directed at supporters of the proposition, with social media campaigns advocating for the boycott of businesses whose owners made donations to the "Yes on 8" campaign. Post-election protests received heavy coverage in the media, while less attention focused on Proposition 8 supporters (CNN staff 2008; Garrison and Knoll 2008).

While many felt defeated, some advocates for same-sex marriage were noticeably upbeat, even positive. They cited the proportion of voters who supported same-sex marriage and noted that it had never been higher in the state's history. Projecting the support for the issue over years, the trajectory seemed clear.

Mark Leno, one of the first openly gay members of the California State Assembly, stated "We gained 18 points, they lost 18 points. Momentum is on our side" (Fagan and King 2008).

Neil Giuliano, President of the Gay and Lesbian Alliance Against Defamation (GLAAD), commented, "It's a setback and we have to work hard now to keep moving on our question for equality and the fundamental rights that our Community deserves...[but] there has been progress. There has been cultural change" (Robinson 2008).

Advocates also turned toward thinking about the strategies used by their opposition, and how to do better. Karin Wang with the Asian Pacific American Legal Center admitted that civil rights groups could have "done more" to engage with communities of color in the campaign against Prop 8 (James 2008). Neil Giuliano with GLAAD noted that proponents of the "Yes on 8" campaign had financial resources earlier than the opponents and were able to "inundate the media and control the message and essentially put the 'No on 8' campaign on the defensive in the beginning" (Robinson 2008).

From the court of public opinion, the venue for policy change shifted to the California Supreme Court. More accurately, the fight looped back to the court, which had first ruled in May 2008 that the state constitution guaranteed gay and lesbian couples the "basic civil right" to marry, which spurred opponents of gay marriage to propose Proposition 8 (CNN staff 2009). *Strauss v. Horton* brought together three legal cases on behalf of same-sex couples who were married or intended to marry, represented by a legal team from The National Center for Lesbian Rights, Lambda Legal and American Civil Liberties Union. The respondent in the lawsuit was the state of California, and the court allowed ProtectMarriage. com to join the litigation. Sixty-three *amicus curiae* friend-of-the-court letters were received by the court, 43 opposed to Proposition 8, including one signed by 44 members of the California Legislature, about 1/3 of its membership (Associated Press 2008). In May 2009, the California Supreme Court upheld the passage of Proposition 8 but also ruled that the 18,000 marriages conducted between May and November 2008 were valid (CNN staff 2009).

The judicial drama continued to play out through a series of US Federal Court cases under *Hollingsworth v. Perry*. The case eventually made its way to the US Supreme Court in June 2013, which held that supporters of a proposition did not have standing to appeal a federal court ruling if the state did not choose to do so. The effect of this decision was to uphold a 2010 federal court ruling in *Perry vs Schwarzenegger* that invalidated Proposition 8. The US Supreme Court also issued a ruling striking down the federal Defense of Marriage Act (DOMA) as unconstitutional (Peralta 2013). The federal appeals court issued an order allowing gay and lesbian couples to marry in California, with legal marriages carried out from June 28, 2013 (Go 2013).

## Why Policy Advocacy?

This book was first inspired by the drama of the Proposition 8 fight. Advocacy for social change can be daunting and mysterious, with potential setbacks along the way that can make change seem impossible. What, besides preferable policy change, do advocates expect to get from their advocacy efforts? How do advocates view the process of changing policy, and what strategies do advocates use to get those changes? These questions are important because their answers can help policy advocates learn from the broader community of advocates, rather than only their own individual networks. They can also help the academic community better understand the processes of policy change from the perspectives of policy advocates.

Nonprofit organizations that work toward achieving policy change through advocacy use a wide variety of tactics, as will be discussed in this book, including those in the campaign against Proposition 8, such as media work, protests, and litigation. Nonprofit organizations involved in policy advocacy are frequently playing a long game and they need to have a sense of an overarching plan to sustain motivation and course correct. This book is based on empirical evidence and theory drawn from policy studies, providing guidance on how nonprofit organizations can draw from a set of tactics to plan long-range strategies that account for potential short and long-term outcomes along the path to policy impact.

There are normative reasons for nonprofit organizations to conduct policy advocacy. In the United States, nonprofit organizations have developed in relation to the state, deriving the preponderance of their funding through contracts to deliver government-mandated services. While both service delivery and advocacy address human suffering, the latter is more radical because it seeks to address causes, not simply alleviate suffering (Valentinov et al. 2013). Nonprofit organizations are likely to engage in advocacy for the social benefit of the vulnerable populations they serve as well as to promote increased government spending on favored issues (Garrow and Hasenfeld 2014).

While service delivery responds to the problems as they are represented under the status quo, advocacy holds an imaginative space of how things could be. Nonprofit organizations do "moral" work, driven by missions that generally aim to promote a more just society and serve groups with relatively little political power. They play an essential societal role by acting as agents of social change, "[stimulating] ideational innovation and social reform" by bringing in new ideas and creating new social institutions (Valentinov et al. 2013, p. 6).

All nonprofit organizations can engage in advocacy for policy change (though there are limitations to lobbying as a registered American nonprofit, discussed in Chapter 1). The intention of this book is to help nonprofit organizations and their staff think through their strategy for policy advocacy. As a first step, it is helpful for organizations to think through the following questions (Mason 2018): the *what* of their advocacy (the cause for which they will advocate), the *why* (how this work fits within the organization's mission), the *who* (the staff or volunteers who will be involved), and the *how* (the tactics in which the organization will engage to meet its goal). It is the "how" that this book will address, describing strategies using a variety of tactics that have been derived from empirical research and are supported by policy studies theory and have been employed by a range of nonprofit organizations working toward social change.

## Preview of the Book

**Chapter 1, Nonprofit Advocacy in the United States** provides context for the chapters that follow by introducing major concepts and policy frameworks. The chapter opens by recounting the campaign by The National Centre for Lesbian Rights to ban sexual orientation "reparative therapy," followed by discussion of how this campaign raises questions about the strategic advocacy choices of nonprofit organizations. The chapter then describes how advocacy by nonprofit organizations functions within the American political system, and how separation of powers and federalism creates opportunities for influence at the local, state and national levels, particularly in light of devolution, which has shifted greater authority over social policy to the state and local levels. The policy process model highlights how nonprofit organizations can contribute at different stages of policymaking, including problem definition, formulating policy, and monitoring implementation. The chapter concludes by providing a broad overview of nonprofit organizations in the United States that are active in advocacy, in a variety of topic areas.

**Chapter** 2, **Tactics and Strategies** describes the empirical research underpinning the book, drawing upon a random survey of 811 American nonprofit organizations, and 31 case studies drawn from interviews employing Q-methodology, document analyses, and media audits. The authors have identified categories of tactics, which are defined as advocacy activities intended to achieve specific outcomes. These tactics can be combined together with their assumed short- and long-term outcomes into overarching strategies, depending on the viewpoint of the advocate about how to achieve desired policy change. The strategies fall along a spectrum in terms of whether they emphasize influencing formal policy actors or grassroots citizens; they are presented in order along this spectrum in the chapters that follow.

**Chapter** 3, **Public Lobbying** strategy seeks to affect broad improvements in physical and social conditions and to make the policy process more responsive to public interest by developing long-term relationships with policymakers. These are generally collegial relationships in which advocates seek to educate and sway policymakers toward policy that the organization has defined as in the public's interest. They accomplish these goals by lobbying policymakers—which may be legislators or government administrators—as they see these policymakers as the key to policy change. Their approach is less confrontational than others, preferring the development of long-term relationships with policymakers. Also, although they charge themselves to promote public interests, those interests are generally determined by themselves, not through direct community engagement. Indeed, influencing the public's views is not a part of the strategy.

**Chapter** 4, **Institutional Partnership** strategy seeks specific policy changes through partnerships with government institutions. To make a case for their desired policy alternatives, these organizations provide policymakers with organized public support, research, messaging, and sometimes pilot programs. The purpose is to educate and guide policymakers in constructive ways that lead to the policy outcome. Advocacy organizations employing this strategy view government institutions as central to policymaking, and they pursue policy changes by collaborating with them. These advocates see themselves as partners with the government institutions, not adversaries of them. Indeed, they generally avoid public debates, litigation, and other confrontational tactics that might deteriorate their relationships with the policymakers. They also avoid indirect tactics such as media work that they don't completely control. Because these advocates work primarily with decision makers directly, they view their purpose more narrowly focused on specific policy changes, and not more broadly on social changes or democratic enhancement.

**Chapter 5, Inside-Outside** strategy is distinguished by its two-prong approach to achieving favorable policy change. Organizations indirectly influence decision makers by applying public pressure through information campaigns and media work, constituting the "outside" component of the strategy. At the same time, organizations nurture relationships with one or a few "inside" influential issue champions from within the decision-making body, such as a legislator or an executive, helping them to sway their peers with information and shows of public support. Together, these two tactics lead to their ultimate objective, which is favorable policy change.

**Chapter 6, Direct Reform** strategy is a way to seek a specific policy change that bypasses legislative processes in favor of judicial or administrative processes. Advocates using this strategy may be litigants using the judicial system to seek policy relief for those they represent, or may engage administrative processes to get changes in the implementation of policies. Advocates supplement this work with information campaigns aimed at building general awareness and support for their causes. Even so, their aim is not a more democratic or responsive system, nor is it to mobilize the public or create coalitions around their causes. Instead, this strategy focuses on specific policy changes to improve social or physical conditions of their represented interests.

**Chapter 7, Indirect Pressure** strategy aims to achieve desired policy changes by indirectly pressuring policymakers. These advocates convey public opinion of the groups already mobilized around the issue, use the media, and implement policy programs to create pressure on policymakers. Advocates using this strategy affect policy change by influencing policymakers, but they do so indirectly rather than through lobbying or other direct tactics. These advocates believe that with these pressures, policymakers will affect their desired policy changes to improve social and physical conditions.

**Chapter 8, Popular Power** strategy seeks to advance the public's interest and democratic policymaking by influencing public opinion. Commonly used tactics include coalition building, public mobilizations, media and information campaigns, framing and messaging, and rebutting opposing views to stimulate broad public demand for policy change and more responsive policymaking systems. Like the public lobbying strategy, the popular power strategy is also aimed at advancing the public's interests and democratic policymaking. However, its approach is completely different. While the public lobbying strategy focuses its activities on formal policymakers, the popular power strategy eschews them. Instead, organizations adopting the popular power strategy aim to engage and mobilize the public to create public demand for change.

**Chapter** 9, **Considerations for Strategic Policy Advocacy** concludes by summarizing the viewpoints of advocates associated with each of the six strategies and then considering some of the unique challenges of advocacy before turning to methods for evaluating advocacy. The nature of advocacy work means that the best conceived strategy may not result in success, with many influential factors outside of the advocates' control. A logic model can be useful for planning and monitoring advocacy, though there is value in maintaining flexibility for adaptations that may emerge. Flexibility is also required for evaluation. Rather than rigidly following an evaluation plan, developmental evaluation is an approach relevant to initiatives that are emergent and complex. A range of methods can be used to evaluate the efficacy of an advocacy effort, using approaches that capture the views of relevant stakeholders about how advocacy activities may have contributed toward observed outcomes.

San Francisco, USA                                                                    Sheldon Gen
Sydney, Australia                                                         Amy Conley Wright

# References

Associated Press. (2008, November 10). Political protest: Lawmakers join Prop 8 fight. *NBC Bay Area Online.*

Ballotpedia (n.d.). California Proposition 8, the "Eliminates Right of Same-Sex Couples to Marry" Initiative (2008). Retrieved from https://ballotpedia.org/.

CNN Staff. (2008, November 8). Gay marriage supporters take to California streets. *CNN.com.*

CNN Staff. (2009, May 27). California high court upholds same-sex marriage ban. *CNN.com.*

Fagan, K., & King, J. (2008, November 16). Bay Area demonstrations condemn Prop 8. *SF Gate.*

Garrison, J., & Knoll, C. (2008, November 11). Prop. 8 opponents rally across California to protest gay-marriage ban. *Los Angeles Times.*

Garrow, E. E., & Hasenfeld, Y. (2014). Institutional logics, moral frames, and advocacy: explaining the purpose of advocacy among nonprofit human-service organizations. *Nonprofit and Voluntary Sector Quarterly, 43*(1), 80–98.

Go, K. (2013, June 28). Prop. 8 officially out—SF weddings begin. *SF Gate.*

James, S. D. (2008, November 19). Prop. 8 sparks gay-black divide. *ABC News.*

Los Angeles Times Staff. (2013, November 20). Gay marriage. *Los Angeles Times.*

Mason, D. P. (2018). Yes, you can—And should! Nonprofit advocacy as a core competency. *Nonprofit Quarterly.*

People Staff. (2008, September 23). Steven Spielberg gives $100,000 to fight gay marriage ban. *People Magazine.*

Peralta, E. (2013, June 26). Court overturns DOMA, sidesteps broad gay marriage ruling. *NPR.com.*

Robinson, C. (2008, December 14). GLAAD president speaks out on Prop 8. *Huffington Post.*

Valentinov, V., Hielscher, S., & Pies, I. (2013). The meaning of nonprofit advocacy: An ordonomic perspective. *The Social Science Journal, 50*(3), 367–373.

The original version of the book was revised: All the abstracts have been corrected. The correction to the book is available at https://doi.org/10.1007/978-3-030-43696-4_10

# Acknowledgments

We are deeply grateful to the several outstanding MPA students at San Francisco State University who provided critical assistance in the development of the research reported in this book.

Amelise Lane provided extensive assistance with general research, including the market research for the book. Amanda Akers and Tory Taylor helped implement the national survey of nonprofit organizations, which included the arduous task of developing the sample and extracting contact information from Guide-Star. About half of the interviews with nonprofit leaders were conducted by Yasya Berezovskiy, Suzanne El Gamal, Richard Gregory, Ana Guzina, Jaime Kemmer, Joseph Lapka, Ching Fang Lin, Mary McGinty, Chris Rosenlund, Maria Sakata, Carrie Slaughter, Kenneth Songco, Jill Talmage, Linda Tran, Maggie Weadick, and Brian K. Wilson. Background research on individual cases was assisted by Lyndsey Ballinger, Jessica Bank, Nicole Barcan, Anissa Basoco-Villarreal, Michelle Capobres, Danielle Carey, Noel Chow, Chris Corgas, Xu Han, Samantha Kelman, Katie Kirk, Saidah Leatutufu, Jasmine Moore, Norah Mutuma, Hilary Near, Tijen Sahin, Andrea Schiavoni, and Amanda Trescott.

We also thank Dr. Joel Kassiola and Dr. Jennifer Shea for their guidance and feedback on the book proposal and key parts of this research. Dr. Ayse Pamuk also provided us expert assistance with data mapping.

Finally, it has been a pleasure to work with Palgrave Macmillan to produce this book. We are grateful for the anonymous reviewers and we benefited greatly from their questions and helpful suggestions. Our editor Michelle Chen expressed enthusiastic interest in the proposal and provided invaluable support and advice. We are also grateful to Rebecca Roberts who managed the production.

# Contents

**1 Nonprofit Policy Advocacy in the United States**................ 1
"It Does Not Repair, and It Is Not Therapy".................... 3
Strategic Advocacy ......................................... 5
Nonprofit Advocacy in the Context of American Public Policy ........ 6
Political Context of Policy Advocacy ........................... 9
Policy Advocacy by Nonprofit Organizations in the United States:
Scope and Scale ........................................... 15
Discussions ............................................... 18
References................................................ 18

**2 Tactics and Strategies** ...................................... 23
A Menu of Tactics for Policy Advocacy........................ 23
Strategies of Policy Advocacy Organizations.................... 37
Discussions ............................................... 40
References................................................ 41

**3 Public Lobbying** ........................................... 45
The Public Lobbying Strategy ................................ 46
Books Not Bars............................................ 57
"Power Grab" ............................................. 64
Discussions ............................................... 69
References................................................ 69

**4  Institutional Partnership** . . . . . . . . . . . . . . . . . . . . . . . . . . . . . . . . .   73
   The Institutional Partnership Strategy. . . . . . . . . . . . . . . . . . . . . . . . . .   75
   Over-Incarceration . . . . . . . . . . . . . . . . . . . . . . . . . . . . . . . . . . . . . . .   84
   Foster Youth Emancipation. . . . . . . . . . . . . . . . . . . . . . . . . . . . . . . . . .   89
   Discussions . . . . . . . . . . . . . . . . . . . . . . . . . . . . . . . . . . . . . . . . . . . . .   94
   References. . . . . . . . . . . . . . . . . . . . . . . . . . . . . . . . . . . . . . . . . . . . . .   94

**5  Inside-Outside** . . . . . . . . . . . . . . . . . . . . . . . . . . . . . . . . . . . . . . . . .   97
   The Inside-Outside Strategy . . . . . . . . . . . . . . . . . . . . . . . . . . . . . . . . .   99
   Banning Plastic Bags . . . . . . . . . . . . . . . . . . . . . . . . . . . . . . . . . . . . .  108
   Evaluating Teacher Performance . . . . . . . . . . . . . . . . . . . . . . . . . . . . .  111
   Raising the Tobacco Tax . . . . . . . . . . . . . . . . . . . . . . . . . . . . . . . . . . .  114
   Discussions . . . . . . . . . . . . . . . . . . . . . . . . . . . . . . . . . . . . . . . . . . . . .  117
   References. . . . . . . . . . . . . . . . . . . . . . . . . . . . . . . . . . . . . . . . . . . . . .  118

**6  Direct Reform** . . . . . . . . . . . . . . . . . . . . . . . . . . . . . . . . . . . . . . . . . .  121
   The Direct Reform Strategy . . . . . . . . . . . . . . . . . . . . . . . . . . . . . . . . .  123
   Banning Trans Fats . . . . . . . . . . . . . . . . . . . . . . . . . . . . . . . . . . . . . . .  133
   Closing Coal-Fired Power Plants . . . . . . . . . . . . . . . . . . . . . . . . . . . . .  140
   Discussions . . . . . . . . . . . . . . . . . . . . . . . . . . . . . . . . . . . . . . . . . . . . .  147
   References. . . . . . . . . . . . . . . . . . . . . . . . . . . . . . . . . . . . . . . . . . . . . .  148

**7  Indirect Pressure** . . . . . . . . . . . . . . . . . . . . . . . . . . . . . . . . . . . . . . .  151
   The Indirect Pressure Strategy . . . . . . . . . . . . . . . . . . . . . . . . . . . . . . .  155
   Enhancing Local Parks . . . . . . . . . . . . . . . . . . . . . . . . . . . . . . . . . . . . .  164
   Discussions . . . . . . . . . . . . . . . . . . . . . . . . . . . . . . . . . . . . . . . . . . . . .  168
   References. . . . . . . . . . . . . . . . . . . . . . . . . . . . . . . . . . . . . . . . . . . . . .  168

**8  Popular Power** . . . . . . . . . . . . . . . . . . . . . . . . . . . . . . . . . . . . . . . . . .  171
   The Popular Power Strategy . . . . . . . . . . . . . . . . . . . . . . . . . . . . . . . . .  171
   Bring Our War $$ Home. . . . . . . . . . . . . . . . . . . . . . . . . . . . . . . . . . . .  181
   Parent Engagement in Public Schools. . . . . . . . . . . . . . . . . . . . . . . . . . .  185
   Discussions . . . . . . . . . . . . . . . . . . . . . . . . . . . . . . . . . . . . . . . . . . . . .  189
   References. . . . . . . . . . . . . . . . . . . . . . . . . . . . . . . . . . . . . . . . . . . . . .  190

**9  Considerations for Strategic Policy Advocacy** . . . . . . . . . . . . . . . . .  191
   Creative and Strategic Policy Advocacy . . . . . . . . . . . . . . . . . . . . . . . . .  191
   The Challenges of Policy Advocacy . . . . . . . . . . . . . . . . . . . . . . . . . . . .  194
   Measuring and Evaluating Advocacy Performance . . . . . . . . . . . . . . . . .  195
   Conclusion . . . . . . . . . . . . . . . . . . . . . . . . . . . . . . . . . . . . . . . . . . . . .  207

Discussions . . . . . . . . . . . . . . . . . . . . . . . . . . . . . . . . . . . . . . . . . . . . . . .   208
References. . . . . . . . . . . . . . . . . . . . . . . . . . . . . . . . . . . . . . . . . . . . . . . .   208

**Correction to: Nonprofits in Policy Advocacy** . . . . . . . . . . . . . . . . . . . . . .   C1

**Appendix A: Derivation of the Composite Logic Model**
            **of Policy Advocacy** . . . . . . . . . . . . . . . . . . . . . . . . . . . . . . . .   213

**Appendix B: Methods** . . . . . . . . . . . . . . . . . . . . . . . . . . . . . . . . . . . . . . .   217

**Index** . . . . . . . . . . . . . . . . . . . . . . . . . . . . . . . . . . . . . . . . . . . . . . . . . . .   235

# List of Figures

Fig. 1.1    Agents and avenues of policymaking .....................    11
Fig. 3.1    Public lobbying strategy ...............................    49
Fig. 3.2    Importance of key outcomes in the public lobbying strategy ....    51
Fig. 3.3    Advocates' usage of key tactics in the public lobbying strategy ....    52
Fig. 3.4    Importance of policy advocacy to mission of public lobbying
            strategists.........................................    52
Fig. 3.5    Public issues engaged by public lobbying strategists ..........    54
Fig. 3.6    Levels of government targeted by public lobbying strategists ...    55
Fig. 3.7    Branches of government targeted by public lobbying strategists....    55
Fig. 3.8    Memberships of public lobbying strategists ................    56
Fig. 3.9    2013 Income distribution of public lobbying strategists........    57
Fig. 4.1    Institutional partnership strategy........................    75
Fig. 4.2    Advocates' usage of key tactics in the institutional
            partnership strategy ..................................    79
Fig. 4.3    Importance of policy advocacy to mission of institutional
            partnership strategists ...............................    80
Fig. 4.4    Public issues engaged by institutional partnership strategists....    81
Fig. 4.5    Levels of government targeted by institutional partnership
            strategists.........................................    82
Fig. 4.6    Branches of government targeted by institutional partnership
            strategists.........................................    82
Fig. 4.7    Memberships of institutional partnership strategists...........    83
Fig. 4.8    2013 Income distribution of institutional partnership
            strategists.........................................    84
Fig. 5.1    Inside-outside strategy................................    102
Fig. 5.2    Advocates' usage of key tactics in the inside-outside strategy ...    104

Fig. 5.3    Importance of policy advocacy to mission of inside-outside
            strategists......................................................... 105
Fig. 5.4    Public issues engaged by inside-outside strategists............ 106
Fig. 5.5    Levels of government targeted by inside-outside strategists..... 107
Fig. 5.6    Branches of government targeted by inside-outside strategists... 108
Fig. 5.7    Memberships of inside-outside strategists................... 109
Fig. 5.8    2013 Income distribution of inside-outside strategists ........ 109
Fig. 6.1    Direct reform strategy ................................... 124
Fig. 6.2    Advocates' usage of key tactics in the direct reform strategy .... 128
Fig. 6.3    Importance of policy advocacy to mission of direct reform
            strategists......................................................... 128
Fig. 6.4    Public issues engaged by direct reform strategists ............ 130
Fig. 6.5    Levels of government targeted by direct reform strategists...... 131
Fig. 6.6    Branches of government targeted by direct reform strategists ... 131
Fig. 6.7    Memberships of direct reform strategists ................... 132
Fig. 6.8    2013 Income distribution of direct reform strategists .......... 132
Fig. 7.1    Indirect pressure strategy............................... 158
Fig. 7.2    Importance of key advocacy outcomes in the indirect pressure
            strategy............................................................ 159
Fig. 7.3    Importance of policy advocacy to mission of indirect pressure
            strategists......................................................... 160
Fig. 7.4    Public issues engaged by indirect pressure strategists......... 161
Fig. 7.5    Levels of government targeted by indirect pressure strategists... 162
Fig. 7.6    Branches of government targeted by indirect pressure
            strategists......................................................... 162
Fig. 7.7    Memberships of indirect pressure strategists................. 163
Fig. 7.8    2013 Income distribution of indirect pressure strategists ....... 164
Fig. 8.1    Popular power strategy ................................. 174
Fig. 8.2    Advocates' usage of key tactics related to the popular
            power strategy..................................................... 175
Fig. 8.3    Importance of policy advocacy to mission of popular
            power strategists .................................................. 176
Fig. 8.4    Public issues engaged by popular power strategists ........... 178
Fig. 8.5    Levels of government targeted by popular power strategists .... 179
Fig. 8.6    Branches of government targeted by popular power strategists ... 179
Fig. 8.7    Memberships of popular power strategists ................. 180
Fig. 8.8    2013 Income distribution of popular power strategists ........ 180
Fig. B.1    Locations of organizations surveyed....................... 227
Fig. B.2    Founding years of organizations surveyed ................. 228
Fig. B.3    2013 Incomes of organizations surveyed .................. 228

# List of Tables

Table 2.1   Composite logic model for policy advocacy . . . . . . . . . . . . . . .   25

Table 2.2   Theoretical links among inputs, activities, outcomes
and impacts . . . . . . . . . . . . . . . . . . . . . . . . . . . . . . . . . . . . . . . .   27

Table 2.3   Q-method statistics on the resulting six policy advocacy
strategies . . . . . . . . . . . . . . . . . . . . . . . . . . . . . . . . . . . . . . . . . .   40

Table 3.1   Factor array for public lobbying strategy . . . . . . . . . . . . . . . . .   47

Table 3.2   Resources devoted to policy advocacy by public lobbying
strategists. . . . . . . . . . . . . . . . . . . . . . . . . . . . . . . . . . . . . . . . . . .   53

Table 4.1   Factor array for institutional partnership strategy . . . . . . . . . . .   76

Table 4.2   Resources devoted to policy advocacy by institutional
partnership strategists . . . . . . . . . . . . . . . . . . . . . . . . . . . . . . . . .   80

Table 5.1   Factor array for inside-outside strategy. . . . . . . . . . . . . . . . . . .   101

Table 5.2   Resources devoted to policy advocacy by inside-outside
strategists. . . . . . . . . . . . . . . . . . . . . . . . . . . . . . . . . . . . . . . . . . .   105

Table 6.1   Factor array for direct reform strategy . . . . . . . . . . . . . . . . . . .   125

Table 6.2   Resources devoted to policy advocacy by direct reform
strategists. . . . . . . . . . . . . . . . . . . . . . . . . . . . . . . . . . . . . . . . . . .   129

Table 7.1   Factor array for indirect pressure strategy. . . . . . . . . . . . . . . . .   157

Table 7.2   Resources devoted to policy advocacy by indirect
pressure strategists . . . . . . . . . . . . . . . . . . . . . . . . . . . . . . . . . . .   160

Table 8.1   Factor array for popular power strategy . . . . . . . . . . . . . . . . . .   172

Table 8.2   Resources devoted to policy advocacy by popular power
strategists. . . . . . . . . . . . . . . . . . . . . . . . . . . . . . . . . . . . . . . . . . .   177

Table 9.1   Viewpoints associated with policy advocacy strategies . . . . . . .   192

Table 9.2   Example indicators for interim outcomes of policy
advocacy . . . . . . . . . . . . . . . . . . . . . . . . . . . . . . . . . . . . . . . . . . .   201

Table B.1    Sample of nonprofits in the Q-methodology portion
             of the study . . . . . . . . . . . . . . . . . . . . . . . . . . . . . . . . . . . . . . . . . .    219
Table B.2    Factor loadings matrix from 6-factor extraction . . . . . . . . . . . .    220
Table B.3    Extracted factor arrays for 24 policy advocacy statements. . . . .    222

# Nonprofit Policy Advocacy in the United States

Kate Kendell had spent most of her career advocating for civil rights for lesbian, gay, bisexual, and transgender (LGBT) people. She started with the American Civil Liberties Union (ACLU) in Utah as a staff attorney working on LGBT issues. She later became legal director for the National Center for Lesbian Rights (NCLR) in 1994, and ultimately Executive Director in 1996 and stayed in that position until 2018 (Gray 2018). NCLR is a national nonprofit organization whose mission is to advance "the civil and human rights of lesbian, gay, bisexual, and transgender people and their families through litigation, public policy advocacy, and public education" (NLCR 2020, Mission & History).

We were in the throes of collecting data for this research on nonprofit policy advocacy, and we had set an appointment to interview Kendell about her work. The appointment was for the afternoon of June 25, 2013. That morning, the US Supreme Court announced that on the next day they would issue their rulings on two cases affecting same-sex marriage: a challenge against the Defense of Marriage Act (DOMA), and another against California's Proposition 8.

The former was a 1996 federal law signed by President Bill Clinton that only recognized marriage between a man and a woman. It was challenged in a case that highlighted the numerous legal benefits conferred by over a thousand federal laws to married couples—benefits such as tax savings, Social Security benefits, health insurance coverage, pension protections, and many more. DOMA effectively constrained those benefits to only heterosexual married couples. At the time, nine states had already recognized same-sex marriage, creating the legal conflict (Totenberg 2013).

The latter was a 2008 ballot proposition in California, adopted with 52% of the votes, that changed the state's Constitution to define marriage as only between a man and woman. It followed an earlier state law that attempted to do the same

© The Author(s) 2020
S. Gen and A. C. Wright, *Nonprofits in Policy Advocacy*,
https://doi.org/10.1007/978-3-030-43696-4_1

thing, but was struck down by the state's Supreme Court. That law, in turn, was an attempt to stop cities such as San Francisco from issuing marriage licenses to same-sex couples. That city had initially started doing so in 2004, when then-Mayor Gavin Newsom returned from President George W. Bush's State of the Union address in Washington, DC, in which the president promised to defend DOMA (Rose 2004). Newsom reflected that the event "sparked a real sense of responsibility to do something" for his progressive city.

We arrived at Kendell's office just before our appointed time, when she met us at the front door. She kindly asked us to postpone our interview, because she was "busy" with media requests from across the country, who wanted her opinions on the Supreme Court's pending rulings. There were already local reporters at the front door with us, wanting Kendell's views. We quickly rescheduled our appointment and let her return to her work.

On June 26, 2013, the Supreme Court announced their rulings. In a 5-4 vote, DOMA was essentially struck down, thus requiring the federal government to recognize—and confer federal benefits to—same-sex couples who were legally married. On Proposition 8, the ruling was less decisive. The court upheld a federal appellate court's ruling that had struck down the constitutional amendment, but based their ruling on the plaintiff not having legal standing. Their decision effectively legalized same-sex marriage in California, but the court avoided the broader question of whether same-sex marriage must be recognized by all states. Neither decision legalized same-sex marriage nationally.[1] Instead, they required the federal government to recognize same-sex marriages, while allowing individual states to continue to discriminate between heterosexual and homosexual couples.

When we finally met with Kendell a month and a half later, we asked what her life had been like since those court rulings. She replied that the organization has struggled with what to do next, following the "tipping point" of winning in California. She had no doubt that there was much more hard work ahead on same-sex marriage, as the ruling only affected California, and most states at the time did not license or recognize same-sex marriage. But the issue had just passed the metaphorical crest of the hill, and the issue's speed would now accelerate, she correctly predicted. "We're still a long way from the finish line. We're not done by any means. But we definitely have the wind at our back now, and that is a different dynamic, and feels differently in our bones, than the grueling climb up the

---

[1]That decision would come in 2015, with the US Supreme Court case *Obergefell v. Hodges.*

hill." The Supreme Court's rulings on these two cases weren't a complete victory to Kendell or NCLR. But "striking down Prop 8 on standing, and striking down Section 2 of DOMA have transformed the landscape."

Their policy advocacy strategies had to change as a result of the transformation, she said. NCLR is a legal organization, and as such their main approach to policy change is through the courts, both state and federal. It was the approach that inspired her to become a lawyer. "State legislatures did bad things. They passed discriminatory laws. And it was the courts that vindicated the rights of minorities." That setting is changing, she said. "It's now the case that courts have in many ways retreated from this role largely because of conservative appointments to the judiciary. So our strategies have to broaden. It's not just about courts anymore. It's state legislatures, it's Congress, and it's federal agencies, which we're now able to advocate with in ways we were never able to."

At the time, there were 37 states with no recognition of same-sex marriage, and about 32 with no protections for them. "You can be fired from your job," Kendell explained, "in the vast majority of states in this country simply for putting a picture of your partner on your desk. Most people have no idea this is the case. They think it's illegal. Well, it's perfectly legal in most states. So our work now is really going to shift to the states where LGBT people are feeling left behind."

## "It Does Not Repair, and It Is Not Therapy"

While the weight of the court's historic rulings was still palpable, Kendell wanted to tell us about another issue that she and NCLR had been working on for years. *Sexual orientation change efforts* first came to Kendell's attention when she worked with the ACLU. The legal director at NCLR contacted her to ask if the ACLU would work with NCLR on a case involving a lesbian girl in Utah. The girl's parents had put her in a psychiatric institution when she came out to them at age 15. Kendell agreed to the work, and they met with the girl and the institution's staff, who admitted that the parents wanted the girl's sexual orientation changed. Kendell was surprised to learn that there were several institutions like that one, throughout the state. There methods were "barbaric," she said. For a boy, they would place a plethysmograph on his penis to measure blood flow while the boy was shown pornography. If the boy responded to pictures of two men, he would get shocked. It was aversion therapy, said Kendell, but misapplied. "Can you imagine the scarring this would do to you as a 12 or 13 year old?" she asked. This was in 1992, decades after the American Psychiatric Association removed homosexuality from its *Diagnostic and Statistical Manual of Mental Disorders* (DSM) in 1973. NCLR filed a lawsuit on behalf of the girl, and she was eventually released from the institution.

Kendell carried that experience with her throughout her career, and when she joined the NCLR staff, the organization began work with multiple psychiatric organizations to condemn these practices, which proponents called "reparative therapy." The problem is, Kendell told us, "it does not repair, and it is not therapy." Some psychiatric associations at that time confirmed that it was ineffective and harmful, but few would condemn the practice, said Kendell.

For years, NCLR monitored the practice "privately," meaning they advocated behind the scenes to debunk the practice, but they did not bring new lawsuits against it. Kendell explained that it was difficult to bring cases for those who had undergone sexual orientation change efforts, because many were ashamed and did not want to revisit the experiences. Plus, it was legal. At the time, no state had barred the practice.

In 2011, a window of opportunity opened for a legislative remedy to the issue. Representative Michele Bachmann of Minnesota was one of several Republicans vying for that party's nomination for the 2012 presidential election, and her popularity among Republicans was rising quickly in national polls (Horowitz 2011). This brought heightened attention to her husband's counseling center, which included sexual orientation change efforts. The public's level of consciousness on the issue was raised, said Kendell. So NCLR took advantage of the situation to sponsor a California bill with State Senator Ted Lieu. Senate Bill 1177 was introduced in February, 2012, and originally sought an outright ban on sexual orientation change efforts in the state (California Legislative Information 2011–2012).

Kendell said this was NCLR's first time being centrally involved with legislation. Usually, the organization had only gone so far as to provide "expert advice, memos, research, and testimony." This was the first time they helped draft the bill and advocate for its passage. NCLR devoted significant time and resources to the public education component of the campaign. Initially, psychiatric associations did not want to co-sponsor the bill, because they did not want to constrain their members' practices. But when the bill's sponsors agreed to change it from an outright ban to one that only banned the practice on minors, they earned more support. So NCLR mobilized LGBT youth to tell their stories. "Kids who have gone through this have suicidal tendencies and problems with substance abuse," said Kendell, "and this is generally a bad predictor for mental health."

The modified bill passed and was signed by then-Governor Jerry Brown on September 20, 2012. It was a remarkably fast and successful campaign, as policy advocacy goes. But the war was not over. Shortly after its passage, it was challenged in court, and the processes of policy change continued. The ban was eventually upheld in court, and today, several other states have implemented similar bans.

## Strategic Advocacy

For NCLR, this case caused them to stretch their practices in policy advocacy. "This not only has been a huge multi-decade effort," said Kendell, "but every aspect of our work has been engaged in it. Public education, community education, litigation, and legislative advocacy." The same-sex marriage case also caused them to advocate at different levels of government, and different branches. In short, NCLR was *strategic* in their policy advocacy, thoughtfully considering varied tactics and venues that could help them achieve their policy goals.

Their experience raises several relevant questions about policy advocacy that are common among nonprofit organizations:

- *What are the tactics and strategies used by policy advocacy nonprofits, and how do they deploy them in campaigns?*
- *Whom do they target? Which levels of government, and which branches?*
- *What do they expect from their efforts? Certainly favorable policy change, but are there other objectives of policy advocacy?*
- *And what kinds of policy issues are nonprofits engaged in?*

These are the questions that have guided the research reported in this book. Their answers, we hope, can help two distinct groups of readers. First, this book can help policy advocates in nonprofit organizations more effectively engage policymaking processes, by introducing six distinct strategies that are based upon viewpoints and tactics of nonprofits working in a wide variety of issues and at different levels of government. These strategies can guide advocates' campaigns and help them track the outcomes of their efforts. Second, this book can help students and academicians of policy studies understand the viewpoints of advocacy practitioners, and how their views and actions fit into major theories of policy change. While those theories are often based on empirical study of policy advocacy efforts, the practitioners' perspectives are largely missing. In this book, the voices of nonprofit advocates take center stage, and their viewpoints enrich our understanding of their associated theories.

But first we need to describe the American context in which this research was conducted, because it shapes the answers we found.

## Nonprofit Advocacy in the Context of American Public Policy

Policy advocacy by nonprofit and voluntary organizations has an important history in the United States. As illustrated in the NCLR case, policy advocacy by nonprofits is characterized by an organization representing a group, and engaging the policy process to protect or promote their interests. While there is no universally agreed-upon definition of advocacy in the nonprofit sector (Pekkanen et al. 2014), the following defining characteristics of policy advocacy emerge from the academic and professional literature. First, policy advocacy is *initiated by citizens*, acting individually or as a collective (Reid 2001) often represented by nonprofit organizations (Reid 2006). The citizens represented may have less relative power in society or may be unable to represent their own interests, such as the poor or children (Jansson 2010). Second, the method of policy advocacy involves a *deliberate process* (Sprechmann and Pelton 2001) *of influencing decision makers* (Jenkins 1987) *or influencing a social or civic agenda* (Schmid et al. 2008) in order to build political will around action (Grantmakers in Health 2005). Finally, the aim of advocacy ultimately is a *change to policy* (Reisman et al. 2007) *or the policy-making process*, generally to make it more accessible and transparent to the public. This latter goal has been called "participatory advocacy" rather than policy advocacy (Chapman and Wameyo 2001). In terms of policy change, the goal may be to adopt, modify, or reject certain policy options (Moore 2011). Thus, to summarize the main characterizations across the academic and professional literature, for our purposes in this book, *policy advocacy is defined as intentional activities initiated by the public to affect the policymaking process*. And when members of the public come together in a group to influence public policy, they are known as an *interest group*, also called public interest group or pressure group.

Policy advocacy is a means toward social change, one in which government authority is central to the change. There are two sides to public engagement in policymaking processes, from the perspectives of government and the public. Policy advocacy is "bottom-up" public engagement (McLaverty 2011). The public initiates interactions, selecting from a wide variety of structures and mediums for input to policy decisions. The public's right to influence policy is established in the Bill of Rights in the American Constitution. The First Amendment protects the rights of citizens to join together through freedoms of speech, assembly, and petition. In some states, ballot initiatives allow for members of the public to initiate legislation through collecting signatures on a petition. By contrast, "top-down" public engagement is initiated by the government (McLaverty

2011). Government routinely collects public input to inform decisions, dictating the structure and mediums of input. This is particularly common in bureaucratic policy processes, such as the process of public comment and revision codified in Code of Federal Regulations, but is also seen in all the branches of government in varied forms.

Voluntary organizations have been part of the American system of governance since its formalization through the establishment of the Constitution. Debates among the American founders about the tensions between the majoritarian style of government and individual liberty recognized that voluntary associations could give voice to the concerns of citizens, outside their opportunity to exercise voice through voting for elected members. The granting of a charter provided a form of legal personhood, allowing an organization to function by making contracts, holding funds, and owning real estate, transforming voluntary actions into a durable voluntary association (Clemens and Guthrie 2010). Notable social movements such as anti-slavery relied upon voluntary associations organizing to mobilize public opinion and influence political leaders (see Box 1.1). Gradually from the mid-nineteenth century, social and economic changes influenced the scope of family and community responsibility and led to growing reliance on associations and organizations for education and care. The Progressive Era of the early 1900s saw a rise in reformist activism for women with education, but few career opportunities (Hall 2006), with voluntary associations providing significant opportunities for managerial and financial leadership (Clemens and Guthrie 2010).

Formalization of voluntary associations as not-for-profit entities proliferated in the twentieth century, with dual roles of provider of government-funded service and advocate for policy change. When a voluntary group formally registers with the government, they can accept charitable donations in support of their work. The term nonprofit refers to a tax status as classified in section 501(c) of the Internal Revenue Code of 1954 and subsequent revisions, including 501(c)(3) and 501(c)(4) entities established for charitable, educational, religious, and civic purposes that are tax-exempt and to which individuals can make tax-deductible contributions. Nonprofits are characterized by: (1) voluntary nature without the coercive powers of the state; (2) reinvestment of profits (if any) into the organization's mission, rather than distribution to enrich shareholders; and (3) broad public accountability and ownership rather than the clear definitions of the government and corporate sectors (Vaughan and Arsenault 2013).

Post-World War II economic expansion led to a growth in resources for social causes and new opportunities for professionalizing the role of the policy advocate (McCarthy and Zald 1973). Large membership-driven religious and civic organizations of the 1940s and 1950s engaged in multiple rather than specialist pursuits, often combining social activities with community services, mutual aid, and involvement in national issues (Skocpol 2003). The social upheavals of the 1960s led to an "advocacy explosion" (Berry 1997) with social movements initiated in this decade subsequently becoming formalized as organizations (Minkoff 2002). Charitable organizations increasingly 'professionalized' by relying less on volunteers and hiring professionals—a transition "from members to managers" (Skocpol 2003). Over the 1960s and 1970s, "a veritable nonprofit public interest industry" (p. 2) emerged, championing causes such as the civil rights movement, women's liberation, environmental protection, and consumer rights, through a diversity of tactics including investigating social issues, producing reports, testifying before Congress, and organizing demonstrations (Salamon 2002).

In the second half of the twentieth century, the total number of nonprofit organizations in the United States increased by almost fourfold, according to listings in the Encyclopedia of Associations (Skocpol 2003). Rights-based organizations championing groups that had been politically marginalized—including African-Americans, Hispanic Americans, Asian Americans, and women—grew at a rate of at least sixfold over the period. The numbers increased dramatically in the 1970s and 1980s, outpacing the percentage of US population growth, until plateauing at around 22,000–23,000 in the 1990s (Skocpol 2003).

Changes in the legal sector to allow class action lawsuits opened up a new avenue for policy change through the judicial system, requiring specialist legal skills. With policy advocacy becoming an increasingly professionalized role through institutionalized social movements, downsides have been noted as the diminishment of active democracy contributed by a broadly based constituency, who support social causes with money but without further engagement (Putnam 2000; Skocpol 2013). Yet the voluntary and nonprofit sector through its policy advocacy activities continues to play a central role as mediating structures that contribute to democratic society (Salamon 2002), promoting civic engagement, political discourse, and furthering democratic ideals (LeRoux and Feeney 2014).

---

### Box 1.1 Landmark American Non-profit Advocacy Victories

- The first national advocacy group calling for the abolition of slavery, American Anti-Slavery Society, was established in 1833. Its membership was estimated to be 250,000, nearly 2% of the nation's population at the time.
- Founded in 1915, the National Women's Party organized for women's suffrage, including the Silent Sentinels who picketed the White House from January 1917 to June 1919, when the 19th amendment was passed.

- The National Association for the Advancement of Colored People (NAACP) Legal Defense and Educational Fund, led by civil rights attorney Thurgood Marshall, successfully argued against racial segregation of public schools in *Brown v. Board of Education* in 1954.
- Ralph Nader and his 'Nader's raiders' through nonprofits he established under the umbrella of Public Citizen Inc. in 1971 won important protections in the auto industry and pioneered consumer activism.
- The passage of the Americans with Disabilities Act in 1990 resulted from years of advocacy by people with disabilities, their families, and allies. When the bill was stalled in committee, the nonprofit ADAPT organized sixty disability activists with physical disabilities to shed their assistive devices and crawl up the steps of the Capitol.

## Political Context of Policy Advocacy

The exercise of political engagement through groups is known as *pluralism*. According to this theory, interest groups compete in a marketplace of ideas, with policies resulting from equilibrium reached in their struggles for political dominance (Truman 1971; Baskin 1970). Social critics have long pointed out that those with concentrations of economic and political power have greater potential for influence, with business interests holding greater sway in the American context than the nonprofit sector (Baumgartner and Leech 2001; Berry 2006; Gilens and Page 2014). The political arena is shaped by structures associated with federalism, separation of powers, and devolution of policymaking to local levels. This section provides background on the American political system, to contextualize tactics, strategies, and case studies of policy advocacy by nonprofit organizations shared in the book.

## Federalism and Devolution

Policymaking takes place at different levels of government—the federal or national level, the state level, and the local level. The US Constitution lays out this division of power between the federal and state levels, which has been clarified through the US Supreme Court. The division of power between states and the federal government is called *federalism*. The allocation of power has changed over time, from what has been described as "dual federalism," with relatively distinct spheres of power, to "cooperative federalism," with greater collaboration in policymaking between the federal and state levels (Vaughan and Arsenault 2013). This model of cooperative federalism became popular in the 1960s and 1970s, with the establishment of large-scale federal programs that devolved implementation to the states.

Devolution from the federal government to the state and local levels has increased their power when it comes to social policy. The general model is that the federal level sets standards and allocates funding through block grants or categorical grants and the state or local levels implement policy through delivering services, administering regulations or other implementation actions. Block grants allow for some discretion in how funding is used to meet policy goals, while categorical grants are more restricted. Yet all too frequently the federal government can impose unfunded mandates, placing federal requirements on states without allocating federal tax dollars, despite legislation to limit this (e.g., the 1995 federal Unfunded Mandates Reform Act) (Kraft and Furlong 2017).

The nature of federalism creates space for nonprofit organizations to influence policymaking through efforts including framing public problems, advocating policy approaches, and funding pilot initiatives. Nonprofits are also often implementers of policy through government-contracted service provision (Vaughan and Arsenault 2013). Salamon (1995) termed this complex interdependence of federal, state, and local governments with nonprofit organizations "nonprofit federalism," highlighting the critical role of nonprofits in addressing complex social problems.

## Separation of Powers

Power over policymaking is intentionally dispersed in the American system of government over multiple actors and complex interactions. This creates numerous potential points of access for potential policy advocates (see Fig. 1.1). Separation of powers is mandated in the Constitution, distributing policymaking responsibilities among the executive, legislative, and judicial branches and requiring some level of cooperation. There are parallels between the structure of government at the federal, state, and local levels, with a similar tripartite with the role of executive held by the president at the national level, governor at the state level, and mayor or local administrator at the local level (Kraft and Furlong 2017).

The role of the executive branch is to enforce policy, but it also plays a role in policy development. The president is involved in setting agenda, policy formation and adoption, and implementation. The attention and popularity of a

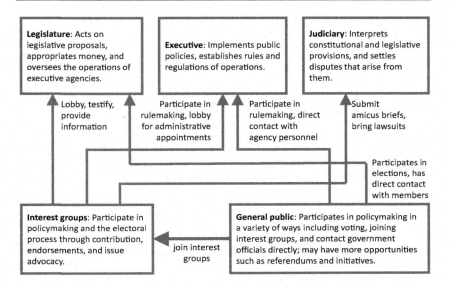

**Fig. 1.1** Agents and avenues of policymaking (adapted from Kraft and Furlong 2017)

president can have enormous influence on policymaking. The executive branch is also made up of fifteen cabinet-level departments, each managed by a secretary appointed by the president, with the mission of developing and implementing policy in various speciality areas. The bureaucratic structure attached to these cabinets is charged with interpreting legislative language and developing regulations that are essential to policy implementation. Thus, the bureaucrats who work within these departments can have considerable influence over policy. These positions are nominated by the president and confirmed by Congress, while some are appointed positions.

The legislative branch makes policy with the hundreds of statutes or laws it enacts each year. The United States has a bicameral system, with two houses: Senate and House of Representatives (collectively known as Congress). Federal policy sets the framework for state policy. Ideas for new laws or amendments of current laws are submitted by members of Congress as bills. After bills are introduced, they are referred to a committee for consideration. A lot of the work gets done in committees. The party in charge holds the chair of committees. Committees hold hearings, at which they invite experts to testify in order to learn more about the issue. A committee may accept, modify, or reject a bill. In some states, laws may be proposed directly by the public. A state's constitution may be amended either by public petition or by the legislature submitting a proposed constitutional amendment to the electorate. The process of allowing the public to propose legislation or constitutional amendments is called an initiative. The process of the state legislature proposing constitutional amendments is called a referendum.

Federal, state, and local courts establish policy through interpretation of the law, by clarifying what they mean and adjudicating differences in opinion. This branch of law is reactive in the sense that it does not initiate laws—it reacts to cases brought by others. The Supreme Court has been involved in landmark cases that have had sweeping impact on public policy—for example, *Roe vs. Wade* and abortion policy, and *Brown vs. Board of Education of Topeka*, which was intended to end school segregation (see Box 1.1).

While not part of the formal government structure, media and public opinion also plays a role in policy formation. For this reason, the media is called the "fourth estate." Politicians care about public opinion, because it can influence their reelection. Public opinion polls are used by politicians to take the pulse of the public on a given issue. There are two important concepts with regard to public opinion: saliency, how centrally important an issue is for an individual, and intensity, how strongly an opinion is held. Both of these dimensions play into how likely people are to act upon their opinions (Miller et al. 2016). If people choose to act on their opinions, they can do so by voting, attempting to influence their representatives or bureaucrats involved in setting out rules for legislation, proposing an initiative in some states like California, or joining an interest group.

Highly specialized policy actors in particular issues areas, such as defense or agriculture, form issue networks. These can also be known as iron triangles, emphasizing the interconnections and interdependence between government elected officials, bureaucracy, and special interests. An example would be decisions about defense procurement involving the congressional armed services committee, Department of Defense, and corporate entities in the defense industry, where interests align to support spending on weapon systems and where there may be little oversight or input from interests outside the issue network (Kraft and Furlong 2017).

## Policy Cycle

Policies do not just happen; rather they are the products of a regular pattern of events. This process has been pictured as a circle, because it is cyclical and iterative, rather than one-time actions. Changing conditions, new information, formal evaluations, and shifting opinions often lead to reconsideration and revision of policies through this cycle. In real life, stages may overlap or may be skipped, but understanding the stages informs advocates about the evolution of policy change. These stages are: (1) problem recognition and definition; (2) policy formulation; (3) policy legitimation; (4) policy implementation; and (5) policy evaluation and change (Gerston 2008). It is necessary to understand the policy cycle and roles of the different government branches, to understand potential opportunities for influence. Changing existing policy also involves going back through this process.

## Problem Recognition and Definition

Policy intervention to solve a social problem begins with broad recognition that the problem exists. This stage of the policy cycle—sometimes called agenda setting—is about raising awareness among formal players and the public that a social problem warrants government intervention and should advance to the policy agenda. Usually there is not a single agreed-on definition of a problem. The act of defining and framing a problem is political. Policy advocates engage in this stage by drawing attention to problems, providing information and expert testimony at hearings, issuing reports drawing attention to social problems, and other awareness-raising tactics. In Chapter 8, the Bring Our War $$ Home campaign by Codepink aimed to raise awareness of the opportunity costs of the war in Iraq. In Chapter 6, a one-person nonprofit was able to dramatically raise the public debate on transfats, and help set into motion a chain of events that would eventually lead to their ban in the United States.

## Policy Formulation

In this stage, varied stakeholders propose alternative solutions to the social problem identified in the problem recognition stage. Government stakeholders such as legislators and bureaucrats may certainly contribute their ideas, but oftentimes ideas originate from interest groups with expertise in the issue. Competing proposals vie for support and get feedback, as they evolve to more effectively address the social problem. Advocates in this stage develop courses of action and promote them to the public and policymakers. They articulate the problem as they see it, and the policy solution to solve it. For example, in Chapter 5 the American Lung Association proposed a new tobacco tax to enhance a state's tobacco control initiatives. While their original proposal was rejected by the public, they learned from their experience and modified their proposal in a subsequent cycle.

## Policy Legitimation

Also called policy adoption, this is the stage in which formal players—those required by law or constitution to participate in policymaking—formally select one or more policy proposals to address the social problem. Legislatures vote on bills, executives sign or veto them, bureaucracies adopt regulations, courts adjudicate legal disputes, and the public votes on ballot initiatives. In all these cases, the decisions earn legal force as adopted policies. Advocates actions in this stage aim to influence the decisions of the formal players, through lobbying, public pressure, information campaigns, and other tactics. Interest groups may also challenge the legitimacy of policy by bringing class action lawsuits. For example, in Chapter 4, the California Youth Connection organized foster youth to lobby legislators at the state capital to pass a bill that would extend their eligibility for care and assistance from age 18 to 21.

## Policy Implementation

Implementation is about putting a policy into effect, a stage that is dominated by bureaucratic agencies. Once a policy is passed, the executive branch implements it by developing procedures and regulations, allocating personnel and other resources, setting up programs, and other activities. Legislatures often oversee the process, to ensure their intents are carried out effectively. This stage is often slow and long, because social problems to be solved are often complex. Nonprofits are often involved in policy implementation as service providers supported by government. But they can also be involved as policy advocates, when they help monitor progress or develop programs based upon their expertise. In Chapter 3, the Books Not Bars campaign by the Ella Baker Center for Human Rights aimed to help California move away from its system of incarcerating juvenile offenders to more restorative alternatives. While there are legislative processes involved in their campaign, the focus is on the bureaucratic practices that need improvement.

## Policy Evaluation and Change

After a policy has had the opportunity to be implemented, it can be evaluated to judge its effectiveness in addressing the original social problem, and the findings of the evaluation can inform and influence the policy's future. On one extreme, a completely successful policy would fully solve the social problem and could be terminated because it is no longer needed. This is a rare occurrence. On the other extreme, a policy that is completely ineffective would have no impact on the ongoing social problem, so it too might be terminated because it is wasteful, and other alternative solutions can be considered. This, too, is rare, though many more might claim to know of such policies. More commonly, an evaluation would find that a policy has made some progress in addressing the original social problem, but that the problem still persists. It also often finds ways the policy could be refined to more effectively address the problem. Thus, the issue moves forward to problem identification and agenda-setting stage in the next cycle, where policy reforms are considered. The evaluation stage sets up the next cycle in the evolutionary life of policy.

The evaluations themselves are often done by formal players, through budget audits or legislative oversight. For example, the US Government Accountability Office is Congress's investigative body charged with audits and evaluations of programs and policies. Informally, policies are often evaluated by interest groups, investigative journalism, and academic researchers, etc. One way interest groups force the evaluation of policies is through lawsuits. In Chapter 7, we recount a case in which Our Children's Earth Foundation filed a lawsuit to determine whether a utility company had complied with environmental law when it modified and expanded its facilities. The judicial action forced the utility's actions to be evaluated against standards established in law.

## Policy Advocacy by Nonprofit Organizations in the United States: Scope and Scale

While nonprofits play many vital roles in the United States, advocacy is among the most critical (Salamon 2002). Nonprofit organizations are active in the United States at every level of policymaking, across different sides of issues. They represent interests, values, and preferences of diverse constituencies, from mainstream to minority views, secular and religious (Reid 2006). Nonprofits may engage in policy advocacy as a regular activity, or as required when decisions by government affect their service provision or other central activities (Minkoff 2002).

Nonprofits engaging in advocacy take various structures, including ones that run at the grassroots level by volunteers with minimal budgets, and others that attract donations and other funding and employ professional staff. Nonprofits may have a membership, of individuals or other organizations that they represent by consulting members on their views and acting as a vehicle for their interests. Nonprofits may also band together as a coalition to engage in collective advocacy. While policy advocacy by nonprofits is common, many nonprofit organizations encounter barriers, due to limitations in resources, time, and leadership (LeRoux and Feeney 2014). Some types of advocacy require specialist skills in law and regulatory processes (Reid 2006).

The tax status of nonprofits regulates how they can lobby political representatives (see Box 1.2), establishing a set of limits. For public charities established as 501(c)(3), these rules include barring nonprofits from endorsing candidates and using public funds for lobbying. Compliance is assessed through a set of rules, the Substantial Part Test or the Expenditure Test, establishing whether lobbying accounts for a "substantial part" of the organization's activities or expenditures. Nonprofits may instead choose classification as a "social welfare" organization 501(c)(4), or labor and business organizations 501(c)5 and 501(c)6, which are free to lobby, engage in partisan messaging, and support candidates. Some organizations create multiple nonprofit entities to reap tax benefits while maximizing policy advocacy options. For example, Sierra Club is a 501(c)(4) membership organization with the primary goal of lobbying for environmental issues, which is linked with the Sierra Club Foundation, a 501(c)(3) charity and educational entity (LeRoux and Feeney 2014). Most countries have fewer legal constraints on nonprofit advocacy and lobbying than the United States (Salamon 2006).

---

**Box 1.2 Lobbying and Advocacy—What's the Difference?**

The terms lobbying and advocacy are often used interchangeably. However, advocacy is a broader concept encompassing a variety of tactics, as discussed in Chapter 2. *Lobbying* is a specific tactic to influence policy by engaging with politicians. Nonprofit organizations representing social welfare interests, labor, and business that are classified as 501(c)(4), 501(c) (5), and 501(c)(6) are more often engaged in lobbying than other nonprofits (LeRoux and Feeney 2014).

---

**Box 1.3 Causes Championed by Nonprofit Organizations**

Overview: Nonprofit organizations can be searched in the Guidestar database using the National Taxonomy of Exempt Entities (NTEE) codes developed by the National Center for Charitable Statistics. When nonprofits annually file their financial information with the Internal Revenue Service, they self-identify their mission or primary issues of concern using these codes (Guidestar 2019):

A. Arts, Culture, and Humanities                 P. Human Services
B. Educational Institutions                       Q. International, Foreign Affairs,
                                                  and National Security

C. Environmental Quality Protection, Beautification
D. Animal related
E. Health-General & Rehabilitative
F. Mental Health, Crisis Intervention
G. Disease, Disorders, Medical Disciplines
H. Medical Research
I. Crime, Legal Related
J. Employment, Job Related
K. Agriculture, Food, Nutrition
L. Housing, Shelter
M. Public Safety, Disaster Preparedness, and Relief
N. Recreation, Sports, Leisure, Athletics
O. Youth Development
R. Civil Rights, Social Action, Advocacy
S. Community Improvement, Capacity Building
T. Philanthropy, Voluntarism, and Grantmaking
U. Science and Technology Research Institutes
V. Social Science Research Institutes
W. Public, Society Benefit
X. Religion, Spiritual Development
Y. Mutual/Membership Benefit Organizations, Other
Z. Unknown

The nonprofit landscape of the United States is massive and diverse. While the national picture is in constant flux, with new organizations being established while others cease, the Guidestar database is the best source of fairly up-to-date data on nonprofits. Guidestar reports data from the tax files of registered nonprofit organizations, which includes 501(c)(3) and 501(c)(4) organizations. These organizations identify their primary cause through the use of National Taxonomy of Exempt Entities (NTEE) codes. Organizations can self-classify their causes using letter prefix codes and their activities using number suffix codes. For example, the "R Civil Rights, Social Action and Advocacy" code can be paired with the "01 Alliance/Advocacy Organizations" code—resulting in code R01—to identify a nonprofit organization engaging in civil rights advocacy as their primary activity. See Box 1.3 for a list of causes championed by nonprofit organizations. While these codes are useful for identifying the broad swath of organizations involved in advocacy across causes, it may undercount organizations which engage in policy advocacy but not as their primary activity. The research presented in the rest of book relied on Guidestar and these NTEE codes to sample nonprofit advocacy organizations and to characterize the participating organizations.

With this contextual understanding of nonprofit policy advocacy in the United States, we can turn back to the questions raised by the National Center for Lesbian Rights case. The next chapter describes our approach to answering these questions empirically, by surveying and studying nonprofits that say policy advocacy is their primary mission.

**Discussions**

1a. Scholars such as Robert Putnam and Theda Skocpol argue that the public
    has ceded active participation in civic activities and substituted charitable
    giving for investing time working alongside others for community better-
    ment. What do you see as the upsides and downsides to the professionaliza-
    tion of nonprofit organizations and decline in reliance on volunteer labor?

1b. Voluntary associations and nonprofits have been behind many of the
    major policy changes in American history. Research the history of a
    piece of legislation (state or federal) on a topic of interest to you and
    see if and how nonprofit organizations were involved in advocating for
    or against the legislation.

1c. Where do you think power lies in the American government sys-
    tem? Federalism divides political responsibilities between the federal
    and state levels, and much of the implementation for social policy is
    devolved from the federal to state and local levels. On the causes that
    interest you, which level of government holds most sway?

1d. The media is a powerful informal actor in American policymaking.
    What are ways that you have observed policy advocates attempting to
    harness media to influence public opinions or decision makers?

1e. To learn more about the landscape of nonprofit organizations involved
    in policy advocacy, select a topic area (see Box 1.3) and look at the
    organizations associated with that area that also identify as 01 (Alli-
    ance/advocacy organization). Look at the range of organizations by
    overall budget and location. Select one to investigate further, by look-
    ing for their website and searching for annual reports. Consider top-
    ics like the history of the organization, their annual budget and if that
    reflects staffing by professionals or reliance on volunteers, the parts of
    the policy process in which the organization engages and the primary
    activities of the organization, such as research, lobbying, and litigation.

# References

Baskin, D. (1970). American pluralism: Theory, practice, and ideology. *The Journal of Pol-
    itics, 32*(1), 71–95.
Baumgartner, F. R., & Leech, B. L. (2001). Interest niches and policy bandwagons: Interest
    group involvement in national politics. *Journal of Politics, 63*(4), 1191–1213.
Berry, J. M. (1997). *The Interest Group Society* (3rd ed.). New York: Longman.

Berry, J. M. (2006). Nonprofit organizations as interest groups: The politics of passivity. In A. Cigler & B. A. Loomis (Eds.), *Interest Group Politics* (7th ed., pp. 235–255). Washington, DC: CQ Press.

California Legislative Information. (2011–2012). *SB-1177 Sexual Orientation Change Efforts*. California Legislative Information. Retrieved from https://leginfo.legislature.ca.gov/faces/billTextClient.xhtml?bill_id=201120120SB1172.

Chapman, J., & Wameyo, A. (2001). *Monitoring and Evaluating Advocacy: A Scoping Study*. ActionAid. Retrieved from https://justassociates.org/sites/justassociates.org/files/monitoring_and_evaluating_advocacy.pdf.

Clemens, E. S., & Guthrie, D. (Eds.). (2010). *Politics and Partnerships: The Role of Voluntary Associations in America's Political Past and Present*. Chicago: University of Chicago Press.

Gerston, L. N. (2008). *Public Policymaking in a Democratic Society: A Guide to Civic Engagement* (2nd ed.). Armonk, NY: M. E. Sharpe.

Gilens, M., & Page, B. (2014). Testing theories of American politics: Elites, interest groups, and average citizens. *Perspectives on Politics, 12*(3), 564–581.

Grantmakers in Health. (2005). *Funding Health Advocacy* (GIH Issue Brief No. 21). Washington, DC: Grantmakers in Health. Retrieved from http://www.gih.org/usr_doc/issuebrief21_Funding_Advocacy.pdf.

Gray, L. (2018). *NCLR's Kate Kendell Will Step Down After 22 Years*. National Center for Lesbian Rights. Retrieved from http://www.nclrights.org/press-room/press-release/nclrs-kate-kendell-will-step-down-after-22-years/.

Guidstar. (2019). *National Taxonomy of Exempt Entities (NTEE) Classification System*. Guidestar. Retrieved from https://learn.guidestar.org/help/ntee-codes.

Hall, P. D. (2006). A historical overview of philanthropy, voluntary associations, and nonprofit organizations in the United States, 1600–2000. In W. W. P. R. Steinberg (Ed.), *The Nonprofit Sector: A Research Handbook* (pp. 32–65). New Haven: Yale University Press.

Horowitz, J. (2011, July 5). Michele Bachmann's husband shares her strong conservative values. *The Washington Post*. Retrieved from https://www.washingtonpost.com/lifestyle/style/michele-bachmanns-husband-shares-her-strong-conservative-values/2011/06/21/gIQAyNmvzH_story.html.

Jansson, B. (2010). *Becoming an Effective Policy Advocate: From Policy Practice to Social Justice* (5th ed.). Belmont, CA: Thomson Brooks/Cole.

Jenkins, J. C. (1987). Nonprofit organizations and policy advocacy. In W. W. Powell (Ed.), *The Nonprofit Sector: A Research Handbook* (pp. 296–315). New Haven, CT: Yale University Press.

Kraft, M. E., & Furlong, S. R. (2017). *Public Policy: Politics, Analysis, and Alternatives*. Washington, DC: CQ Press.

LeRoux, K., & Feeney, M. K. (2014). *Nonprofit Organizations and Civil Society in the United States*. London: Routledge.

McCarthy, J. D., & Zald, M. N. (1973). *The Trend of Social Movements in America: Professionalization and Resource Mobilization*. Morristown, NJ: General Learning Press.

McLaverty, P. (2011). Participation. In M. Bevir (Ed.), *The Sage Handbook of Governance* (pp. 402–417). Thousand Oaks, CA: Sage.

Miller, J. M., Krosnick, J. A., & Fabrigar, L. R. (2016). The origins of policy issue salience: Personal and national importance impact on behavioral, cognitive, and emotional issue engagement. In *Political Psychology* (pp. 139–185). New York: Psychology Press.

Minkoff, D. C. (2002). The emergence of hybrid organizational forms: Combining identity-based service provision and political action. *Nonprofit and Voluntary Sector Quarterly, 31*(3), 377–401.

Moore, S. (2011). Can public policy advocacy be taught? Or learned? *The Philanthropist, 23*(4), 471–480.

NCLR. (2020). *Mission & History*. National Center for Lesbian Rights. Retrieved from http://www.nclrights.org/about-us/mission-history/.

Pangrazio, P. (n.d.). *A Brief History of Disability Rights & The Americans with Disabilities Act*. Retrieved from https://ability360.org/livability/advocacy-livability/history-disability-rights-ada/.

Pekkanen, R. J., Smith, S. R., & Tsujinaka, Y. (Eds.). (2014). *Nonprofits and Advocacy: Engaging Community and Government in an Era of Retrenchment*. Baltimore: John Hopkins University Press.

Putnam, R. D. (2000). *Bowling Alone: America's Declining Social Capital*. New York: Palgrave Macmillan.

Reid, E. J. (2001). Understanding the word 'advocacy': Context and use. In *Nonprofit Advocacy and the Policy Process: Structuring the Inquiry into Advocacy* (Vol. 1, pp. 1–7). Washington, DC: The Urban Institute.

Reid, E. J. (2006). Nonprofit advocacy and political participation. In E. T. Boris & C. E. Steuerle (Eds.), *Nonprofits and Government: Collaboration and Conflict* (pp. 343–372). Washington, DC: Urban Institute.

Reisman, J., Gienapp, A., & Stachowiak, S. (2007). *A Guide to Measuring Policy and Advocacy*. Seattle: Organizational Research Services.

Rose, C. (2004, March 3). *Mayor Gavin Newsom*. Charlie Rose LLC. Retrieved from https://charlierose.com/videos/15061.

Salamon, L. M. (1995). *Partners in Public Service: Government-Nonprofit Relations in the Modern Welfare State*. Baltimore: Johns Hopkins University Press.

Salamon, L. M. (2002). *Explaining Nonprofit Advocacy: An Exploratory Analysis* (Working Paper Series, 21). Center for Civil Society Studies.

Salamon, L. M. (2006). Government-nonprofit relations from an international perspective. In E. T. Boris & C. E. Steuerle (Eds.), *Nonprofits & Government: Collaboration & Conflict* (pp. 399–436). Washington, DC: The Urban Institute Press.

Schmid, H., Bar, M., & Nirel, R. (2008). Advocacy activities in nonprofit human service organizations: Implications for policy. *Nonprofit and Voluntary Sector Quarterly, 37*(4), 581–602.

Skocpol, T. (2003). *From Membership to Management in American Civic Life*. Norman: University of Oklahoma.

Skocpol, T. (2013). *Diminished Democracy: From Membership to Management in American Civic Life* (Vol. 8). Norman: University of Oklahoma Press.

Sprechmann, S., & Pelton, E. (2001). *Advocacy Tools and Guidelines: Promoting Policy Change*. CARE. Retrieved from https://resources.peopleinneed.cz/documents/15-advocacy-tools-and-guidelines-promoting-policy-change.pdf.

Totenberg, N. (2013, March 26). *DOMA Challenge Tests Federal Definition of Marriage.* National Public Radio. Retrieved from https://www.npr.org/2013/03/27/175295410/doma-challenge-tests-federal-definition-of-marriage.

Truman, D. B. (1971). *The Governmental Process.* New York: Alfred A. Knopf.

Vaughan, S. K., & Arsenault, S. (2013). *Managing Nonprofit Organizations in a Policy World.* London: CQ Press.

# Tactics and Strategies

**2**

This chapter introduces the concepts of tactics and strategies used in policy advocacy, and discusses how the strategies and case studies presented in the following chapters of the book were derived. Policy advocacy strategies are comprehensive, long-range approaches to policy change, while tactics are the specific advocacy activities employed within the strategies intended to achieve specific outcomes (Ganz 2009; Berry 1977). The metaphor of military operations is apt in this context: A tactic is a specific action undertaken within a war, such as a battle plan, while a strategy is the long-range plan of how to win a war. A strategy includes a set of tactics, and the objectives of the tactics lead to the achievement of the strategy's goals. In the context of policy advocacy, the list of tactics was synthesized from practitioner literature and policy studies, and the strategies that combine them were measured through empirical research with nonprofit organizations, drawing on a national survey and interviews employing Q-methodology. The resulting set of six strategies falls along a spectrum in terms of whether they attempt to influence formal policy actors or grassroots citizens. They are presented in order along this spectrum in the chapters that follow.

## A Menu of Tactics for Policy Advocacy

Advocates have an extensive menu of tactics for seeking their policy advocacy goals, which include tactics that aim to engage, inform, and influence other advocates, decision makers, policy implementers, and the public. These activities may result in short-term/proximal outcomes, such as responsive democratic environment that enables advocacy, greater public awareness and support of an issue, and decision makers' awareness and support. These outcomes, in turn, support

© The Author(s) 2020
S. Gen and A. C. Wright, *Nonprofits in Policy Advocacy*,
https://doi.org/10.1007/978-3-030-43696-4_2

long-term or distal goals of public policy advocacy, which is, of course, affecting change in the policy domain through policy adoption and changes to policy implementation. Policy advocates may also pursue defensive actions to shield the status quo. Ultimately, policy itself is a means to an end, and that end is societal impact (Knowlton and Phillips 2009), whether on people, services and systems, or the political system (Chapman and Wameyo 2001).

The best source of information on the types of tactics used by policy advocates is the materials produced by policy advocacy organizations themselves and foundations that fund these organizations. These tactics were identified by searching for practitioner literature suggesting links between policy advocacy activities and possible outcomes, using logic models. Logic models are visual depictions of social programs or change efforts, diagramming the connections between inputs (resources and necessary conditions), the activities they enable (in this case, specific to policy advocacy), the short- and longer-term outcomes that may arise from these activities, as well as the ultimate desired impact (Knowlton and Phillips 2009). Logic models' more general use in program planning and evaluation are well established, but their application to policy advocacy is more recent. For example, in 2006, Hoefer provided an early prescription for logic models to plan advocacy efforts of social workers.

Logic models from an adequately representative sample (Cooper 1988) of nonprofit policy advocates were identified. The sources of the logic models included a mix of major national foundations in the areas of health (Grantmakers in Health) and child welfare (Annie E. Casey Foundation), academia (Harvard Family Research Project), and research and evaluation institutes (Center for Community Health and Evaluation and Innovation Network). One organization (Action Aid) is an international humanitarian organization. After identifying these logic models, themes identified in the logic models became repetitious and we determined that saturation of ideas had been reached (Glaser and Strauss 1967). The breadth of activities identified captured all those identified by Baumgartner and Leech's (1998) comprehensive review of interest group activities, further confirming the representative scope of our sample of logic models. Elements from these logic models were coded and reduced to a combined logic model (see Table 2.1), with three major categories of elements: inputs, activities, and outcomes. More detail on the derivation of the composite logic model can be found in Appendix A.

The combined logic model guided a review of the academic literature, to seek theoretical support for the activities and outcomes identified and the connections between them. To be plausible, the hypothesized connections between elements of a theory of change or logic model require an underlying foundation of theory

**Table 2.1** Composite logic model for policy advocacy

| Inputs/competencies[a] (necessary conditions) | Activities (actions) | Proximal outcomes[b] (indirect and near-term) | Distal Outcomes (indirect and long term) | Impacts |
|---|---|---|---|---|
| • Sense of 'agency' in the political process as manifested by<br>– Sense of empowerment and political power[c]<br>– Will to challenge status quo<br>– Ability to identify and define problems<br>• People and Relationships<br>– Leadership<br>– Staffing<br>– Ability to organize collective action<br>– Strategic partnerships<br>• Specialized knowledge and skills:<br>– Strategy<br>– Research<br>– Media<br>– Public relations<br>– Lobbying<br>• Material resources<br>– Financial | • Coalition building<br>– Networking<br>– Forming coalitions/Federations<br>• Engaging and mobilizing the public<br>– Community organizing, outreach<br>– Voter registration<br>– Rallies, convenings, protests, writing letters<br>• Engaging decision makers<br>– Lobbying<br>– Relationship building<br>• Information campaigning<br>– Research, policy analysis, white papers<br>– Refining and framing message; labeling<br>– Education<br>– Briefings, presentations<br>– Media advocacy<br>• Reform efforts<br>– Pilots, demonstrations<br>– Litigation<br>• Defensive activities<br>– Read and react to opponents<br>– Read and react to climate<br>• Policy monitoring<br>– Evaluation | • Democratic environment<br>– Governance: Transparency/accountability improved<br>– Civil society: Power and capacity enhanced<br>• Changes in public views<br>– Changes in awareness, beliefs, attitudes, values, salience of issues, behaviors<br>– Strengthened base of support: Increased public involvement, levels of action<br>• Changes in decision makers' views<br>– Getting on political agenda<br>– Political will | • Policy adoption<br>– Changed, improved policy<br>– Policy blocking<br>• Implementation change<br>– Improved implementation<br>– Policy enforcement | • Desired changes for target population<br>• Desired changes in services and systems<br>• People-centered policymaking |

[a]Group or individual level

[b]Excluded agency-specific goals (e.g., increased funding, collaboration, recognition) as not central to policy advocacy mission

[c]Sub-bullets are examples of the items in the major bullets; they are not comprehensive lists

and research, rather than just assumptions or anecdotal evidence (Knowlton and Phillips 2009). The sources of the combined logic models presented lists of activities and outcomes, without specifying linkages between them. To hypothesize the linkages between activities and outcomes, we turned to the theoretical and empirical academic literature in policy studies and related academic disciplines, including public administration, political science, and social work. We searched for theories and empirical studies that discussed the possible connections between an activity and an outcome. For example, public participation theory suggests that engaging and mobilizing the public can lead to a more democratic policymaking environment and people-centered policymaking. Table 2.2 identifies hypothesized theoretical connections between policy advocacy activities and intended outcomes. The next section discusses the practitioner-identified tactics and applies and interprets relevant theories to the context of public policy advocacy. In some cases, application involves extrapolation, as theories originally devised in other contexts of public policy and political science are extended to advocacy.

## Coalition Building and Mobilizing the Public

The first two types of activities in the combined logic model are coalition building and engaging the public. Coalition building involves bringing together individuals, groups, and organizations with mutual interests, to amplify their influence. An example would be a network of environmental organizations with various emphases (e.g., clean air, preservation of marine habitat, renewable energy) to work together to block a new coal-fired energy plant. Engaging the public encompasses a range of activities that promote awareness and coordinated action among a segment of the public. This may involve grassroots organizing, to work with people affected by a policy to act on their own behalf, voter mobilization to "get out the vote" for a candidate or issue, or organizing rallies and marches for a visible demonstration of public views on an issue (Coffman et al. 2007). Grassroots organizing occurs at a local level, to address issues that affect people in a particular geographic area. For example, grassroots organizing for tenants' rights in San Francisco has resulted in strong protections against eviction. Voter mobilization is often organized by political parties in advance of an important election of a candidate, or may be organized by a coalition around a ballot initiative, such as increasing funding available for public education. Rallies and marches have played an important role in coalescing and demonstrating public views on issues in American history, including marches for civil rights and rallies demonstrating anti-war and other sentiments. The activities of coalition

**Table 2.2**   Theoretical links among inputs, activities, outcomes and impacts

| Activities | Theoretical link | Outcomes and impacts |
|---|---|---|
| Coalition building; Engaging and mobilizing the public; information campaigning | Advocacy Coalition Framework; interest group studies | Changes in public views; changes in decision makers' views; policy adoption |
| Engaging decision makers | Institutionalism; elite theory | Changes in decision makers' views; Policy adoption |
| Information campaigning: research and analysis | Rational decision making | Changes in public views; changes in decision makers' views; policy adoption |
| Information campaigning: rhetoric (e.g., issue framing, labeling, anecdotes, etc.) | Rhetoric studies | Changes in public views; changes in decision makers' views; policy adoption |
| Information campaigning: media work | Media studies | Changes in public views; changes in decision makers' views; sets policy agenda; raises political will to act; shortens time frame for action |
| Reform efforts: litigation | Adversarial legalism | Policy adoption |
| Reform efforts: pilots, demonstrations | Incrementalism | Changes in public views; changes in decision makers' views; policy adoption |
| Defensive activities | Public dialectic; Policy-oriented learning | Changes in public views; changes in decision makers' views |
| Policy monitoring | Bottom-up implementation theories | Changes in bureaucrats' actions |
| Policy monitoring | Evaluation theory | Setting the policy agenda |
| Information campaigning; Engaging and mobilizing the public; Engaging decision makers | Multiple streams theory | Setting the policy agenda; policy adoption |
| Engaging and mobilizing the public | Public participation | Democratic environment; people-centered policymaking |

building and engaging the public share a common characteristic of coordinating with organizations and individuals with similar policy goals. These types of activities share a pluralistic view of democracy (Dahl 1967) in which policy power is dispersed among many competing groups and interests. In this view, an organization's own policy preferences are more likely to be enacted if greater support for them can be demonstrated.

The theoretical literature on coalitions, issue networks, and interest groups most directly applies here. The Advocacy Coalition Framework claims that policy subsystem, made of participating coalitions of interests, is the most relevant unit of analysis for understanding policy change (Sabatier 1988), even more so than government players, because it is the coalitions within these subsystems, and their interactions with each other, that drive policy change. Furthermore, these coalitions are formed around common policy beliefs and interests, and their goals are to translate those beliefs into public policies (Nowlin 2011; Sabatier 1988; Sabatier and Jenkins-Smith 1999). They attempt to do so through exchanges of information and views among the coalitions, resulting in relevant learning about the policy issue, and changes in policy preferences. Thus, the theory appears to link coalition building, public engagement, and information campaigning to changes in the public's and decision makers' awareness and support, leading further to policy change. The Advocacy Coalition Framework originated from observations of environmental policy change, but has since been applied to numerous policy issues, including transportation, biotechnology, national intelligence, and disasters, among others (Weible et al. 2011). Complementing this framework are interest group studies that describe the characteristics of groups that affect their relative influence on policy (Baumgartner and Leech 1998). These focus on their ability to coordinate collective communication and mobilize members for actions (Cahn 1995, p. 208), their size (e.g., membership, budgets) and expertise (Cahn 1995, p. 208; Sabatier 1988), and their status or prestige in the policy issue (Truman 1993).

Mobilizing the public to act is difficult and has drawn its own attention in policy studies. Olson's (1965) theory of latent groups claims that large groups are ineffective (latent) in achieving common goals unless the individuals in them are coerced or induced to act. Thus, in policy advocacy, large groups of engaged citizens must be mobilized to vote, protest, rally, etc., because most individuals in the group will not be on their own. The purposes of such mobilization may depend upon the specific organized activity. Protests are meant to draw attention to an issue, to spur policy actions. Thus, they can be seen as focusing events to set the policy agenda (Kingdon 1984). While Birkland (1997) limited his study of focusing events to natural disasters (e.g., hurricanes) and human accidents (e.g., nuclear power plant meltdowns), focusing events can be intentional, particularly from the viewpoint of policy advocates. Protests and rallies are examples of these.

In general, mobilization activities at a minimum increase the capacities of individuals in the policy process. Putnam (1976) identified a stratification of policy power with six levels, ranging from bottom to top: nonparticipants, voters, attentive public, activists, influentials, and proximate decision makers. One purpose of mobilizing the public, therefore, could be to move individuals to higher strata of policy influence. Indeed, one normative criticism of this stratified, elitist policy power structure is the lowest strata support elitism by not participating in the process (Walker 1966). Through inaction, nonparticipants tacitly delegate their authority to the existing power holders. In contrast, developing broader participation in the lower strata essentially redistributes power more equitably across the strata.

## Lobbying and Building Relationships with Decision Makers

In contrast to engaging the public to build broad-based support is a set of advocacy activities that focus on building support within small groups of key policy players. Lobbying is about communicating with a person in position of power, to attempt to influence his or her actions with regard to legislation and policy decisions. It may be proceeded by broader activities to build relationships with decision makers, through regular interaction, and to educate decision makers to promote their awareness of a particular issue (Coffman et al. 2007). Interest groups representing industries, professions, or social issues may employ a lobbyist to regular engage with decision makers and share information encouraging them to espouse a particular view. The Senate Office of Public Records notes over 10,000 lobbyists are registered (Center for Responsive Politics 2017). Organizations may also build relationships with decision makers by inviting them to events and preparing policy briefs and other communiques targeted to decision makers, so that they become a known and trusted source of information. There are many well-known examples of organizations that employ these tactics involved in US federal policymaking. On the right of the political spectrum, the National Rifle Association, and on the left of the political spectrum, Planned Parenthood, are just two examples.

This type of activity of lobbying and building relationships with decision makers evokes the view of institutionalism in which power to change policy is wielded directly by those formal players who are required to participate in the policy process: legislatures, executives, courts, and even government agencies

(Cahn 1995; Theodoulou and Kofinis 2004). While engaging those who are required to participate and have direct influence seems like an obvious advocacy strategy, rival theories of the policy process do not place primary power with the institutional players. Instead, they view the decisions and the actions of institutional players to be reactions to more powerful, noninstitutional players that influence them. In institutionalism, however, policy advocates attempt to influence the formal players directly, rather than through public pressure, media, or other intermediate players.

Still, advocacy work with key policy players is not limited to institutional players. There may be powerful individuals or groups, inside and outside of government institutions, that dominate the policy process, and policy advocates may attempt to build relationships with them in order to influence policy. Elite theory substantiates this strategy. It claims, like institutionalism, that policy power is concentrated in a relatively small group of people. But unlike institutionalism, that group is not necessarily government players. Instead, they are an upper social class of people who are relatively homogenous, self-aware, and self-perpetuating (Mills 1956; Putnam 1976). Advocates holding this view of power distribution conclude that any policy change necessarily requires the actions of the elite. Thus, educating them on issues and swaying their preferences is a proximal goal toward policy change. Admittedly, elite theory itself does not leave much room for non-elite advocates to influence the elite class. In fact, a tenant of elite theory is their relative autonomy (Putnam 1976) and their ability to mold the opinions of the public to follow their own (Edelman 1964; Herman and Chomsky 2002). Even so, in Putnam's (1976) pyramid of political stratification, he opens the possibility of the elite class being influenced by the activists and public below it.

## Information Campaigning

The tactic of information campaigning entails conducting analysis and research on an issue, as well as how the information generated is pitched to various audiences. Issue or policy analysis and research involves systematically investigating a topic, to provide definition and inform possible policy solutions (Coffman et al. 2007). Research outputs may be shared through reports, journal publications, or verbal presentations and briefings. Common elements that appear in policy analyses include defining the problem, providing evidence, recommending alternatives, and analyzing these alternatives based on common criteria such as efficiency, efficacy, and equity (Bardach and Patashnik 2015). Advocates can also use elements of persuasion when making their case. The classic elements of persuasion are *logos* (invoking logic), *pathos* (invoking emotion), and *ethos* (establishing the credibility of the messenger) (Ramage and Bean 1998). For example, an advocate representing children's issues could provide statistics that demonstrate the scale and consequences of a problem (*logos*), share stories about children who are personally affected by the problem (*pathos*), and demonstrate why the advocate is to be trusted on the issue, due to credentials or experience (*ethos*) (Wright and Jaffe 2013).

Academic theories and empirical evidence identify a broad range of expected outcomes related to information campaigning. This literature can be divided into two broad categories: research and rhetoric. Research activities in this context include the analysis of empirical data as well as the construction of arguments based upon rationality (e.g., the practices described in Bardach and Patashnik 2015; Weimer and Vining 1992). Indeed, many theories of policy decision making are derived from the classic normative theory of rationality. In this view, research and analyses play an important role in policy processes by providing relevant information to produce better decisions (Lindblom and Cohen 1979; Weiss and Bucuvalas 1980). Thus, some advocacy groups—especially think tanks—engage in policy research to inform stakeholders of relevant information needed for optimal policy selections. The audiences of the research may range from the decision makers themselves, for direct influence on policy change, to the at-large public, for indirect influence. Rationality as a descriptive theory, however, has come under unrelenting empirical criticism. Many have observed the sub-optimal realities of policy decision making and derived more grounded theories, such as Lindblom's incrementalism (1959) and Simon's (1945) bounded rationality and satisficing. Even so, these theories assume a normative desire for rationality, so research remains a vital aspect of these theories. Even normative critics of a rational approach to decision making do not refute the role that research can play. They simply don't give it the place of honor that it finds in rational approaches (e.g., Stone 2002).

The other major category of information campaigning is rhetoric, carefully crafted language meant to persuade. Products of rhetoric used in policy advocacy are varied, but a few are supported by academic research. For example, framing is the practice of presenting an issue from a particular perspective that supports the framer's preference. Schneider and Ingram (1993) found that framing policy targets in a favorable light is an effective tactic for gaining policy support. They described this practice as the social construction of policy target populations. Anecdotes, in contrast, are stories that convey policy-relevant information (Nowlin 2011) that help audiences better understand the contexts, stakeholders, and values surrounding a policy issue (Jones and McBeth 2010). So far, the academic literature on rhetoric in policy advocacy lacks an overarching theory of impact, but the individual studies of specific rhetorical tools appear to mostly aim to change people's perspectives and understandings of policy issues.

## Engaging and Using Media

Turning from the creation of information to its dissemination, engaging and using media provide a powerful platform to get out advocacy messages. Earned media involves pitching a topic and receiving coverage on the advocacy issue. For example, an advocacy campaign can "earn" media when its spokesperson is quoted in the newspaper, or a rally is covered by local news. Another powerful form of earned media is opinion pieces and letters to the editor. Opinion pieces are pitched to media outlets and are often printed in response to current political issues in the news. An opinion piece can be a way for an advocacy campaign to make a persuasive case for or against a piece of legislation, or bring attention to a social problem. Paid media is coverage that is paid for, to convey a message to a particular audience, such as a public service announcement or "open letter" in a newspaper. Increasingly, social media is an important way to gain awareness, through posting to one's own networks through channels such as Twitter and Facebook, or having one's posts shared by others through their networks.

Media studies provide a wide range of expected outcomes for policy advocates who engage media. Overall, mass media are engaged by advocates for the obvious reason of raising public awareness of, and support for, advocates' issues (Nowlin 2011). But some researchers have identified more specific outcomes. Iyengar and Kinder (1987), for example, found that issues covered by mass media can set the policy agenda by drawing public attention to it. Similarly, Linsky (1988) found that media coverage of policy issues raises the issue to higher levels of policymakers and increases their political will to act on these issues. He also found that media coverage can shorten the time for policy change.

## Litigation

Policy advocates can also attempt to more directly and actively reform policy. The most direct path is through litigation, which can force the judiciary to review the advocate's case and applicable policies themselves. Strategic or impact litigation is about using a particular case to bring about broader change, and can be brought on behalf of a group or individual. A famous example is the *Brown vs. Board of Education Topeka, Kansas* US Supreme Court case that overturned racial segregation in schools. The case was brought by the National Association for the Advancement of Colored People (NAACP). Previous cases brought by NAACP required that school districts simply address the "tangible" aspects of their segregated schools to be equivalent to white-only schools. NAACP selected the Topeka school district because it had taken measures to improve black schools, allowing NAACP to bring segregation itself as the focus as inherently unequal because of depriving black students of equal protection under the law. This decision led to guidelines for federal district courts to oversee the nation-wide desegregation of schools (Foner and Garraty 1991).

Litigation as an advocacy tool is based less on academic theory as it is on judicial process. However, as an advocacy strategy that tends to be pursued by groups, scholars have considered activism through judicial channels to be a type of group pressure. Epstein and colleagues (1995) conclude that the decision-making process of whether to pursue litigation as a strategy relates to the internal features of a group, the external social/political environment, and the perceived interplay between these. Key internal features include: the autonomy of group leaders to make decisions on the use of litigation; resources (money, time, staff, and contacts), with litigation requiring significant financial expenditure and time; organizational maintenance (or efforts to sustain the organization's existence), in terms of how the organization's constituency views litigation; and the foci or interests that the advocacy group is positioned to promote or defend, with organizations focused on issues such as discrimination and good governance tending to make greater use of litigation. The external environment is the broad social/political context, and whether it is favorable, unfavorable, or malleable (not yet decided) on the issue. The final decision of whether to act through litigation comes down to perceived institutional and organizational reasons. Acting through the courts can be an appropriate institutional avenue to achieve goals, such as under circumstances when groups perceive that they do not have influence in the executive or legislative branches. For organizational reasons, litigation may be an attractive approach due to the availability of attorneys, the value of publicity for the organization, and the opportunity to challenge ideological opponents.

Overall, the study of group litigation has been criticized as being overly focused on examining substantive issues and failing to produce generalizable theory (Epstein et al. 1995). Still, adversarial legalism has been advanced by Kagan (1991, 1999) as a theory of the role of the courts in the policymaking process, focused less on groups than on the (perhaps uniquely American) role of aggressive lawyers. One emphasis of this theory is on litigant activism, with claimants represented by lawyers, asserting their claims with the support of evidence.

According to this theory, the upside of litigation is the opportunity for "have nots" to triumph, while the downside is the cost (in terms of time and money) and the uncertainty of outcome (due to fragmented legal authority and variability of the courts) (Kagan 1999). While Kagan favors European approaches that put more policy control in the hands of bureaucrats, others defend the role of the courts in the policymaking process as promoting balance among policymaking authorities (Busch et al. 1998–1999).

## Pilot and Demonstration Projects

Pilot or demonstration projects are another way advocates may try to directly reform policies and programs. This approach entails implementing a policy proposal on a small scale, to show how the approach could work and the outcomes that could be achieved (Coffman et al. 2007). Policy that is later implemented on a wide scale often begins as a pilot—for example, the Supplemental Nutrition Assistance Program, often informally referred to as food stamps, was first initiated as a pilot in the early 1960s (USDA 2014).

The use of pilot or demonstration projects is supported by incrementalism. Lindblom (1959) first identified incremental decision making in a negative light, as "muddling through," in which comprehensive rational decision making is abandoned in lieu of low-risk, low-impact decisions based upon series of "successive limited comparisons (p. 81)." According to Lindblom, this approach is taken because the necessary information and institutional support for comprehensive rational analyses are often lacking. He was describing a sub-optimal decision-making process, not prescribing one. But low-risk incremental decision making can be an effective strategy for policy advocates when high-risk comprehensive reforms are politically infeasible. In such cases, pilot projects can demonstrate the efficacy of a reform on small scales, thereby building support for more comprehensive reforms without imposing high risks to stakeholders. Thus, pilot projects can be seen as a strategic use of incrementalism to advocate for larger policy changes.

## Defensive Activities

Defensive activities may include a range of advocacy activities already described. The key point of distinction is that defensive activities are aimed at preserving current policy, rather than advancing a policy alternative. For example, a policy advocate could defend a current policy through earned media, describing what would happen if a policy was repealed. Or a policy advocate could defend current policy through engaging the public through grassroots organizing of those who would be negatively affected. Policy processes seldom have an end. Even when favorable policies are adopted, advocacy activities often need to continue (Baumgartner and Leech 1998) to ensure meaningful implementation, monitor progress, and defend gains against opposition. Nelson (1986) identified "issue maintenance" as a critical part of policy advocacy, to sustain public interest and government support.

The defensive activities in the combined logic model assume a pluralistic democracy (Dahl 1967) in which policymaking influence is distributed among multiple competing factions. In this setting, engaging opposing factions in public discourse or debate is necessary to counter or lessen the oppositions' influence. The public dialectic among the factions transforms observers into informed stakeholders, influencing their perspective on the issues and perhaps gaining their alliance (Majone 1989). For example, in the Advocacy Coalition Framework, policy change follows policy-oriented learning among participants in the policy subsystem. Such learning refers to enduring changes in participants' understandings of the issues and their values placed on them, and the learning occurs through the exchange of information and views among policy participants (Sabatier 1988). Operationally, this could include varying forms of public debate.

## Influencing Policy Implementation

The passage of legislation marks the beginning of a process to put the policy into effect, to ensure that the policy's objectives and goals are attained. This is a process involving development of a program, regulation, payment, or other tool of government that is intended to achieve the policy's goals. In other words, this is when the actual intervention and impact upon the public are achieved. For example, there is relatively little detail in federal legislation on how the Occupational Safety and Health Administration protects workers' safety, and the agency has been criticized for weak implementation of worker safety provisions (Kraft and Furlong 2017).

Activities that monitor policy implementation may serve different purposes for policy advocates. On the one hand, they may be used to apply pressures on government agencies to implement policies as adopted. This function adopts the bottom-up view of policy implementation, in which bureaucrats have substantial discretionary power to interpret and apply policies as they see fit (Hill and Hupe 2011). Bardach (1977) and Pressman and Wildavsky (1984) famously described how bureaucrats and bureaucracies can thwart best intentions of adopted policies. In this view, bureaucrats are effectively policymakers themselves (Lipsky 2010). Thus, savvy policy advocates may recognize the opportunity to influence bureaucrats' implementation activities by holding them accountable to the advocates' preferences in the adopted policies (Riley and Brophy-Baermann 2006). On the other hand, monitoring can be viewed as an evaluation activity, meant to measure and judge how well-adopted policies are achieving their goals. The purpose here is to improve policy, though sometimes it is used as a symbolic act to appease stakeholders (Nachmias 1980). For policy advocates, each of these outcomes may be relevant: the former to change policy and the latter to defend policy status quo. But in both cases, the target of their advocacy is not the bureaucrats directly, but the policy agenda. That is, the monitoring is meant to get the policy back on the agenda for reform, or keep it off the agenda to maintain its current form.

The academic literature applied above all focuses on the elements of our combined logic model that are advocacy activities, projecting what advocacy outcomes might be expected from them. Complementing this are a few theories from the policy studies literature that focus on specific outcomes in the combined logic model, and identify their antecedents. These too can help understand what policy advocates expect from their efforts. First, Kingdon's (1984) multiple streams theory describes how policy change can occur when three streams of events converge: a problem stream in which a social problem ascends the policy agenda, a policy stream that identifies solutions to the problem, and a political stream that dictates the political feasibility of policy change at a given time. The theory opens up several points of access for advocates to influence policy change. Indeed, each of Kingdon's streams might be influenced by activities in the combined logic model. For example, information campaigning can build public awareness of a problem or promote a favored solution. Similarly, citizen mobilizations, such as protests, can serve as focusing events that build awareness of a problem and set the policy agenda. Also, lobbying and campaigning might increase political will among policymakers to act.

Second, studies on public participation in policymaking, as described earlier, identify outcomes that strengthen democracies, independent of the specific policies adopted. These include legitimization of the policymaking process through broader input and support for adopted policies (Bryson and Anderson 2000; Smith and Huntsman 1997; Xu 2005), more effective polices (Kastens and Newig 2008), and broader distribution of policy benefits among stakeholders (Gallagher and Jackson 2008). For some policy advocates, these democratic outcomes may be as important, if not more so, as specific policies.

## Strategies of Policy Advocacy Organizations

These theoretical linkages between policy advocates' activities and expected outcomes provide a menu of hypothesized tactics that have been empirically tested with nonprofit organizations, to determine how organizations combined these tactics into distinct strategies. Q-methodology was employed, with interviews of 31 individuals who manage their respective organizations' policy advocacy efforts, to identify strategies that fit their organizations. The resulting six factors identify unique viewpoints of nonprofit organizations on the processes of policy change and how they seek to influence those processes—these factors are henceforth described as strategies. These strategies were further supported by a national survey of 821 randomly selected US nonprofits engaged in policy advocacy as a primary activity. The strengths of this methodological approach include in-depth examination of policy advocacy through qualitative interview and Q-methodology, complemented by breadth exploration of policy activity strategies by a range of organizations. A limitation of the research is that it is a cross-sectional study at a particular point in time and may not reflect modifications in policy advocacy strategies due to changing political and economic conditions. A detailed discussion of the study population, sampling frame, and methodology is included in Appendix B.

Q-methodology is a "...systematic and rigorously quantitative means for examining human subjectivity" (McKeown and Thomas 1988, p. 7). It employs factor analysis to identify underlying structures of viewpoints collected from structured surveys. However, its application of factor analysis is opposite that typically found in survey research. In the typical R-method that is dominant in social sciences, the variables being analyzed are statements in a survey, while the cases are the respondents. The resulting factors are clusters of statements that reveal underlying meanings among them. In contrast, factor analysis in Q-methodology treats the statements as the cases and the respondents as variables. Respondents rank the relative importance of the statements based on their internal point of view, and the resulting factors are clusters of respondents with related viewpoints on the phenomenon represented by the statements. Watts and Stenner (2012) succinctly label Q-methodology a "by-person" factor analysis, in contrast to the more common "by-variable" (or by-statement) factor analysis of R-methodology (pp. 10–13). In the research informing this book, the statements are opinions about advocacy activities and their resulting outcomes, and respondents sorted them by their relative importance to their organizations.

Factor analysis was conducted four times, to extract four, five, six, and seven factors from the data. These extractions were compared by the cumulative variances they explained, the numbers of different organizations loading onto each factor, the numbers of confounding sorts (i.e., organizations that load onto more than one factor), and the numbers of nonsignificant sorts (i.e., organizations that do not load onto any factor). The six-factor extraction was the most efficient in that it loaded the most organizations onto the fewest factors. It explained 61% of the variance in the data while loading at least five organizations onto each factor and accounting for all but one organization, at the 95% level of confidence (see Appendix B summarizing the organizations significantly loading onto each of the six factors). These loadings can be interpreted like correlation coefficients, in that the closer the loading is to 1.0000, the stronger the relationship between the organization's strategy and the factor. No organization's strategy is perfectly represented by any of the factors. Instead, an organization's strategy might overlap with a factor or two. That is, the factors represent commonalities in the strategies among the organizations, but each organization might employ more than one strategy in their advocacy campaigns.

The survey of US nonprofits engaging in policy advocacy provides context on frequency with which these tactics and strategies are used and the types of organizations that employ these strategies. A representative of each organization ($n = 821$) was asked how often activities (reflecting column 1 of Table 2.2) are used as part of their policy advocacy campaigns and the importance of this outcome (reflecting column 3 of Table 2.2) to the organization's policy advocacy campaigns. Background questions about the organization included its annual budget, total number of full-time equivalent staff, geographic location, number of years of operation, and issue area as identified by IRS National Taxonomy of Exempt Entities (NTEE) code.

The remainder of the book draws upon these two data sources in the discussion of six policy advocacy strategies. Each chapter explores a strategy in depth, drawing upon case studies, policy studies theory, and empirical data on the characteristics of organizations associated with each strategy. To preview these chapters, the six strategies are described here in brief. They are presented in order from most closely targeting policymakers to most closely partnering with community members.

Each strategy description includes a summary of its key statistics from Q-methodology. These statistics report how the 24 Q-sample statements (see Q-sample in Appendix B) are sorted in the factor, on the same scale of $-3$ to $+3$. Interpretation of these arrays was guided by the "crib sheet" procedure prescribed by Watts and Stenner (2012). This process systematically focuses attention on not only the lowest and highest rated statements in each array, but also those statements with ratings that are relatively low or high among all the factors, no matter the absolute value of the rating. Doing so highlights the relative differences between the factors. In these descriptions, statement numbers and their ratings are referenced parenthetically (e.g., 11:+2 means statement 11 has a rating of +2 in the factor array). Schematic pathways are also included in these descriptions, to graphically summarize the causal relationships assumed in each factor. Statistics are also reported on how the factors relate to the 31 organizations in the research sample. An eigenvalue is the sum of squared factor loadings, a measure of the variance explained by the factor. The eigenvalue of 1.00 is generally accepted as threshold above which factors are deemed reliable and worthy of interpretation, because the factor would explain more variance than a single Q-sort would on its own (Watts and Stenner 2012). Each factor had at least five organizations' Q-sorts loading significantly.

The strategies in the table below and in the chapters that follow are ordered from those most reliant on institutional players to the least. *Public lobbying strategy* uses the tactics of building long-term relationships with decision makers to educate and persuade them to pursue policy change that the advocates perceived as being in the public's best interests. *Institutional partnership strategy* also works closely with decision makers in critical institutions, by organizing public support, research and messaging, and sometimes pilot programs for the desired policy change. *Inside-outside strategy* takes a two-pronged approach, of collaborating with a policy champion within the decision-making structure, while applying outside pressure through information campaigns and media work. *Direct reform strategy* circumvents legislative policymakers by going through the channels of judicial or administrative processes, by engaging in litigation or implementation monitoring while also doing information campaigns to raise awareness of their work. The *Indirect pressure strategy* focuses on an already formed constituency, conveying the views of this mobilized group, using the media, and implementing pilot programs to pressure decision makers to enact their desired policy changes. *Popular power strategy* harnesses the influence of the public rather than policy decision makers, influencing their views through a variety of tactics including coalition building, public mobilizations, media and information campaigns, framing and messaging, and rebutting opposing views. Table 2.3 includes the Q-method statistics for each of the six strategies, which are elaborated and illustrated in the chapters that follow.

**Table 2.3**  Q-method statistics on the resulting six policy advocacy strategies

| Strategy | Schematic pathways | | | |
|---|---|---|---|---|
| | Eigen value | Variance explained | Organizations associated at 99% confidence | Organizations associated at 95% confidence |
| Public lobbying | *Policy advocacy* → *democracy, people-centered policies, effective policies* *Lobbying* → *policymakers' views* → *policy change* → *social/physical conditions* | | | |
| | 7.12 | 11% | 4 | 7 |
| Institutional partnership | *Coalitions, research, messaging, lobbying* → *policymakers' views* → *policy change* | | | |
| | 1.84 | 9% | 3 | 6 |
| Inside-outside | *(Information campaigns, media work, rebuttals) + (lobbying, coalitions)* → *policymakers' views* → *policy change* | | | |
| | 3.12 | 12% | 6 | 7 |
| Direct reform | *(Litigation, monitoring) + information campaign* → *policy change* → *social/physical conditions* | | | |
| | 2.95 | 11% | 3 | 7 |
| Indirect pressure | *Public's views, media, pilot programs* → *policymakers' views* → *policy change* → *social/physical conditions* | | | |
| | 1.52 | 8% | 3 | 5 |
| Popular power | *Coalitions, media work, rebuttals/debate* → *public views* → *policy agenda, change* → *social/physical conditions* *Coalitions, media work, rebuttals/debate* → *responsive policies/democracy* | | | |
| | 2.23 | 10% | 4 | 5 |

### Discussions

2a. The policy studies theories reviewed in this chapter highlight a tension about where political power lies in the US political system: institutional players, elites, or with the people. Have a class discussion or debate about which of the entities possesses the greatest share of political power in specific policy issues, using evidence to support your arguments.

2b. Logic models, like the one shown in Table 2.2, are often used to depict the inputs, activities, and outcomes associated with social programs serving a specific population. Do you think they are useful for planning policy advocacy—why or why not? How are the approaches to planning a social program similar to planning an advocacy campaign and how are they different?

2c. Do an Internet search to look for policy advocacy organizations active in your geographical area, or on a topic about which you are passionate. Which of the tactics described in this chapter relate to the organizations' work? Find 1–3 examples.

2d. In this study, Q-methodology was used to identify distinct viewpoints among advocates on how they influence policy change. Consider a nonprofit with which you are associated or familiar. Which viewpoint, and associated strategy, does it seem to hold? Your answer may span more than one viewpoint.

# References

Bardach, E. (1977). *The Implementation Game: What Happens After a Bill Becomes a Law*. Cambridge: MIT Press.

Bardach, E., & Patashnik, E. M. (2015). *A Practical Guide for Policy Analysis: The Eightfold Path to More Effective Problem Solving*. Thousand Oaks: CQ Press.

Baumgartner, F. R., & Leech, B. L. (1998). *Basic Interests: The Importance of Groups in Politics and in Political Science*. Princeton, NJ: Princeton University Press.

Berry, J. M. (1977). *Lobbying for the People: The Political Behavior of Public Interest Groups*. Princeton, NJ: Princeton University Press.

Birkland, T. (1997). *After Disaster: Agenda Setting, Public Policy, and Focusing Events*. Washington, DC: Georgetown University Press.

Bryson, J. M., & Anderson, S. R. (2000). Applying large-group interaction methods in the planning and implementation of major change efforts. *Public Administration Review, 60*(2), 143–153.

Busch, C. B., Kirp, D. L., & Schoenholz, D. F. (1998–1999). Rights, politics, and expertise: Righting the balance. *New York University Journal of Legislation and Public Policy, 2*(2), 247–263.

Cahn, M. A. (1995). The players: Institutional and noninstitutional actors in the policy process. In S. Z. Theodoulou & M. A. Cahn (Eds.), *Public Policy: The Essential Readings* (pp. 201–211). Englewood Cliffs, NJ: Prentice Hall.

Center for Responsive Politics. (2017). *Lobbying Database*. Retrieved from https://www.opensecrets.org/lobby/.

Chapman, J., & Wameyo, A. (2001). *Monitoring and Evaluating Advocacy: A Scoping Study*. ActionAid. Retrieved from http://www.actionaid.org/assets/pdf/Scoping%20 advocacy%20paper%202001.pdf.

Coffman, J., Hendricks, A., Kaye, J. W., Kelly, T., & Masters, B. (2007). *The Advocacy and Policy Change Composite Logic Model*. Seattle, WA: Advanced Practice Institute conducted at the 58th Annual Conference of the Council on Foundations. Retrieved from http://www.gse.harvard.edu/hfrp/eval/issue34/index.html.

Cooper, H. M. (1988). Organizing knowledge synthesis: A taxonomy of literature reviews. *Knowledge in Society, 1,* 104–126.

Dahl, R. A. (1967). *Pluralist Democracy in the United States: Conflict and Consent*. Chicago: Rand McNally.

Edelman, M. J. (1964). *The Symbolic Uses of Politics*. Champaign: University of Illinois Press.

Epstein, L., Kobylka, J. F., & Stewart, J. F. (1995). A theory of interest groups and litigation. In S. Nagel (Ed.), *Research in Law and Policy Studies*. Greenwich, CT: JAI Press.

Foner, E., & Garraty, J. A. (1991). *The Reader's Companion to American History*. New York: Houghton Mifflin Harcourt.

Gallagher, D. R., & Jackson, S. E. (2008). Promoting community involvement at brownfields sites in socio-economically disadvantaged neighborhoods. *Journal of Environmental Planning and Management, 51*(5), 615–630.

Ganz, M. (2009). *Why David Sometimes Wins*. New York: Oxford University Press.

Glaser, B., & Strauss, A. (1967). Grounded theory: The discovery of grounded theory. *Sociology the Journal of the British Sociological Association, 12,* 27–49.

Herman, E., & Chomsky, N. (2002). *Manufacturing Consent: The Political Economy of the Mass Media*. New York: Pantheon.

Hill, M., & Hupe, P. (2011). *Implementing Public Policy* (2nd ed.). London: Sage.

Hoefer, R. (2006). *Advocacy Practice for Social Justice*. Chicago: Lyceum Books.

Iyengar, S., & Kinder, D. (1987). *News That Matters*. Chicago: University of Chicago Press.

Jones, M. D., & McBeth, M. K. (2010). A narrative policy framework: Clear enough to be wrong? *Policy Studies Journal, 38*(2), 329–353.

Kagan, R. A. (1991). Adversarial legalism and American government. *Journal of Policy Analysis and Management, 10*(3), 369–406.

Kagan, R. A. (1998–1999). Adversarial legalism: Tamed or still wild? *New York University Journal of Legislation and Public Policy, 2*(2), 217–245.

Kastens, B., & Newig, J. (2008). Will participation foster the successful implementation of the water framework directive? The case of agricultural groundwater protection in Northwest Germany. *Local Environment, 13*(1), 27–41.

Kingdon, J. W. (1984). *Agendas, Alternatives and Public Policies*. New York: Longman.

Knowlton, L. W., & Phillips, C. C. (2009). *The Logic Model Guidebook: Better Strategies for Great Results*. Thousand Oaks: Sage.

Kraft, M. E., & Furlong, S. R. (2017). *Public Policy: Politics, Analysis, and Alternatives*. Washington, DC: CQ Press.

Lindblom, C. E. (1959). The science of muddling through. *Public Administration Review, 19*(Spring), 79–88.

Lindblom, C. E., & Cohen, D. K. (1979). *Usable Knowledge: Social Science and Social Problem Solving*. New Haven: Yale University Press.

Linsky, M. (1988). *Impact: How the Press Affects Federal Policy Making*. New York: W. W. Norton.

Lipsky, M. (2010). *Street-Level Bureaucracy: Dilemmas of the Individual in Public Services* (30th anniversary expanded ed.). New York: Russell Sage.

Majone, G. (1989). *Evidence, Argument and Persuasion in the Policy Process*. New Haven: Yale University Press.

McKeown, B., & Thomas, D. (1988). *Q Methodology* (Sage University Paper Series on Quantitative Applications in the Social Sciences, Series Number 07-066). Beverly Hills: Sage.

Mills, C. (1956). *The Power Elite*. New York: Oxford University Press.

Nachmias, D. (1980). The role of evaluation in public policy. *Policy Studies Journal, 8,* 1163–1169.

Nelson, B. J. (1986). *Making an Issue of Child Abuse*. Chicago: University of Chicago Press.

Nowlin, M. C. (2011). Theories of the policy process: State of the research and emerging trends. *Policy Studies Journal, 39*(S1), 41–60.

Olson, M. (1965). *The Logic of Collective Action: Public Goods and the Theory of Groups*. Cambridge, MA: Harvard University Press.

Pressman, J. L., & Wildavsky, A. B. (1984). *Implementation: How Great Expectations in Washington Are Dashed in Oakland; or, Why It's Amazing That Federal Programs Work at All, This Being a Saga of the Economic Development Administration as Told by Two Sympathetic Observers Who Seek to Build Morals on a Foundation of Ruined Hopes*. Berkeley: University of California Press.

Putnam, R. D. (1976). *The Comparative Study of Political Elites*. Upper Saddle River, NJ: Prentice Hall.

Ramage, J. D., & Bean, J. C. (1998). *Writing Arguments: A Rhetoric with Readings* (4th ed.). Boston: Allyn.

Riley, D. D., & Brophy-Baermann, B. E. (2006). *Bureaucracy and the Policy Process: Keeping the Promises*. Lanham, MD: Rowman & Littlefield.

Sabatier, P. A. (1988). An advocacy coalition framework of policy change and the role of policy-oriented learning therein. *Policy Sciences, 21,* 129–168.

Sabatier, P. A., & Jenkins-Smith, H. C. (1999). The advocacy coalition framework: An assessment. In P. A. Sabatier (Ed.), *Theories of the Policy Process* (pp. 117–166). Boulder, CO: Westview Press.

Schneider, A. L., & Ingram, H. M. (1993). Social construction of target populations: Implications for politics and policy. *The American Political Science Review, 87*(2), 334–347.

Simon, H. (1945). *Administrative Behavior: A Study of Decision Making Processes in Administrative Organizations*. Mankato, MN: Free Press.

Smith, G. E., & Huntsman, C. A. (1997). Reframing the metaphor of citizen-government relationship: A value-centered perspective. *Public Administration Review, 57*(4), 309–318.

Stone, D. A. (2002). *Policy Paradox: The Art of Political Decision Making* (Revised ed.). New York: W. W. Norton.

Theodoulou, S., & Kofinis, C. (2004). *The Art of the Game: Understanding American Public Policy Making*. Belmont, CA: Thomson Wadsworth.

Truman, D. (1993). *The Governmental Process: Political Interests and Public Opinion* (2nd ed.). Berkeley: University of California Press.

United States Department of Agriculture. (2014). *Supplemental Nutrition Assistance Program: A Short History of SNAP*. Retrieved from https://www.fns.usda.gov/snap/short-history-snap.

Walker, J. L. (1966). A critique of the elitist theory of democracy. *American Political Science Review, 60,* 285–295.

Watts, S., & Stenner, P. (2012). *Doing Q Methodological Research: Theory, Method & Interpretation*. Thousand Oaks, CA: Sage.

Weible, C., Sabatier, P., Jenkins-Smith, H., Nohrstedt, D., Henry, A. D., & deLeon, P. (2011). A quarter century of the advocacy coalition framework: An introduction to the special issue. *Policy Studies Journal, 39*(3), 349–360.

Weimer, D. L., & Vining, A. R. (1992). *Policy Analysis: Concepts and Practice* (2nd ed.). Englewood Cliffs, NJ: Prentice Hall.

Weiss, C. H., & Bucuvalas, M. J. (1980). Truth tests and utility tests: Decision-makers' frames of reference for social science research. *American Sociological Review, 45*(2), 302–313.

Wright, A. C., & Jaffe, K. (2013). *Six Steps to Successful Child Advocacy: Changing the World for Children*. Thousand Oaks, CA: Sage.

Xu, J. (2005). Why do minorities participate less? The effects of immigration, education, and electoral process on Asian American voter registration and turnout. *Social Science Research, 34*(4), 682–670.

# Public Lobbying

# 3

> We [advocates] have a tradition of going up to the building and screaming, but we need a different approach if we want to get inside the building and have a meeting.
> —Brad Erickson, Executive Director of Theatre Bay Area

In the morning of his first day at a new job as executive director of a regional theater arts nonprofit, Brad Erickson received a phone message marked urgent. The message wasn't even addressed to him by name, because he was new to the post. It was from the California Arts Council, an arts advocacy organization, asking Erickson to contact key state legislators to defend the state's arts budget against massive cuts. He had never done that kind of advocacy before, but understood that he had to quickly learn. "I was thrown into the fire." He did what little he could in the short-term, based upon guidance from his board members and senior staff, and based on his prior work in nonprofits. "These experiences were my training." That early effort was not successful, and the state—facing severe budget constraints—made massive cuts to its arts agency. On the other hand, Erickson learned that policy advocacy would be a major part of his job, and building relationships with lawmakers would be more effective than just making demands on them.

In the following years, Erickson grew into his job and embraced the policy advocacy part of it. Advocacy is important to his organization, which claims that "the performing arts are an essential public good, critical to a healthy and truly democratic society" (Theatre Bay Area, n.d., Who we are). Indeed, his organization's advocacy goals include making arts accessible to everyday people, not just the privileged, and to make arts education a part of students' school days. These goals require government funding, so he has to engage those policy processes that affect funding.

© The Author(s) 2020
S. Gen and A. C. Wright, *Nonprofits in Policy Advocacy*,
https://doi.org/10.1007/978-3-030-43696-4_3

It wasn't a smooth ride for Erickson. After the budget gash to the state's arts agency, Erickson worked with the California Arts Council to advocate for its restoration.[1] They advocated for the restoration, applying a strategy centered on lobbying: identify and develop a working relationship with a legislator who will sponsor and develop the bill; work with the appropriate legislative committee staff to hone the bill; "shop" the bill around the capital for co-sponsors; lobby legislative leadership and the governor's office; and testify at legislative hearings. When their proposal failed in their first year of advocacy, they tried again in the second year, finding new sponsors and updating the proposal to fit current budgetary and political circumstances. And when it failed in the second year, they tried again in the third. "It's a frustrating example" to talk about, said Erickson, "but in talking with my colleagues over time, as I've grown into this job, it's that pattern of persistence [that] eventually leads to success." Indeed, the state arts agency's budget has grown steadily since 2013, though it still lags behind 37 other states in level of arts public funding per capita (Brown 2018). So Erickson's lobbying work continues.

## The Public Lobbying Strategy

When we think about people who advocate for policy changes, a common image is the classic lobbyist. These are often individuals representing commercial interests that seek to gain and maintain economic advantage, and their key mode of influence is showering legislators with junkets and campaign funds, as depicted in Birnbaum's (1995) exposé. In our study of nonprofit policy advocates, however, we found a much deeper view of lobbying than that flat stereotype conveys. Nonprofits employing the public lobbying strategy view themselves as champions of public interest issues (not commercial) and engage the policy process in order to effect broad improvements in society (not private economic gain). Also, their lobbying tactics are different and more varied than those of Birnbaum's lobbyists.

The public lobbying strategy scored the highest eigenvalue (7.12) of all the strategies, indicating a strong explanatory power of this strategy among our advocacy organizations. Table 3.1 displays the factor array of the public lobbying strategy, and it clearly expresses the means and purposes of the strategy. Eight of nine statements rated +1 or higher focus on changing policymakers' views or

---

[1]Erickson is currently a board member of the California Arts Council.

**Table 3.1** Factor array for public lobbying strategy

| Tactic (advocacy activity and its expected outcome) | Factor array | Relative extreme |
|---|---|---|
| 02: Lobbying and building relationships with policymakers can change their views | +3 | High |
| 08: Policies can change social and physical conditions | +3 | High |
| 11: Policy advocacy in general builds legitimacy in a democracy | +2 | High |
| 22: Changes in policymakers' views can change policies | +2 | High |
| 24: Policy advocacy in general produces more effective policies | +2 | High |
| 01: Developing messages, framing issues, labeling and other strategies of rhetoric can change policymakers' views | +1 | |
| 06: Using the media to disseminate information can change policymakers' views | +1 | |
| 15: Research and analyses can change policymakers' views | +1 | |
| 16: Using the media to disseminate information can hasten policy change | +1 | |
| 10: Building coalitions and networks with like-minded organizations and individuals can change policymakers' views | 0 | |
| 12: Policy advocacy in general makes policymaking more people-centered | 0 | High |
| 19: Changes in the public's views can change policymakers' views | 0 | Low |
| 20: Developing messages, framing issues, labeling and other strategies of rhetoric can change the public's views | 0 | Low |
| 21: Public mobilizations (e.g., protests, letter writing campaigns, voter registration) can build democracy | 0 | |
| 23: Research and analyses can change the public's views | 0 | High |
| 04: Building coalitions and networks with like-minded organizations and individuals can change the public's views | −1 | Low |
| 07: Monitoring and evaluating existing policy can set the policy agenda | −1 | |
| 09: Using the media to disseminate information can change the public's views | −1 | Low |

(continued)

**Table 3.1** (continued)

| Tactic (advocacy activity and its expected outcome) | Factor array | Relative extreme |
|---|---|---|
| 13: Pilot programs and demonstration projects can lead to policy change | −1 | |
| 03: Monitoring and evaluating existing policy can change how it is implemented | −2 | Low |
| 05: Rebutting opposing views can change policymakers' views | −2 | |
| 14: Public mobilizations (e.g., protests, letter writing campaigns, rallies) can set the policy agenda | −2 | |
| 17: Litigation can change policy | −3 | Low |
| 18: Rebutting opposing views can change the public's views | −3 | Low |

*Note* See Chapter 2 for an explanation of the factor array scores

social outcomes, and they include all but one statement about how to change policymakers' views.

These advocates use lobbying (02:+3), framing and messaging (01:+1), media (06:+1), and research and analysis (15:+1) to sway policymakers. From our interviews with these nonprofit advocates, it was clear that the act of "lobbying" centered around *educating* policymakers about their issues, and it included these abovementioned activities. None of our interviewees described the material influences of Birnbaum's lobbyists. Public lobbying advocates generally avoid tactics to sway policymakers through building public support (10:0, 19:0). Indeed, all of the tactics aimed at swaying the *public's* views are rated 0 or lower (20:0, 23:0, 04:−1, 09:−1, 18:−3). Instead, these advocates' tactics focus on the *policymakers* because the policymakers are seen as the key component for policy change (22:+2), which in turn results in changes in social and physical conditions (08:+3). Their strategy is less confrontational than others (03:−2, 05:−2, 17:−3), preferring the development of long-term relationships with policymakers.

That said, one variation of this strategy uses existing public support to back policymakers, complementing lobbying efforts to educate them. This is subtly different than other strategies' use of public pressure to *sway* policymakers' decisions. Instead, public mobilization in this strategy is to provide decision makers with *cover* for their stances. One advocate described this as an "insider's game" in which he provided legislators with not only technical research to justify a policy, but also the public support to make the policy politically helpful for the

a. Policy advocacy → (democracy, people-centered policies, effective policies)
b. Lobbying → policymakers' views → policy change → social/physical conditions

**Fig. 3.1** Public lobbying strategy

legislators. Another variation is the target of the lobbying. While much of the lobbying targets legislators, this strategy is also applied to administrative processes. The two cases described later in this chapter each included this variation.

Public lobbying strategists see themselves as holding the public's trust on their issues. The factor array shows this in the high ratings for their policy advocacy in building legitimacy and democracy (11:+2) and producing more effective policies (24:+2). The issues they work on are consistent with this view and are generally those in which the public can benefit, but is not well informed or mobilized. For example, issues that public lobbyists promote include child welfare, juvenile justice, power supply, open lands, arts, etc. In these issues, public lobbyists view their jobs as advocates on behalf of the public's interests (Fig. 3.1).

## Theoretical Foundations

The distinguishing tenets of the public lobbying strategy are its focus on direct interaction with formal policymakers (e.g., legislators, administrators), and lobbying as its primary mode of interaction. Distinct strands of policy studies clearly support these tenets. One is institutionalism, which is the traditional view of policymaking that sees power in the policymaking process as concentrated in the government players who must formally select policies (Cahn 1995; Selznick 1996). It is a formal view of policymaking in which policies are outputs of the officials and their processes established by Constitution or law. While this view can support a variety of advocate tactics engaging policymakers, this strategy prefers lobbying through the development of congenial relationships. This, in turn, is clearly supported by a second group of studies represented by Walker's (1991) inside strategy and Baumgartner et al. (2009) study of lobbying. These writings describe advocates' building positive relationships with policymakers in order to influence them.

Indeed, in our study these advocates described building "one-on-one" relationships with policymakers and providing them with credible research and information to support proposals. One policy director described her job as a "teacher" of legislators, with whom she worked hard to build and maintain positive relationships.

Another described with pride her organization's reputation and relationships with city staff and council members, and those relationships allowed her to advocate for children's programming. Brad Erickson clearly explained the rationale behind these collegial relations when he said, "We [advocates] have a tradition of going up to the building and screaming, but we need a different approach if we want to get inside the building and have a meeting... You have to translate the urgency that makes you want to be loud and scream, and translate this into persistence and diplomacy."

A third strand of policy studies that resonate with this strategy, and makes it distinct from the more traditional lobbying by commercial interests, is theories of civic engagement in policy processes. The normative and descriptive theories on public engagement in policymaking claim that such engagement can legitimize the policy processes (deLeon 1992), make government more responsive to public concerns (Frederickson 1982; Nalbandian 1999), and produce policy outcomes that are more effective (e.g., Kastens and Newig 2008) and fair (e.g., Gallagher and Jackson 2008). Advocates employing the public lobbying strategy clearly embrace these views, even when compared with the popular power strategy (Chapter 8). This is evident in the factor array displayed in Table 3.1 and was clearly expressed in interviews with advocates using this strategy. A director of a land conservation organization described her organization as a trustee of national land, working to keep the land accessible for the whole public. A program director at a well-established child welfare organization situated her work on behalf of children who lack direct political influence. In these examples, the advocates have a strong sense of responsibility to represent the public's interest, even if they do not directly engage the public in their advocacy tactics.

## Current Usage

These core components of the public lobbying strategy are popular among advocacy organizations in general. Just over half of respondents to our national survey engage policy decision makers always or often. Public lobbying strategists complement that key tactic with research, issue framing, and media work, but only issue framing is done always or often by more than half of our respondents. Another key characteristic of the public lobbying strategy is its view that it works on behalf of public interests, especially those that are complex or not well mobilized. They expect their representation of those interests to result in real changes in people's conditions. Figure 3.2 shows the importance of three advocacy outcomes most closely related to this strategy. Among all the advocacy organizations we surveyed, clear majorities rated these outcomes as very or extremely important.

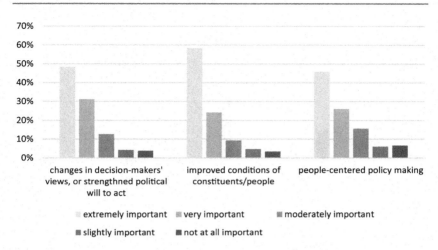

**Fig. 3.2** Importance of key outcomes in the public lobbying strategy

We cross-tabulated advocates who engage policy decision makers often or always with any of the three above expected outcomes of advocacy, to estimate the popularity of the public lobbying strategy among advocacy organizations. We focused just on the tactic of engaging policy decision makers because it is a defining tactic of this strategy. The other tactics displayed in Fig. 3.3 are complementary to the lobbying tactic. Of the 672 organizations that responded to the relevant questions in the survey, 47% (316) use the public lobbying strategy in some form often or always.[2] The following analyses compare these public lobbying strategists against those who do not use this strategy often.

Organizations using this strategy often or always view policy advocacy as central to their mission. As Fig. 3.4 illustrates, over 90% of public lobbying strategists rate their policy advocacy as very or extremely important. In contrast, only 62% of other organizations do. The importance of policy advocacy is also

---

[2]Note that a policy advocacy organization may use any number of strategies described in this book, so it may be included in the analyses of more than one strategy in Chapters 3–8. Therefore, the percentages of organizations using each of these strategies total more than 100%.

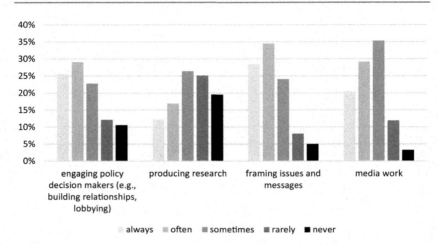

**Fig. 3.3**  Advocates' usage of key tactics in the public lobbying strategy

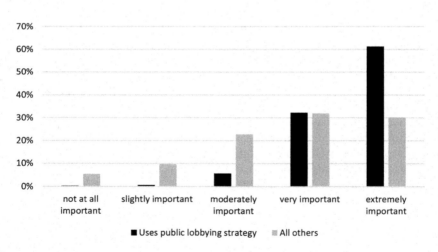

**Fig. 3.4**  Importance of policy advocacy to mission of public lobbying strategists (*Note* $\chi^2_{(4)} = 101.4, p = 0.00$)

reflected in the resources that organizations invest in it. Table 3.2 shows that public lobbyist strategists allocate significantly more staff time to policy advocacy, averaging 51%, compared to an average of 38% by other advocacy organizations

**Table 3.2** Resources devoted to policy advocacy by public lobbying strategists

|  | Staff devoted to policy advocacy (%) | Financial resources devoted to policy advocacy (%) |
| --- | --- | --- |
| Uses public lobbying often or always | Mean = 51<br>S.D. = 30 | Mean = 43<br>S.D. = 32 |
| All others | Mean = 38<br>S.D. = 33 | Mean = 35<br>S.D. = 34 |

$(t_{(522)} = 5.05, p = 0.00)$. Similarly, public lobbying strategists also allocate significantly more financial resources to their advocacy efforts, averaging 43% of their budgets, compared to 35% by all others $(t_{(519)} = 2.84, p = 0.01)$.

Figure 3.5 charts the proportions of advocacy organizations engaged in several policy issues, comparing the rates of public lobbying strategists to all others. Of course, advocacy organizations can engage in many different issues, so the sums for each of the two groups far exceed 100%. The chart shows that public lobbyists are most engaged in issues of health and mental health (50%), education (49%), social welfare and poverty (45%), and civil rights (41%). Those issues are also among the most popular among all advocacy organizations in our study, however, so we identified the issues in which public lobbying strategists are significantly more or less likely than others to engage. We confirmed that the public lobbying strategy is significantly more associated with some interests that can be considered in the public interest but complex or not well mobilized: social welfare and poverty (45% versus 31%, $\chi^2_{(1)} = 13.21$, $p = 0.00$), crime and criminal justice (41% versus 30%, $\chi^2_{(1)} = 9.11$, $p = 0.00$), housing and shelter (25% versus 17%, $\chi^2_{(1)} = 6.67$, $p = 0.01$), immigration and immigrants (24% versus 13%, $\chi^2_{(1)} = 13.06$, $p = 0.00$), transportation (19% versus 10%, $\chi^2_{(1)} = 13.03$, $p = 0.00$), and public safety and emergency preparedness (17% versus 10%, $\chi^2_{(1)} = 7.60$, $p = 0.01$). Other issues significantly more associated with public lobbying are health and mental health (50% versus 36%, $\chi^2_{(1)} = 13.30$, $p = 0.00$); civil rights (41% versus 30%, $\chi^2_{(1)} = 9.16$, $p = 0.00$); economy, jobs, and business (29% versus 14%, $\chi^2_{(1)} = 23.86$, $p = 0.00$); and taxes and monetary policy (12% versus 7%, $\chi^2_{(1)} = 5.02$, $p = 0.03$). One issue was significantly less associated with public lobbying than other strategies: arts, culture, and religion (9% versus 17%, $\chi^2_{(1)} = 9.28$, $p = 0.00$). Still, arts advocates were among the cases in this study who use this strategy.

An overwhelming majority of public lobbying strategists in our study target state governments, nearly doubling the rate of all other policy advocates (82% versus 45%, $\chi^2_{(1)} = 102.19$, $p = 0.00$). See Fig. 3.6. Public lobbying strategists

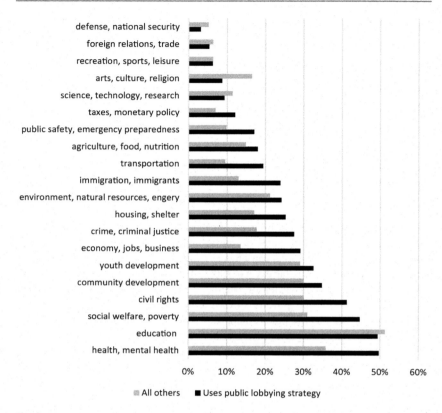

**Fig. 3.5**  Public issues engaged by public lobbying strategists

are also more likely than others to target local governments (65% versus 47%, $\chi^2_{(1)}=22.19$, $p=0.00$) and national governments (50% versus 31%, $\chi^2_{(1)}=24.23$, $p=0.00$). Very few using the public lobbying strategy target no government body (1% versus 19%, $\chi^2_{(1)}=63.33$, $p=0.00$), which is consistent with the strategy's focus on formal actors in the policy process. Turning to the branches of government targeted, public lobbying strategists are significantly more associated with each branch of government, when compared to all other advocates. See Fig. 3.7. They most target the legislative branch (88% versus 48%, $\chi^2_{(1)}=127.84$, $p=0.00$), followed by the bureaucracy (69% versus 38%, $\chi^2_{(1)}=64.27$, $p=0.00$), the executive branch (60% versus 26%, $\chi^2_{(1)}=77.76$, $p=0.00$), and the judicial branch (28% versus 16%, $\chi^2_{(1)}=15.98$, $p=0.00$).

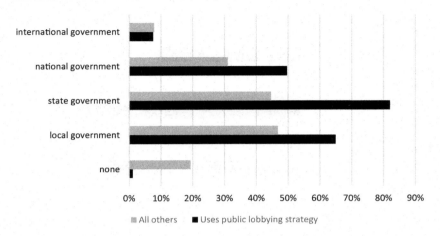

**Fig. 3.6** Levels of government targeted by public lobbying strategists

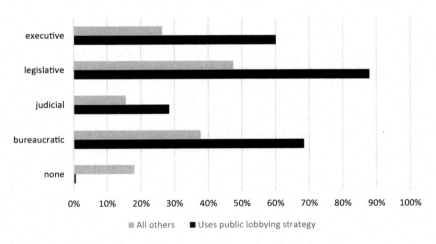

**Fig. 3.7** Branches of government targeted by public lobbying strategists

Lastly, the resources associated with organizations using this strategy also distinguish them. Compared to all other organizations, those employing the public lobbying strategy are more often membership organizations. See Fig. 3.8. They have higher rates of individual memberships (44% versus 33%, $\chi^2_{(1)} = 9.26$,

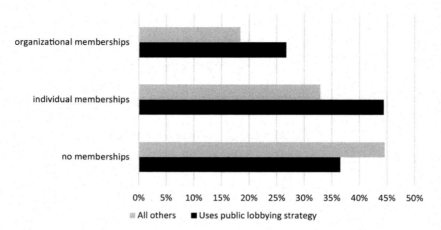

**Fig. 3.8** Memberships of public lobbying strategists

$p = 0.00$) and organizational memberships (27% versus 18%, $\chi^2_{(1)} = 6.61$, $p = 0.01$). Correspondingly, they have no memberships at a lower rate (37% versus 45%, $\chi^2_{(1)} = 4.57$, $p = 0.03$). These findings are somewhat surprising because of the strategy's lack of dependence on mobilizing supporters and coalitions. However, their use of this strategy does not preclude them also using other strategies, including those that depend more on memberships.

Finally, Fig. 3.9 compares the income levels of advocacy organizations using the public lobbying strategy with all others. The proportions of these strategists trail all others at all the income categories below $500,000, and they lead at all the income categories above $500,000. This might reflect the strategy's relative dependence on paid professional staff (e.g., government affairs, research, communications). Still, public lobbying strategists are amply represented at the lower income levels too.

Two cases that follow illustrate how the public lobbying strategy is implemented in diverse issues. The first tracks a human rights organization's continued efforts to fundamentally reform a state's juvenile justice system. The second relays the experiences of a nonprofit focused on making the complex regulations over power supplies (e.g., electricity, natural gas) more aligned with consumer interests.

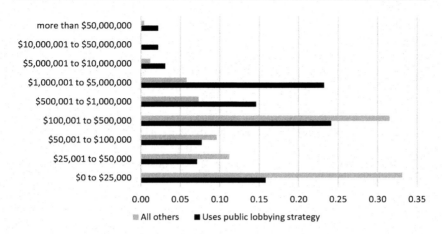

**Fig. 3.9**   2013 Income distribution of public lobbying strategists

## Books Not Bars

A distinguishing characteristic of the public lobbying strategy is the advocates' view that they work on behalf of the public's interests, especially when the public does not, or cannot, act on its own behalf. That trustee-like perspective is particularly applicable to issues related to vulnerable populations that lack their own mobilized political voice, such as children, the poor, or the incarcerated.

The Ella Baker Center for Human Rights is one organization that speaks for some of these populations, on behalf of the public's interests. It describes itself as a "strategy and action" nonprofit (Ella Baker Center for Human Rights, n.d., Books Not Bars), that advocates with "…Black, Brown, and low-income people to shift resources away from prisons and punishment, and towards opportunities that make our communities safe, healthy, and strong" (Ella Baker Center for Human Rights, n.d., About us). It was co-founded in 1996 by Van Jones, the activist, author, and current CNN television show host, who focused the center on making fundamental reforms in the American criminal justice system.

A centerpiece of this work is their ongoing "Books Not Bars" campaign in California. Its overarching goal is to replace that state's youth prison system, formerly known as the California Youth Authority (CYA), with effective local alternatives that are focused more on the restoration of the youths in their own communities than the removal and incarceration of the offenders. "The path to safer streets," the campaign claims, "starts with redirecting California's resources away from youth incarceration and towards youth opportunities" (Ella Baker Center for Human Rights, n.d., Books Not Bars).

The problems the campaign sees in the state's existing juvenile justice system are not unique to California. Rather, they reflect national trends over the last few decades. Box 3.1 highlights those trends and California's contributions to them. According to Weiss (2013), American juvenile justice has gone through four "waves" of reforms. The first covered the latter half of the 1800s, when the first juvenile courts were established and the states could take legal guardianship of youth offenders. In that era, youths were not considered completely responsible for their offending behaviors, so the states' goals were to rehabilitate the youths with training and education. The second wave, in the mid-1900s, established due process rights for youth offenders and put more accountability on the youths for their offenses. The California Youth Authority was established during this era. The third wave saw the tough-on-crime politics of the late 1900s extend to juvenile justice, with an emphasis on punishment and incarceration rather than rehabilitation. Mandatory minimum sentences proliferated, and prison populations rapidly grew. The CYA's inmate population grew to over 10,000 during this era (Commonweal 2014). The resulting public costs of incarceration, combined with recidivism rates that rose with the lack of rehabilitation, led to the forth and current wave. It refocuses criminal justice, and juvenile justice in particular, toward greater public safety and cost savings by emphasizing the restoration of offenders into productive members of society. In California, this means less reliance on incarcerating youth in CYA prisons, and more reliance on smaller community-based programs aimed at rehabilitation.

---

### Box 3.1 Juvenile Justice Reforms in the United States and California

Overview: The evolution of the juvenile justice system in the United States has passed through four "waves," highlighted below. California's recent history parallels the waves of the national reforms, with organizations like the Ella Baker Center for Human Rights playing key roles in the movement into the fourth wave.

National eras in juvenile justice (Weiss            California Youth Authority's history
2013):

First wave: "child savers" (late 1800s to
early 1900s)

- Children are less responsible for their actions than adults, so adult punishments are not warranted
- First juvenile court established in 1899
- State could be guardian of young offenders
- Rehabilitative approach, in home-like care facilities

- Youth offenders sent to several state-sponsored "reform schools" that focused on trade training and academics (California Department of Corrections and Rehabilitation 2019)

Second wave: due process rights (middle 1900s)

- Actions of juvenile courts criticized as arbitrary, unfair, and informal
- Youth offenders get due process rights
- Juveniles become more accountable for their actions

- CYA established in 1943, when management of three reform schools were transferred to the CYA (California Department of Corrections and Rehabilitation 2019)

Third wave: "backlash" (late 1900s)

- Tough-on-crime politics results in punitive laws; mandatory minimum sentences focused on the offense rather than the offender
- Focus on rehabilitation abandoned; replaced by focus on confinement in secure facilities
- Recidivism became the norm
- Youth of color disproportionately affected

- CYA's focus turns to incarceration. Inmate population peaked in 1996 with over 10,000 juvenile offenders in 11 institutions (Commonweal 2014)
- Youth of color reached 84% of CYA's inmate population (Witness and Books Not Bars 2004)

Fourth wave: youth development (early 2000s)

- High costs of incarceration, combined with high recidivism, led to focus on public safety and positive outcomes for youth offenders
- Young offenders held accountable in developmentally appropriate ways
- Balance youth development, personal accountability, and public safety

- CYA's recidivism rate reached 90% in early 2000s (Anderson et al. 2005)
- Senate Bill 81 (2007) transferred major juvenile justice responsibilities to counties (Commonweal 2014)
- All but 3 youth prisons closed, reducing inmate population to less than 800 in 2013 (Commonweal 2014)

From its start, the Ella Baker Center has been an active advocate for this fourth wave reform of the juvenile justice system in California, through its Books Not Bars campaign. Jennifer Kim led this effort when she was the center's California Justice Director. Trained as an attorney, Kim directed the center's policy work, conducted its legal research, and drafted legislation that the center sponsored in this campaign. This work also required her to cultivate diverse working relationships, not only with legislators, but also with the families of incarcerated youth, to identify the needed reforms that could help restore their youths into productive lives outside of prison, and to get their testimonies heard by legislators. When we met with Kim, she had been working on the Books Not Bars campaign for six years.

The center sees a fundamental flaw in the CYA—known today as the Department of Juvenile Justice—which requires reform. Reflecting the third wave of criminal justice reforms in the United States, the CYA relates to youth offenders as prisoners to be incarcerated and punished. Their physical design, for example, is large centralized warehouse facilities that are "virtually indistinguishable from adult prisons" (Anderson et al. 2005, p. 3). Furthermore, their large size induces anonymity of the youth, which catalyzes more use of force to control their behaviors. Their remote locations also hinder full family involvement, further exacerbating the youths' anonymity. These conditions, focused on imprisonment rather than rehabilitation, contributed to a 90% recidivism rate.

The interpersonal dynamics within the facilities also reflect the third wave viewpoint. According to a 2003 CYA-authorized assessment of their facilities—commissioned in response to a lawsuit filed against the CYA—violence among the youths and against the youths permeates the prisons. Dr. Barry Krisberg, author of the assessment, described the conditions in subsequent legislative hearings. "To me the overriding issue that drives so many of the problems that I observed was the issue of violence. The amount of violence in the California Youth Authority has been allowed to deteriorate to unprecedented levels" (Witness and Books Not Bars 2004). Furthermore, the lack of adequate educational and health services in the facilities diminish the youths' prospects of successful transition after release. Said Krisberg, "We as citizens of this state interested in public safety have a vested interest in making that return home as safe and as positive as we can." Instead, the CYA was making society less safe. Van Jones explained it this way:

> Young people and adults in prison have been thrown away... Once they're outside the circle of people who deserve dignity and respect, then they can be preyed upon... It also destroys communities. When you take a young parent away from a family, leaving behind a two year old who takes years off the lives of grandparents, and then throw that person back into the community with no resources, you're not helping the family reintegrate the person. You're making the community worse. You're making it harder for families to recover from the mistakes anybody makes. (Townsend, n.d.)

With such deeply rooted flaws in the structures and operations of the CYA, the Ella Baker Center for Human Rights seeks not to improve the facilities, but to dismantle them and replace them with alternative programs. "The main objective is to close the Division of Juvenile Justice... the state-run youth prison system," said Jennifer Kim. "California was investing hundreds of millions of dollars each year in a broken system, where we had skyrocketing recidivism rates, poor youth outcomes, and really inhuman conditions." She went on, "The only solution we saw was that we needed to close the system, and look at models working in other states, and try to bring them to California."

At least 10 other state had already begun closing their centralized youth prisons in favor of small-group, community-based rehabilitation centers, which are showing lower recidivism rates and lower costs of operation (Anderson et al. 2005). Missouri, for example, had made such reforms decades earlier and reduced their expenditures per youth offender to "about half" that of California, while decreasing its recidivism rate to 15%. Kim noted that Missouri's success was due in part to that state's transfer of their juvenile justice system from their Department of Corrections to their Department of Health and Human Services, thereby changing their approach to the youth offenders.

The Books Not Bars campaign's solutions for California's system do allow the removal of some youth offenders from the public, but far fewer, and into restorative environments. Most youth offenders, however, could be diverted from incarceration altogether. "America has done such an incredible job of incarcerating people," explained Vincent Shiraldo of Washington DC's Department of Youth Rehabilitation Services, "but the goal of the system is not to have more inmates. It's to have fewer victims. It is about the best way to make our society safe" (Books Not Bars Campaign 2010). That goal can often be served by community alternatives to incarceration. During the pre-adjudication phase, the accused youths could be screened to determine who really should be detained and who could be simply monitored through reporting stations or other mechanisms that allow the youths to be supported by their families. During post-adjudication, screening could identify programs that are most appropriate for each youth's needs and the public's safety. Incarceration would still be an option for those that posed a threat to public safety, but their time separated from the public would be focused on rehabilitation rather than isolation. Missouri's model of therapeutic secure care, for example, uses small facilities near their communities, in which the youths have structured group discussions and access to educational services, health services, and life skills workshops. Most youth offenders, however, would be diverted from incarceration into community-based alternatives like in-home family services, therapeutic group homes, treatment foster care, or more contact with social workers.

To support all these reforms, the Ella Baker Center for Human Rights relies on lobbying as a primary tactic. Their lobbying team consisted of three attorneys, plus two mothers of incarcerated youth who helped the center develop a network of families of incarcerated youth. That network, in turn, helped the center communicate their message to legislators and the public.

The center's brand of lobbying has two key characteristics. The first is that it is focused on education. "So many people don't know about the juvenile justice system," explained Kim, "so there was a huge educational component to the campaign." For example, she estimated that a recent election resulted in thirty percent new members in the state's legislature,[3] all of whom needed to be educated on the CYA and issues in juvenile justice. So those new legislators become the center's students. Drafting relevant bills is a key way the center establishes relationships with new legislators. The bills become opportunities to reach out to legislators and to recruit sponsors for them. "We view bills not as the only way we can be successful," Kim said. "Sometimes it's a way for us to educate the new legislators...." They also produced two films that they use to educate policymakers and the public. The first, *System Failure: Violence, Abuse, and Neglect in the California Youth Authority* (Witness and Books Not Bars 2004), profiled the experiences of CYA inmates and their families. The second, *Learning from Our Mistakes: Transforming the Juvenile Justice System* (Books Not Bars Campaign 2010), looks at the successes of other states' reforms of their youth prison systems. The center hosted screenings of the films with local politicians and other stakeholders of the juvenile justice system.

The second characteristic of the center's lobbying is that it is strategic. They tailor their lobbying to specific targets, based upon the specific outcome they seek from each. Jones compared this style of lobbying to combat. "There's a way of being in conflict like a barbarian, and a way of being in conflict like a ninja. I think that we need a lot more ninja energy and a lot less barbarian energy. When it's time to fight, you want to be as surgical and precise with your intervention as you possibly can. You want to use just as much conflict as required, just as much force as required and no more. There's a call for a wise kind of warrior" (Townsend, n.d.). For example, the center often lobbies legislators with reform bills they draft. But they also do budget advocacy with legislators, because much

---

[3]California has term limits on its legislators.

of any policy's impact is predicated on its funding level. Kim concedes, however, that this can be a more challenging route to reform for policy advocates. "The issue with budget advocacy is it's just not as transparent and linear as just sponsoring a bill. You build your relationships [with legislators], you give your suggestions to someone, and then you don't know what happens until the budget comes out. It's a more challenging space for everyday people to get engaged, even for folks who do regular policy advocacy."

The center also lobbies agencies to change regulations and procedures in the prisons. Kim explained, "In juvenile justice work, there are certain policies that are institutional, that don't have to go through the rigorous process of a legislature. It's more administrative. So we contact the heads of these specific departments... and recommend specific changes." It's not easy to do, because it requires a lot of relationship building with the administrators to establish that trust. Plus, this kind of lobbying regularly faces opposition. The prison guard union has been the center's most consistent opposition.

The center also organizes families and communities of the youth offenders to support their educational efforts with legislators. Their experiences add a human dimension to the fiscal and statistical arguments for reform. Kim explained, "I've always viewed all of those components as elements of one strategy. If I'm just behind my computer working on legislation and research, that's really just for one particular type of audience, and it doesn't really reach the people who will put the pressure on the legislators, or the people behind the bars who can provide the stories."

The Books Not Bars campaign is ongoing, but the center already claims substantial progress. The measures of success are very clear to Kim, because some of the outcomes can be quantified. Most importantly, she wants to see reductions in the numbers of youth in prisons and closures of youth prisons. She feels good about their progress so far. When she started work in this campaign, there were eight youth prisons in the state with a total population of about 4500 youth in them. When we spoke with her in 2011, only three of those prisons remained open with about 800 youth. "I'm not going to say it was all because of us—there was a concerted effort with everyone working on it—but we've been very consistent with our message of closure." Kim certainly took these as a victories and as measures of their work's success. In the intermediate term, while pushing for prison closures, the center looks at the reductions in the populations of youths in prisons. Those reductions precede facility closures, so they make good metrics of progress. They also track local practices, like counties that support local alternatives to the state prisons. "It's been a remarkable process, and the timeline seems relatively quick considering where we started," Kim reflected. "It's just a matter of time now, and there's a general sense in the legislature that the system isn't effective and is actually very harmful. It's more about *how* do we close them down in a responsible way, rather than should we do it."

## "Power Grab"

A mobilized public voice is not limited only by level of social capital, as it often is for youth and criminal offenders. It can also be limited by the complexity of the policy issue and the deep investment of time and learning required to understand an issue enough to engage it politically. When such barriers prevent broad public engagement, the public lobbying strategy can be advantageous by focusing on mobilization of decision makers rather than the general public.

One such policy issue in the United States is electricity provision. The country's power grid is a "complex machine" consisting of over 7300 power plants and millions of miles of power lines operating under many and varied markets and regulatory structures (U.S. Environmental Protection Agency 2017). Individual states establish the retail electricity markets for their jurisdictions, and most have chosen "traditionally regulated" retail markets in which consumers do not choose their providers and are required to purchase electricity from the jurisdiction's provider. Eighteen states, however, have competitive retail electricity markets in which consumers can choose their electricity provider and sometimes even electricity generation options, like renewable sources (e.g., solar, wind).

In California, the situation is even more complex, because its competitive retail market includes public and private utilities competing under different regulatory constraints. About two-thirds of Californians get their electricity from private, for-profit, investor-owned utility companies, which are required to provide service to everyone in their service areas and are regulated by the California Public Utilities Commission (Secretary of State 2010). The largest of these companies is Pacific Gas & Electric (PG&E). Most of the other third are served by local, publically owned utilities such as water and power districts and municipal utility districts. When a local government wants to start-up a publically owned utility or expand its services into areas currently served by private utilities, the state often requires a majority vote of those in the proposed new service area. But it generally does not require any vote of those in the existing area of the public utility. As local governments and public utilities considered these options, private utilities saw threats to their market share of electricity customers.

To minimize the threat, PG&E spearheaded an effort to amend the state's Constitution to make it more difficult for public electricity providers to start-up or expand into territory currently served by privately electricity providers (Ballot-pedia, n.d.). The proposal was Proposition 16, which appeared on the June 2010 ballot. Proposition 16 aimed to curb the expansion of public utilities by requiring a 2/3 supermajority approval by voters in both the existing service area and the new or expanded service area, before a public utility could start or expand their service area (Secretary of State 2010). The proposition was placed on the ballot through California's initiative process. A petition management companied was paid over $2 million by proponents to collect 694,354 valid signatures to qualify for the ballot (Ballotpedia, n.d.). The campaign was largely funded by PG&E, which contributed $46.1 million to the effort. Proponents framed the proposition as the "Taxpayers Right to Vote Act" (Secretary of State 2010), saying that "... taxpayers should have the final say in how government spends our money."

The proposition didn't sit well with Dr. Mark Toney. He is executive director of The Utility Reform Network (TURN), a nonprofit organization that advocates for fair utilities rates, cleaner energy, and consumer projections in California. The advocates for Proposition 16 were promoting it as an issue of voters' rights, but Toney saw it as an attempt to reduce private electricity providers' competition from public providers. "What PG&E was trying to do was to cripple public power as an option for people, and we think that the existence of public power makes the private utilities have to compete for customers and price," he explained. "The public power agencies generally charge less and give better service than companies like PG&E, so it was really to preserve options for consumers that we fought it." He worried that without their opposition, the proposition might pass and reduce consumer choice. He explained, "Consumers can't tell on their own what's good" in policies on electricity supply. Instead, "The grassroots depend on us to have expertise on the policy." Therefore, TURN "fights against regulation in the corporate interest, and fights for regulations in the public interest. That is the framework that guides our work."

Toney came to TURN in 2008, after leading other nonprofits. He studied political science at Brown University and completed a Ph.D. in sociology from the University of California, Berkeley. He founded a nonprofit focused on social welfare issues, and he was executive director of another in which he organized communities around issues of social justice (The Utility Reform Network 2011). He sees his current work with TURN as being very similar. "I still think of myself as an organizer."

The policy issues that TURN primarily engages are energy regulation, telecommunications regulation, consumer rights, and some water resources issues. Their policy advocacy work generally targets the state legislature and the California Public Utilities Commission, the regulatory agency that oversees utilities services. "So much of policy is not made legislatively. It's administrative, [with] all these administrative departments. People have no idea how big the PUC is... They have so many hearings and proceedings that they have forty full-time administrative law judges." Toney said that TURN participates in about 115 PUC proceedings per year. The proceedings cover a wide variety of topics such as energy rates, energy efficiency, renewable energy, and consumer protections.

Despite TURN's portfolio, the case of Proposition 16 presented a unique challenge to the organization: It was not a bill in the legislature, or a regulation in an agency. It was, instead, a ballot initiative that would be decided by the voting public. Who does the public lobbying strategist lobby in this case? The public becomes the legislative body, but lobbying the public on a complex issue could not be done in the same relational ways typical of lobbying state assembly members or agency administrators. Instead, they would lean on the other tactics of public lobbying strategy—particularly framing, messaging, and media work—focusing them on the opinion leaders that the public would trust on this issue.

Toney chaired the statewide "No On 16" campaign, with a steering committee of six people who met weekly, and a volunteer pool of about 25–30 people. The campaign was only able to raise about $130,000 to fund their fight, compared to PG&E's $46.1 million contribution to support the proposition (Ballotpedia, n.d.). "PG&E had enough money to buy television, newspaper ads, send out mailings. We didn't have money for all of that," admitted Toney. It was clear to him that their campaign could not fight PG&E in those mediums. Instead, "...we needed to go after opinion leaders because we didn't have the money to do direct voter contact."

Their campaign lobbied editorial boards, labor unions, chambers of commerce, and other organizations that could sway the opinions of their members. "Every group that endorses us," Toney explained, "is telling their members, they're communicating with their own members, on what to do." He elaborated,

"We got the editorial endorsements of sixty-three newspapers in California, [while] PG&E got three. They claimed to have the support of labor, because they had one union supporting them. We ended up with several labor councils. They had the endorsement of the California Chamber of Commerce. That's how they claimed they had business support. We got the support of twelve chambers of commerce... to break ranks with their state body. That is very unusual... So part of our strategy was to go after their core. We undermined their claims of who supported them."

To earn these endorsements, the No On 16 campaign relied on messaging that succinctly clarified the complex issue. "We were very clearly able to use the 'corporate versus public interest' as a theme throughout the campaign... We got the media to be able to understand what was going on and to gain their support, to gain their editorial support." They used carefully developed messages to negatively brand the proposition as narrowing competition to the benefit of private suppliers.

This tactic is rooted in social science. "Basically, the Benford and Snow framing theory is what I use all the time," explained Toney. Toney has a doctorate in sociology, and his advocacy is guided by his studies on social movements. He was referring to Robert Benford and David Snow's conceptualization of the roles, processes, and outcomes of *issue framing* in social movements. According to Benford and Snow (2000), issue framing constructs meaning for the public on a social problem, its causes, its solutions, and reasons for the public to become engaged. In the case of Proposition 16, a complex proposal whose legal content is challenging to decipher, Toney's campaign needed clear and compelling framing that would resonate with voters and compel them to act. They pushed phrases like "monopoly protection," and the double entendre "power grab."

It was also important for the campaign to get the endorsements of organizations that span the political spectrum. Liberal groups might already be inclined to oppose a proposition sponsored by a large corporation, so the No On 16 campaign had to also focus on more conservative groups. Toney explained, "The business list is the most powerful part of the entire thing because in some ways, the other [supporters] aren't terribly surprising. The Sierra Club? Give me a break! That's not going to shock anybody. But some of those business organizations?" His list included the California Association of Realtors, California Manufacturers & Technology Association, California Farm Bureau, and several chambers of commerce. The campaign also targeted more conservative geographies of the state. "We talked about the need to reach Southern California... We fought with people internally who wanted to waste a lot of time and energy doing literature drops at farmers' markets in the Bay Area, and we're like... that ain't gonna happen! We got the Bay Area, it's over in the Bay Area. The fight's in Southern California." The campaign successfully secured the endorsements of the major newspapers and chambers of commerce in San Diego and other areas of the state that lean toward the political right.

**Key Endorsements in the No On 16 Campaign (No On Prop 16, 2010)**

Overview: To fight a ballot proposition, the No On 16 campaign could not lobby individual voters. Instead, they lobbied opinion leaders across the political spectrum, but concentrated on more conservative organizations. Below are examples of key endorsements the campaign secured.

Newspaper editorial boards
- Los Angeles Times
- San Francisco Chronicle
- Sacramento Bee
- San Jose Mercury News
- San Diego Union Tribune
- Bakersfield Californian
- Fresno Bee

Civic organizations
- California Democratic Party
- Republican Party of Los Angeles County
- American Association of Retired Persons
- League of Women Voters of California
- Consumer Federation of California
- California Tax Reform Association
- Consumer Attorneys of California
- Lutheran Office of Public Policy

Business organizations
- California Association of Realtors
- California Manufacturers & Technology Association
- San Diego Chamber of Commerce
- South Orange County Chamber of Commerce
- California Farm Bureau

Labor unions
- California Federation of Labor
- State Building & Construction Trades Council
- California Federation of Teachers
- California Nurses Association

Environmental organizations
- Sierra Club California
- California League of Conservation Voters
- Earth Island Institute

Their strategy was ultimately successful. Proposition 16 was defeated by the voters, 52.8–47.2% (Ballotpedia, n.d.). Furthermore, the campaign brought much attention to TURN. "Big time!" said Toney. "A lot of people, a lot of groups, saw TURN in a new light after the campaign, especially the public power community, whose hands were tied. PG&E can put as much money as it wants into the campaign. [Public utilities] are prohibited by statute from contributing one penny, so they really saw us as doing the work they couldn't do." Toney sees how that campaign helped him in his continuing effort to develop TURN to a major player in public policy. "The vision I have for TURN is for TURN to drive the public debate and policy outcomes on energy and telecom in California, and provide leadership to U.S. policy in those areas."

## Discussions

3a. Nonprofits that use the public lobbying strategy view themselves as champions of *public goods and interests* that have broad public benefit but are often complex or lack mobilized political representation. Examples of such public goods and interests in this chapter include arts, juvenile justice and restoration, and public utilities. Describe a public good or interest that is complex or may lack an active political voice. What makes it a complex issue? Why does it lack its own political voice? Identify some nonprofits that may be advocating on its behalf.

3b. The key tactic of this strategy is lobbying, in its broadest terms. For the issue you described above, identify policymakers who could be the focus of advocates' lobbying. In which level and branch of government are they? Describe lobbying activities that might be effective with these policymakers.

3c. While lobbying is a popular tactic among multiple strategies, its application in the public lobbying strategy is differentiated by an accompanying viewpoint that the advocate works on behalf of public interests, and their work enhances democratic values. Meanwhile, lobbyists for commercial interests may use similar tactics, but do so on behalf of private economic interests. Do the differences in viewpoints make any difference in the tactic? Do they effect the outcomes, or the meanings of the outcomes? Explain.

3d. Public lobbying strategists that we interviewed took pride in the collegial relationships they developed with key policymakers, and they generally avoid antagonistic approaches. Why might this approach be more effective, and what are the potential drawbacks?

# References

Anderson, C. L., Macallair, D., & Ramirez, C. (2005). *California Youth Authority Warehouses: Failing Kids, Families & Public Safety.* Oakland, CA: Books Not Bars.

Ballotpedia. (n.d.). *California Proposition 16, Supermajority Vote Required to Create a Community Choice Aggregator (June 2010).* Retrieved from https://ballotpedia.org/California_Proposition_16,_Supermajority_Vote_Required_to_Create_a_Community_Choice_Aggregator_(June_2010).

Baumgartner, F. R., Berry, J. M., Hojnacki, M., Kimball, D. C., & Leech, B. L. (2009). *Lobbying and Policy Change: Who Wins, Who Loses, and Why.* Chicago: University of Chicago Press.

Benford, R. D., & Snow, D. A. (2000). Framing processes and social movements: An overview and assessment. *Annual Review of Sociology, 26,* 611–639.

Birnbaum, J. (1995). *The Lobbyists: How Influence Peddlers Get Their Way in Washington.* New York: Random House.

Brown, K. (2018). *State Budget Includes $8.8 Million One-Time Increase in California Arts Council Funding.* California Arts Council. Retrieved from http://www.arts.ca.gov/news/prdetail.php?id=268.

Cahn, M. A. (1995). The players: Institutional and noninstitutional actors in the policy process. In S. Z. Theodoulou & M. A. Cahn (Eds.), *Public Policy: The Essential Readings* (pp. 201–211). Englewood Cliffs, NJ: Prentice Hall.

California Department of Corrections and Rehabilitation. (2019). *The History of the Division of Juvenile Justice.* Sacramento: California Department of Corrections and Rehabilitation. Retrieved from https://www.cdcr.ca.gov/juvenile-justice/history/.

Campaign, B. N. B. (2010). *Learning from Our Mistakes: Transforming the Juvenile Justice System.* Oakland, CA: Ella Baker Center for Human Rights.

Commonweal. (2014). *Overview: California's Comprehensive Youth Corrections Realignment Reform.* Bolinas, CA: Commonweal Juvenile Justice Program. Retrieved from http://www.comjj.org/realignment/issue-overview/.

deLeon, P. (1992). The democratization of the policy sciences. *Public Administration Review, 52*(2), 125–129.

Ella Baker Center for Human Rights. (n.d.). *About Us.* Oakland, CA: Ella Baker Center for Human Rights. Retrieved from https://ellabakercenter.org/about/about-us.

Ella Baker Center for Human Rights. (n.d.). *Books Not Bars: An Ella Baker Center Campaign.* Oakland, CA: Ella Baker Center for Human Rights.

Frederickson, H. G. (1982). The recovery of civism in public administration. *Public Administration Review, 42*(6), 501–507.

Gallagher, D. R., & Jackson, S. E. (2008). Promoting community involvement at brownfields sites in socio-economically disadvantaged neighborhoods. *Journal of Environmental Planning and Management, 51*(5), 615–630.

Kastens, B., & Newig, J. (2008). Will participation foster the successful implementation of the water framework directive? The case of agricultural groundwater protection in Northwest Germany. *Local Environment, 13*(1), 27–41.

Kim, J. (n.d.). *Division of Juvenile Justice Fact Sheet.* Oakland, CA: Ella Baker Center for Human Rights.

Nalbandian, J. (1999). Facilitating community, enabling democracy: New roles for local government managers. *Public Administration Review, 59*(3), 187–197.

No On Prop 16. (2010, May 20). *No on Prop 16 Key Endorsements.* Pamphlet. Sacramento, CA: No On Prop 16 Stop the PG&E Powergrab.

Secretary of State. (2010). Prop 16. *Tuesday, June 8, 2010, Official Voter Information Guide.* Sacramento: California Secretary of State. Retrieved from http://vigarchive.sos.ca.gov/2010/primary/propositions/16/.

Selznick, P. (1996). Institutionalism 'Old' and 'New'. *Administrative Science Quarterly, 41*(2), 270–277.

The Utility Reform Network. (2011). *Mark Toney.* San Francisco, CA: The Utility Reform Network. Retrieved from http://www.turn.org/staff-board/mark-toney/.

Theatre Bay Area. (n.d.). *Who We Are*. Retrieved from https://www.theatrebayarea.org/page/WhoWeAre.

Townsend, L. (n.d.). A license to be human: An interview with Van Jones. *Orion Magazine*. Retrieved from https://orionmagazine.org/article/a-license-to-be-human/.

U.S. Environmental Protection Agency. (2017). *U.S. Electricity Grid & Markets*. Retrieved from https://www.epa.gov/greenpower/us-electricity-grid-markets.

Walker, J. L. (1991). *Mobilizing Interest Groups in America: Patrons, Professions, and Social Movements*. Ann Arbor: University of Michigan Press.

Weiss, G. (2013). *The Fourth Wave: Juvenile Justice Reforms for the Twenty-First Century*. Washington, DC: National Campaign to Reform State Juvenile Justice Systems. Retrieved from https://nicic.gov/fourth-wave-juvenile-justice-reforms-twenty-first-century.

Witness and Books Not Bars. (2004). *System Failure: Violence, Abuse, and Neglect in the California Youth Authority*. Oakland, CA: Ella Baker Center for Human Rights.

# Institutional Partnership

**4**

We're trying to model more positive approaches to solving crime problems.
—Laura Magnani, Assistant Regional Director of the American Friends Service Committee.

To Jessica Gunderson, *summer slide* isn't a children's playground structure. It's a pernicious problem affecting students from low-income communities, and it was a main target of her work when she was the policy director for Partnership for Children & Youth (PCY). *Summer slide* refers to the well-established pattern of learning gains during the school year followed by learning losses during the summer when students are separated from academic settings (Perry et al. 2018). This learning loss disproportionately affects students from lower-income communities whose access to summer camps and other enrichment programs is less than those from wealthier neighborhoods. While students of all backgrounds generally make similar learning gains during the school year, students from higher-income communities maintain or build upon those gains during the summer through enrichment programs, while students from lower-income communities lose some of those gains and start the following school year with a learning deficit. That deficit starts small in lower grades, but accumulates through the years, resulting in wide achievement gaps in the upper grades. The summer slide also affects the health of lower-income students, due to lost access to school-based nutrition and exercise during summers.

The disproportionate impacts of summer slide made it a key focus for PCY, a nonprofit focused on supporting children in low-income communities in California to have high-quality educational opportunities and to be successful in them. Their advocacy work focuses on "everything outside the classroom," said Gunderson. So they don't work on curricular issues, but rather co-curricular and extra-curricular supports for children and their families that help children in their

© The Author(s) 2020
S. Gen and A. C. Wright, *Nonprofits in Policy Advocacy*,
https://doi.org/10.1007/978-3-030-43696-4_4

learning. These whole-student supports include nutrition, health services, mental health services, and enrichment programs like preschool, after school, and summer school programs.

Gunderson joined PCY in 2011 to manage its policy advocacy work. She brought to the organization her research and planning experiences in nonprofits, and policy experience on the staff of a state legislator. Her experiences were complemented with academic training that includes an MPA degree from New York University. At PCY, Gunderson led their Summer Matters campaign that envisions all California students in low-income communities to have access to high-quality summer programming (Partnership for Children & Youth, n.d., Summer Learning). According to PCY, these communities are "vastly underutilizing" available public funding streams that could support children's educational and social development (Partnership for Children & Youth, n.d., History). So their aim is to link school districts with resources and community-based organizations and to advocate for state and national policies that support such partnerships (Partnership for Children & Youth, n.d., About PCY).

The Summer Matters campaign was originally conceived from research that PCY had conducted on summer opportunity gaps. To measure the prevalence of summer slide, PCY worked with a school boards association to survey superintendents about summer programming in their districts. With the resulting data, they mapped 1700 school sites across California with summer programs and identified geographic gaps representing communities most in need of summertime opportunities for children.

At the underserved communities, PCY's strategy is to help plan and pilot summer programs that the local schools can sustain on their own. Rather than lobby schools and districts to address summer slide on their own, as a public lobbying strategist might, PCY's approach was to partner with schools and local youth serving agencies to design and implement programs at the local level. Gunderson explained that they want these schools to "adopt our vision of summer" and follow their pilot of how it can be implemented through partnerships with local organizations.

PCY developed pilot summer programs with low-income communities, using funding from a multi-year grant they received from the Packard Foundation. Their pilots were focused on elementary and middle schools, rather than high school, to mitigate achievement gaps when they are relatively small. In these communities, PCY conducted local research on services already present and prioritized unmet needs. They then developed local networks of technical assistance and service providers that could work with their local schools. By demonstrating how such programming can be established in low-income communities, and the academic benefits of doing so, PCY advocates for school districts in these communities to invest their own resources to sustain such programming.

This approach to policy advocacy is based upon collaborations. Indeed, Gunderson described her job fundamentally as building relationships with public officials and organizations with whom they partner. "We think that the most effective policy is made from the practitioner level," she explained, so she partners with those practitioners to create policy changes that allow for "flexibility and local innovations" to meet the specific needs of their own communities.

## The Institutional Partnership Strategy

*Partnership* is in PCY's name, and their Summer Matters campaign exemplifies the institutional partnership strategy. Advocacy organizations employing this strategy view themselves as partners with government institutions, investing considerable effort to develop positive relationships with them, and working together toward mutual goals. For example, another nonprofit using this strategy works in the field of gerontology and promotes policies and programs that support people aging in their own communities. They deliver services and interventions that help seniors age in the homes, and they lobby for public funds for their work. But their lobbying is based upon well-established, congenial relationships. Their director highlighted how their board and staff have nurtured personal connections with their city's mayor's office, controller, and key committees. "We tell our connectors, 'This is what we are trying to do, how can you help?'" she explained. They reply, "Well, I know somebody...."

These advocates acknowledge the centrality of government institutions in policymaking and pursue favorable policy changes by collaborating with them (02:+2). They generally avoid public debates (05:−3, 18:−3), litigation (17:−2), and other confrontational tactics favored by other advocates, because such tactics can deteriorate their relationships with policymakers. They also avoid indirect tactics such as media work (06:0, 16:0) or working through the public (19:0, 20:0) that they do not completely control. Instead, institutional partnership strategists directly provide policymakers with organized public support (10:+3), research (15:+3), framing and messaging (01:+2), and sometimes pilot programs (13:+2) to catalyze the policymakers' support. Because these advocates work primarily with the decision makers directly, they view their purpose more narrowly focused on specific policy changes, rather than broader social changes (08:−2) or democratic enhancement (11:−2) (Fig. 4.1 and Table 4.1).

(Coalitions, research, messaging, lobbying, pilot programs) → policymakers' views → policy change

**Fig. 4.1** Institutional partnership strategy

**Table 4.1**  Factor array for institutional partnership strategy

| Tactic (advocacy activity and its expected outcome) | Factor array | Relative extreme |
|---|---|---|
| 10. Building coalitions and networks with like-minded organizations and individuals can change policymakers' views | +3 | High |
| 15. Research and analyses can change policymakers' views | +3 | High |
| 01. Developing messages, framing issues, labeling and other strategies of rhetoric can change policymakers' views | +2 | |
| 02. Lobbying and building relationships with policymakers can change their views | +2 | |
| 13. Pilot programs and demonstration projects can lead to policy change | +2 | High |
| 03. Monitoring and evaluating existing policy can change how it is implemented | +1 | High |
| 04. Building coalitions and networks with like-minded organizations and individuals can change the public's views | +1 | |
| 09. Using the media to disseminate information can change the public's views | +1 | |
| 22. Changes in policymakers' views can change policies | +1 | |
| 06. Using the media to disseminate information can change policymakers' views | 0 | Low |
| 16. Using the media to disseminate information can hasten policy change | 0 | Low |
| 19. Changes in the public's views can change policymakers' views | 0 | Low |
| 20. Developing messages, framing issues, labeling and other strategies of rhetoric can change the public's views | 0 | Low |
| 21. Public mobilizations (e.g., protests, letter writing campaigns, voter registration) can build democracy | 0 | |
| 23. Research and analyses can change the public's views | 0 | High |
| 07. Monitoring and evaluating existing policy can set the policy agenda | −1 | |
| 12. Policy advocacy in general makes policymaking more people-centered | −1 | |

(continued)

**Table 4.1** (continued)

| Tactic (advocacy activity and its expected outcome) | Factor array | Relative extreme |
|---|---|---|
| 14. Public mobilizations (e.g., protests, letter writing campaigns, rallies) can set the policy agenda | −1 | |
| 24. Policy advocacy in general produces more effective policies | −1 | |
| 08. Policies can change social and physical conditions | −2 | Low |
| 11. Policy advocacy in general builds legitimacy in a democracy | −2 | |
| 17. Litigation can change policy | −2 | |
| 05. Rebutting opposing views can change policymakers' views | −3 | Low |
| 18. Rebutting opposing views can change the public's views | −3 | Low |

*Note* See Chapter 2 for an explanation of the factor array scores

The tactics in this strategy include some of the most popularly used ones in many strategies (lobbying, coalition building). What makes this strategy distinct are the few tactics that are much less often used by others—research, pilot studies, and demonstration projects—and the viewpoint expressed in this tactics. These advocates see themselves as partners of governing bodies, helping them to better achieve their mutual goals by providing key support that may be difficult for governments to initiate on their own.

## Theoretical Foundations

Advocates employing the institutional partnership strategy view their participation in governance as an integral part of producing effective and responsive public policies and services. Legislatures and agencies left on their own may be well-intentioned but lack the public's perspectives and values to optimize outcomes. They might also lack the leeway or resources to research options or test innovations that present significant risks. Therefore, these advocates seek partnerships with government institutions to provide complementary support to improve policies and services.

Their viewpoint aligns closely with the public participation literature in both policymaking (e.g., Bryson and Anderson 2000; Smith and Huntsman 1997) and public services (e.g., Roberts 2008).

Those literatures prescribe public participation in policy processes for both systemic and specific reasons. On the systemic side, more and varied public engagement enhances democracy by ensuring that decisions better reflect public values and preferences (Gen and Lugar 2019). On the specific side, public engagement in policymaking has been shown to produce better outcomes. The advocates in our data, however, focused on the latter reason. Their objectives were limited to reforms of specific policies and services, rather than broader democratic processes. This viewpoint also overlaps with the *coproduction* concept found in public administration literature (e.g., Brudney and England 1983), in which service beneficiaries participate in the delivery of public services. However, in our data some of the advocates employing this strategy were not direct beneficiaries of the reforms they sought.

## Current Usage

Coalition building, lobbying, and framing issues are among the most popularly used tactics used by advocates in our dataset (Fig. 4.2), and they are all prominent in the institutional partnership strategy. What sets this strategy apart from others, however, is its additional use of research, pilot studies, and demonstration projects as key tactics. In our dataset, 45% of organizations rarely or never produced research, and 61% rarely or never conduct pilot studies or demonstration projects. For organizations using the institutional partnership strategy, however, such activities allow policy decision makers to learn from the experiences of others without taking the risks of testing interventions themselves.

Not all of these tactics are necessarily used by all institutional partnership strategists. Rather, some combination of them are used, with the aim of influencing policymakers' views and, ultimately, policy decisions. To identify advocates in the survey data who use the institutional partnership strategy, we focused on the two highest scoring tactics in the factor array—coalition building and research—and screened for respondents who use both of those tactics often or always, combined with the outcomes of changing decision makers' views and adoption of favored policy as very important or extremely important. We focused on the combination of coalition building and research not only because of their +3 scores in the factor array, but also because they represent two complementary tactics in the strategy. Coalition building is common across policy advocates and provides broad public support to the government partners, while research is relatively rare and brings evidence to the partnership. Of the 802 organizations

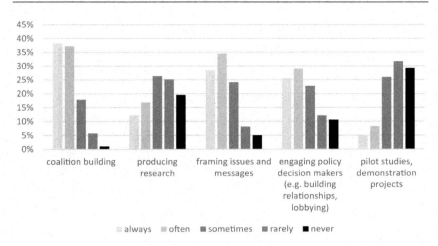

**Fig. 4.2** Advocates' usage of key tactics in the institutional partnership strategy

responding to our survey, 125 of them passed this screening and they are the focus of the following analyses.

When asked how important advocacy is to achieve their organization's mission, almost all institutional partnership strategists said very important or extremely important (99%). Among all other organizations in the survey, only 75% answered similarly. Viewing themselves as partners with government bodies, of course, may require advocacy organizations to more deeply invest in those relationships. That level of investment might only be justified by a stronger organizational commitment to advocacy (Fig. 4.3). Indeed, Table 4.2 shows that advocates using this strategy spend about 15% more staff time and financial resources on policy advocacy than all others in our survey.

When we asked respondents to identify all the policy issue areas in which they advocate, only one issue reached the 50% mark among the advocates using the institutional partnership strategy—health and mental health—and these advocates engage this issue at a significantly higher rate than all other advocates ($\chi^2_{(1)} = 11.13$, $p = 0.00$) (Fig. 4.4). Education, social welfare and poverty, and civil rights come close to half, with rates ranging from 43 to 48%, and the latter two issues are championed by institutional partnership strategists at

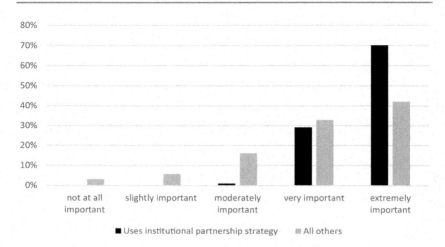

**Fig. 4.3** Importance of policy advocacy to mission of institutional partnership strategists (*Note* $\chi^2_{(4)} = 40.4$, $p = 0.00$)

**Table 4.2** Resources devoted to policy advocacy by institutional partnership strategists

|  | Staff devoted to policy advocacy (%) | Financial resources devoted to policy advocacy (%) |
|---|---|---|
| Uses institutional partnerships often or always | Mean = 57<br>S.D. = 28 | Mean = 53<br>S.D. = 31 |
| All others | Mean = 42<br>S.D. = 32 | Mean = 37<br>S.D. = 33 |

a significantly higher rates than by other advocates ($\chi^2_{(1)} = 12.95$, $p = 0.00$ and $\chi^2_{(1)} = 11.42$, $p = 0.00$, respectively). The other issues that are engaged by institutional partnership strategists at significantly higher rates than other advocates are crime and criminal justice ($\chi^2_{(1)} = 11.65$, $p = 0.00$); economy, jobs, and business ($\chi^2_{(1)} = 8.42$, $p = 0.00$); immigration and immigrants ($\chi^2_{(1)} = 8.93$, $p = 0.00$); public safety and emergency preparedness ($\chi^2_{(1)} = 10.20$, $p = 0.00$); taxes and monetary policy ($\chi^2_{(1)} = 24.48$, $p = 0.00$); transportation ($\chi^2_{(1)} = 3.37$, $p = 0.07$); science, technology, and research ($\chi^2_{(1)} = 4.70$, $p = 0.03$); and foreign relations and traded ($\chi^2_{(1)} = 7.18$, $p = 0.01$). Advocates using the institutional partnership strategy did not engage in any issue at significantly lower rates than other advocates.

Advocacy organizations using the institutional partnership strategy generally target state governments the most (85%), and at a significantly higher frequency

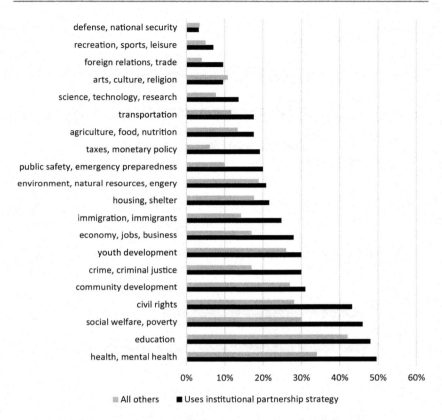

**Fig. 4.4** Public issues engaged by institutional partnership strategists

than other advocacy organizations (49%, $\chi^2_{(1)} = 54.86$, $p=0.00$). See Fig. 4.5. Local and national governments are targeted by 61 and 55% of institutional partnership strategists, also significantly higher than other advocates ($\chi^2_{(1)} = 10.10$, $p=0.00$; $\chi^2_{(1)} = 28.25$, $p=0.00$; respectively).

Looking at the branches of government targeted (Fig. 4.6), a similar pattern emerges. Advocates using the institutional partnership strategy target each branch of government at significantly higher rates than other advocates, but in the same order of frequencies: legislative branch first (90%, $\chi^2_{(1)} = 63.01$, $p=0.00$), bureaucratic branch second (70%, $\chi^2_{(1)} = 34.28$, $p=0.00$), executive branch third (62%, $\chi^2_{(1)} = 37.45$, $p=0.00$), and judicial branch fourth (30%, $\chi^2_{(1)} = 12.63$,

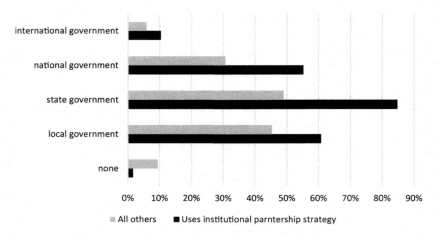

**Fig. 4.5**  Levels of government targeted by institutional partnership strategists

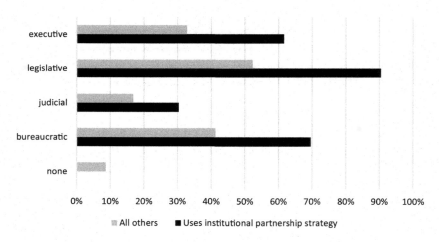

**Fig. 4.6**  Branches of government targeted by institutional partnership strategists

$p = 0.00$). A policy director of one of the significantly associated advocacy organizations succinctly conveyed this pattern when she said, "There are three places to address [policy] issues: legislators, administration, and the courts. [We] are involved with all three." The statement not only identifies the centrality of gov-

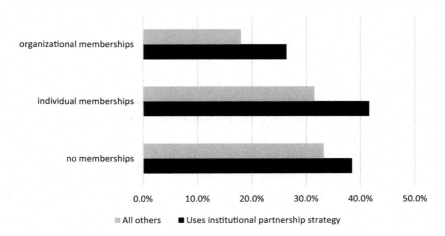

**Fig. 4.7** Memberships of institutional partnership strategists

ernment institutions in policy change, but also the breadth of government institutions this strategy targets. That particular organization, highlighted below, focuses on criminal justice issues, and their key advocacy activities include producing and summarizing research written for legislators, agency administrators, and the courts through *amicus curiae* briefs.

The high rate of targeting bureaucratic institutions might explain this strategy's relatively high use of pilot studies and demonstration projects as key tactics of advocacy. Unlike the more overtly political executive and legislative branches that might respond more to coalitions of support and lobbying, bureaucracies are designed to be more rational in their decision-making processes (Weber 2016), thus responding more to evidence of success that studies and demonstration projects might provide. PCY's Summer Matters campaign illustrates this point.

Figures 4.7 and 4.8 turn to the resources of institutional partnership strategists. A plurality of them are organizations with individual memberships (42%) but nearly as many don't have any memberships (38%). That said, advocates using this strategy are significantly more likely to have individual memberships ($\chi^2_{(1)} = 4.90$, $p = 0.03$) and organizational memberships ($\chi^2_{(1)} = 4.75$, $p = 0.03$) than all other advocates together. Memberships can play an important role in this strategy, to support the coalition building tactic often used in it. Figure 4.8 compares the income levels of institutional partnership strategists with advocates not using this strategy, and it displays a clear pattern. Organizations using this strat-

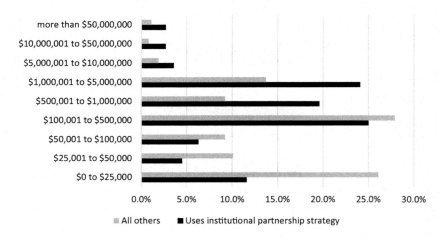

**Fig. 4.8**   2013 Income distribution of institutional partnership strategists

egy have higher representation in higher-income levels and lower representation in the lower-income levels. This might reflect, in part, the resources required to produce research, pilot studies, and demonstration projects.

The two following cases further illustrate the institutional partnership strategy in varied forms. The first describes how the American Friends Service Committee uses research to advocate for policy reform with all three branches of government. The second describes how the California Youth Connection links foster youth with legislators to advocate for reforms to foster care policies.

## Over-Incarceration

Like the Ella Baker Center for Human Rights (Chapter 3), the American Friends Service Committee (AFSC) sees deep flaws in the United States' criminal justice system. Tough-on-crime politics of the late 1900s produced policies focused on the incarceration and punishment of offenders and largely abandoned their rehabilitation (Weiss 2013). Mandatory minimum sentencing, like California's 1994 three strikes law, exemplified such punishment by substantially lengthening prison terms. In California's case, the law required defendants convicted of any second felony to be sentenced to double the term normally applied for the offense, and for defendants convicted of any third felony to be sentenced to

25 years to life in prison (Judicial Council of California 2019). The effects of these policies were the rapid growth of the imprisoned population and the rapid decline of their condition and rehabilitation. However, while the Ella Baker Center's Books Not Bars campaign focuses on the treatment of juvenile offenders, AFSC focuses on the much larger population of adult offenders. And while the Ella Baker Center advocates for reforms by employing a public lobbying strategy that focuses on lobbying decision makers, AFSC uses an institutional partnership strategy that focuses on collaborations with them.

AFSC was founded in 1917 in Washington, DC to provide Quakers committed to nonviolence, and other conscientious objectors to war, with opportunities to provide humanitarian services during war (Nobel Media 2019). Since then, AFSC has expanded to work worldwide in areas of conflict, natural disasters, and oppressed communities. "Real peace is more than the absence of war," they claim. "Rather, we need to change the culture, situations, and systems that lead to violence." AFSC and its British counterpart, the Friends Service Council, won the Nobel Peace Prize in 1947 for their humanitarian work during and in the aftermath of World Wars I and II and the Spanish Civil War. In its hundred-year history, AFSC has moved slightly away from pure service—as emphasized in the organization's name—to put more emphasis on systemic change through policy advocacy, explained Laura Magnani, the Assistant Regional Director of AFSC's Western Region.

Today, the organization has over 30 offices throughout the United States and in Africa, Asia, Central America, and the Middle East. We spoke with Magnani and her colleague Eric Moon at their office, where the two led regional efforts to reform criminal justice policies and practices. Their Healing Justice program is an ongoing campaign seeking reforms in specific areas of California's criminal justice system: mass incarceration, solitary confinement of prisoners, the death penalty, and the advancement of healing alternatives to incarceration (American Friends Service Committee, n.d.). Magnani worked primarily on solitary confinement and restorative justice practices, while Moon focused on death penalty policies. Both worked on the overuse of incarceration as a response to criminal offenses, and they shared with us their experiences in this campaign.

"California has one of the world's largest prison systems," Moon explained, "and it is not serving us well. There's a sense in general that our culture—and California is a prime example of this—*way* overuses incarceration as a response to public safety." Indeed, in 2006, the California Department of Corrections and Rehabilitation (CDCR) reported their inmate population to be over 200% of the design capacities of its prisons (Myers and Sun, n.d.). And the overcrowding causes problems for all stakeholders. Prisoners experience inadequate medical and mental health care, prison staff are placed in greater danger at work, and communities receiving inmates released from overcrowded conditions are more likely to see them recidivate. Moon succinctly summarized, "It doesn't work for the people who are incarcerated, it doesn't work for their families, and it doesn't work for the people out in the streets who imagine that they're safer for this." Magnani added that as AFSC has opposed the overuse of incarceration, they've also been promoting alternatives. This is why AFSC's criminal justice program is called *Healing Justice*. "We're trying to model more positive approaches to solving crime problems," she said. These include restorative justice, and truth and reconciliation processes that exemplify "new paradigms of justice that aren't just punish, punish, punish."

## Supportive Research

A key tactic they use in this advocacy is research. They conduct original research, compile and summarize others' research, and disseminate findings from research to inform and support specific decision makers but also to advance public awareness and discussions on mass incarceration. For example, AFSC partners with former prisoners and current families of prisoners, who share their experiences in the prisons and how they are impacted. From these data and the findings of other researchers, they produce reports on prison overcrowding and propose solutions to alleviate it. These reports are mostly aimed at legislators, but they also take their research and its messages to public forums. In Magnani's view, the isolation of prisons, enhanced by their security and remote locations, shields them from public scrutiny. That "concentration of power and the secrecy" inside the prison system make their operations vulnerable to neglect and abuse. So their research educates stakeholders about the insides of prisons and about reforms that can prevent the abuse. For Magnani, much of this work culminated in a book she co-authored in 2006, titled *Beyond Prisons: A New Interfaith Paradigm for Our Failed Prison System*. It unpacks and details the many problems in the prison system, including the racial conflicts, sentencing problems, and lack of rehabilitation.

The quality of their research has earned AFSC a positive reputation in criminal justice policy circles. "Partly because we've been around so long, partly because we have a lot of experience working in these different arenas… [AFSC] has a good reputation for credibility," claimed Magnani. "For instance, the legislature is actively *asking us* to testify in different arenas, which is based on the fact that they can rely on our information." Moon added, "We're the least objectionable of the grubby activists!"

## Friend of the Court

An example of their establishment as a partner in criminal justice reform was their role in the US Supreme Court case *Schwarzenegger v. Plata and Coleman* (09-1233). Plata and Coleman represented plaintiffs in separate, earlier class action lawsuits that found that the inadequate levels of medical and mental health services, respectively, in California's prisons violated prisoners' Eighth Amendment protections against cruel and unusual punishment (Myers and Sun, n.d.). Despite court orders to rectify the violations, the CDCR failed for years to raise service levels to meet the constitutional standard. In 2007, the plaintiffs in the Plata and Coleman cases argued that overcrowding in the prisons was a primary cause of the CDCR's inability to provide adequate care. Two years later, a federal three-judge court agreed with the plaintiffs and ordered the state to develop a plan to reduce the prison population to no more than 137.5% of design capacity. The state appealed to the US Supreme Court, who heard the case in 2010.

According to Magnani, the lawyers representing the plaintiffs wanted their case accompanied by a variety of *amici curiae* briefs representing different constituencies, such as healthcare experts, mental health organizations, and corrections experts. They specifically asked for a brief from religious organizations who could look at the issue from a moral standpoint, and AFSC was already positioned to lead that effort. AFSC worked with lawyers to write the brief and then helped build a coalition of Christian, Muslim, and Jewish organizations to sign onto the brief. See Box 4.1.

---

**Box 4.1 Amici Curiae Brief Submitted in *Schwarzenegger v. Plata and Coleman* et al.**

Overview: When a federal three-judge panel ordered California in 2009 to address its prison overcrowding, the state appealed the decision to the US Supreme Court. Advocates on both sides of the case submitted briefs to the court, summarizing their arguments in support or opposition of the panel's original decision. Three *amici curiae* briefs were submitted to the Supreme Court requesting a reversal of the appellate court's decision. They represented the Greater Stockton Chamber of Commerce, the Criminal Justice Legal Foundation, and a coalition of 18 states. In support of the panel decision were 7 briefs representing law enforcement, criminologists, the American Bar Association, health organizations, mental health organizations, religious organizations, and civic rights organizations (Rosen Bien Galvan & Grunfeld LLP 2019).

Excerpts from the brief representing AFSC and other religious organizations (Brief for Prison Fellowship et al. 2010):

*"Amici Curiae who submit this brief are religious organizations whose belief systems, while diverse, all emphasize the intrinsic value of every human being and the importance of a legal system that upholds constitutional principles even, or especially, when applied to those whose transgressions would otherwise make them easy targets for maltreatment...."*

*"Despite the subtle, or significant, differences among their beliefs or ministries, these Christian, Muslim, and Jewish Amici agree on two issues relevant to this appeal. First, they share a faith-based duty to ameliorate unnecessary human suffering, especially among the marginalized, such as the inmates in the California prison system. The inhuman conditions in the California prison system, caused primarily by overcrowding, lead to unnecessary deaths, including suicides, and a host of other unjustified and avoidable harms and affronts to human dignity."*

*"Second, Amici share an interest in eliminating the interference with religious freedom that extreme overcrowding causes. The overcrowding, and resultant lockdowns, deprive inmates of opportunities for congregate worship and study, which are central to the practice of the religions most prevalent in the California prisons... When religious practice is crowded out, inmates suffer and prisons become more difficult to manage. Further, the interruption of programs aimed at rehabilitation and redemption impedes inmates' eventual reintegration into society as law-abiding citizens."*

*"Amici's interest in this appeal flows from their concern for the human treatment of prisoners; their desire to attend to the spiritual needs of those who are marginalized, isolated, and even despised; and their commitment to protecting the free exercise of religion in general and in prisons in particular."*

Ultimately, the Supreme Court sided with the plaintiffs in a 5-4 decision in 2011, upholding the panel's original order for California to reduce its prison population substantially. "The US Supreme Court put the State of California under court order to reduce its prison population by 40,000, and we contributed to that court decision," claimed Magnani. "We wrote an *amicus* brief... and then we got a lot of religious organizations to sign the brief. That particular brief was actually cited by the justices in their decision." Moon added, "And the thing we love is the actual decision had a couple of photos [of prisoners in triple bunk beds] that we had contributed… and having a photo in a Supreme Court decision was apparently unprecedented."

*Amici curiae* literally mean "friends of the court," and AFSC's *amici curiae* brief beautifully exemplifies the viewpoint of the institutional partnership strategy that they are assisting the court in its learning and decision-making process.

After the court's ruling, AFSC's attention shifted toward helping the state implement the order, and monitoring their progress. For example, AFSC advocated for "good credit hours" as a legislative reform that could help ease overcrowding. Under this reform, prisoners earn good-time credit that can reduce their sentences. It is a positive incentive that promotes good behavior, instead of the former negative incentive in which bad behavior lengthened sentences. AFSC continues to produce research and materials that explain how the state can lower the prison population, how much money it can save, and how many people will be impacted (American Friends Service Committee, n.d.).

## Why Partnership

AFSC's strategy to work with government institutions on over-incarceration was a driven by practicalities. The state sets criminal justice policies and operates the prison system, explained Moon. "So, if you care about those things, you will find yourself talking to prison administrators and legislators." Magnani added, "There are three places to address issues: legislative, administrative, and the courts. And we've had our hands in all three," depending upon the issue and the amenability or resistance of each, said Magnani. Their challenge is to find "where's the little opening that we can move through?"

## Foster Youth Emancipation

Foster care refers to "24-hour state supervised living arrangements" for children and youth who have been removed from their homes because of neglect or abuse (Youth Law Center 2016). California supports the largest population of foster youth in the United States, with nearly 60,000 in 2018 (kidsdata.org 2019). There, foster care is supervised by the state but administered by counties. County agencies aim to place foster youths in the most family-like environments for the shortest amount of time, with the goal of safely reuniting the youth with their families under improved conditions, or, short of that, placing them in permanent home environments (Danielson and Lee 2010).

Youths exit the foster care system when they reunite with their families, receive guardianship from a relative, are adopted by another family, or are emancipated by aging out of the system (Foster 2001). While a minority of foster youth exit the system through emancipation, those youth experience high risks for homelessness and entering the criminal justice system, and a majority of emancipated foster youth face daunting challenges to self-sufficiency, such as incomplete high school education, unemployment, and unreliable access to healthcare (Danielson and Lee 2010; Foster 2001). This pattern was certainly evident in California. A University of California at Berkeley study reported "...that it is difficult for youth to find stable employment, that many receive means-based cash assistance (welfare), and that in general, youth often are unprepared for life on their own" (Needell et al. 2002). In another study, one emancipated youth succinctly reported, "Basically, they orphan you at the age of eighteen" (Foster 2001, p. 29).

Assembly Bill 12 (AB12), introduced in 2008, aimed to provide some relief to these emancipated foster youth. Taking advantage of a new federal law that offered enhanced federal financial support for state foster care programs, AB12 proposed to extend foster youths' eligibility for care and assistance from age 18–21.

The bill earned significant early support, based on the broad desire to mitigate the personal hardships described above, but there was also early opposition to the bill, based on its fiscal impact. While youth in foster care make up a small portion of children in the broader child welfare system, foster care is the most expensive and involved child service intervention (Danielson and Lee 2010). And while AB12 boasted registered support from over 100 organizations, it faced significant resistance for its projected impact on the state's budget. An early analysis of the original bill estimated a cost to California, even after federal reimbursements, of up to $100 million per year (Salley-Gray 2009).

California Youth Connection (CYC), one of the nine co-sponsoring organizations of AB12 (Courtney et al. 2013), understood the work they would have to do to help the bill get passed. CYC is a statewide membership nonprofit with dozens of county-based chapters across the state. It was established in 1988 by current and former foster youth who, following the model of the successful Youth in Care Canada organization, wanted to improve policies and services that affect foster youth. When we met with them in 2013, they had grown to a staff of 22 plus several interns, but they remained a foster youth-led organization and boasted over 60% of their staff and board of directors being former foster youth.

Jacque Lindeman was one of their few staff were who did not come from a foster care background, but had extensive experience working with disadvantaged youth in southern California, including stints as a drug and alcohol therapist with Orange County and a program director for Boys Hope Girls Hope. Her involvement with CYC began in 2000 when she volunteered as an adult supporter. She eventually joined the staff as a southern regional supervisor in 2006. In 2010 she moved to the organization's headquarters to be its Director of Development. She holds a master of social work degree from the University of Southern California.

CYC's mission is to develop foster youth into leaders "who empower each other and their communities to transform the foster care system through legislative and policy change." According to Lindeman, legislative change refers specifically to statutes adopted in the state legislature, while policy change refers to foster youth services and practices at the county level. To accomplish these parallel roles, CYC's youth leadership includes a legislative committee that oversees CYC's legislative agenda, and a state youth council that provides input and feedback on services and practices led by the California Department of Social Services and the County Welfare Directors' Association. By establishing these standing committees, CYC ensures their foster youth are consistently in partnership with how the state's foster care system operates. For example, in Los Angeles County, CYC foster youth helped develop curricula and training for the county's Department of Children and Family Services. On the legislative side, each year CYC members gather for a leadership and policy conference, in which they prioritize their legislative campaigns for the year. See Box 4.2.

**Box 4.2 Setting the Legislative Agenda for CYC**

Overview: CYC establishes connections between their foster youth members and the state legislature and counties' child welfare services agencies, in order for the youth to improve foster care policies and services. Their legislative agenda is set by their members at their annual leadership and policy conference. At the conference, members also learn about the processes of policy change and advocacy. In 2012, the membership met in Ventura County to set the agenda for 2013. Sade Daniels is a member from Oakland who had already emancipated at age 19. Below is an excerpt from her summary of the conference's processes and conclusions.

Excerpt from the 2012 Summer Policy Conference Report (California Youth Connection 2012):
   *"Approximately 200 youth filled the auditorium at California Lutheran University in Thousand Oaks, CA... Although they traveled from all areas*

*of the state, with some youth traveling as long as 10 hours to be there, the excitement of the attendees was not diminished. The conference began with a rousing ice breaker that showcased the commonalities of the youth's experiences while in care. Questions such as 'Do you feel that your social worker has or had time for you?' or 'Have you ever experienced discrimination while in a placement?' were asked and youth were instructed to step forward if the question or statement applied to them. This activity not only showcased the similarities between the youth's experiences, but it also touched upon the seven policy topics for the conference: finding biological family, foster youth who are parents, social worker and attorney caseloads, mentoring programs for foster youth, foster youth mental health programs, LGBTQQ foster youth, and foster parent accountability. Lastly, the activity gave youth a chance to see which issues were wide scale and those which may be more situational or unique."*

*"For the 2^nd year now, youth were able to learn detailed information about the seven policy topics and pick four of them to create policy recommendations. The seven topics were chosen by the youth curriculum development team who were responsible for creating the vision for all of the workshop activities, so that youth could develop sound policy recommendations over the three day conference. In an effort to expand advocacy efforts through the use of technology and social media, youth were able to text in their votes and watch results come in instantaneously. The four policy topics that were chose by youth were: 1) LGBTQQ Foster Youth, 2) Foster Parent Accountability, 3) Social Worker and Attorney Caseloads, and 4) Mentoring...."*

*"After narrowing topics, youth were able to register for one of three workshops tracks that would further assist them in the creation of their policy recommendations: government, art, or leadership. In the government track, youth were taught the basics of the local, state, and federal branches of government. Youth learned about the legislative process and how federal funding trickles down to the state and local levels for programs such as child welfare. In the art track, youth were introduced to the various ways that art is used to express feelings and/or emotions. Youth participated in various activities that allowed the exploration of how art can be used in advocacy. Youth were then able to create their own art about their chosen policy topics using various mediums such as photography, spoken word, or music. Lastly, the leadership track focused on the qualities that make great*

*leaders and how one possesses those traits. Youth were able to give their own definitions of great leaders and identify ways they were leaders."*

*"The government, art, and leadership tracks provided fundamental knowledge to youth that would not only benefit them in their chapter work but also in the creation and presentation of the policy recommendations...."*

AB12 was introduced to the legislature as a two-year bill, meaning it had two years to be debated and refined before a vote. In that time, CYC youth campaigned for it, conducted press conferences to raise its profile, and presented at community fairs and also at social work trainings.

One key advocacy event was their Day at the Capitol, in which CYC youth met with the 120 state legislators, plus the governor and lieutenant governor. They broke into groups of six to share with the elected officials their personal stories, their experiences in foster care, and their support for AB12. Lindeman said that some legislators go to Sacramento with little exposure to, or understanding of, foster care. For example, she recalled one representative asking a CYC youth "What did you do to get yourself into foster care?" The Day at the Capitol provides elected officials like this first-person perspectives on the contexts, scope, successes, and challenges in the foster care system.

Complementing the Day at the Capitol, CYC also hosted a Shadow Day in which legislators shadowed foster youths for a day, to learn about the youths' backgrounds, living situations, educational and personal development, and the challenges they face in these areas. According to Lindeman, at least one legislator who was not supportive of the foster care system changed his position after Shadow Day and learning how AB12 could help foster youth.

After months of revisions and advocacy, AB12 passed both legislative chambers and was signed by Governor Schwarzenegger in 2010. "We're really proud of the passage of AB12," said Lindeman. "These people were not mentally or emotionally prepared to be an adult at 18 years," she explained. "Many wanted to stay in their foster homes while starting college. [But] they are then turned out on their own, even if they are not ready. Many became homeless." With AB12, their foster care can continue for another three years. AB12 also adds to CYC's long list of legislative victories that they have influenced (California Youth Connection, n.d.). They don't always get their preferred bills passed, but if they oppose a bill it usually dies, said Lindeman.

After the signing of AB12, CYC's advocacy continued with the bill's implementation (California Youth Connection 2012). They worked with the California Department of Social Services to develop youth-friendly materials to explain AB12 and foster youths' expanded services under it. The materials were distributed to social workers, attorneys, and group home staff throughout the state.

**Discussions**

4a. Partnership for Children & Youth, American Friends Service Committee, and California Youth Connection each applied the institutional partnership strategy in different ways. Compare the kinds of partnerships that each developed in their respective cases. How were these partnerships similar and how were they different?

4b. A government agency might be willing to partner with a nonprofit organization to change a policy or program if it lacks the expertise, resources (e.g., money and time), or leeway to so. Identify a public policy, program, or service that needs reform and its responsible government agency. Is it able to make those reforms on its own? How might a nonprofit help it do so?

4c. For a topic of interest, identify a public policy or program that was developed by partnership between a government entity and a nonprofit organization. It might not be obvious which ones were initiated by such partnerships. You may need to investigate several to identify one. Describe the policy or program, and the key partners.

4d. Investigate the key players in the partnership you identified in 4c. What roles does each partner play? Describe how the partners worked together.

4e. Think of a potential policy reform. How might a nonprofit make a case to government decision makers for this reform, considering arguments related to policy analysis criteria such as efficiency, effectiveness, and equity? How could research or pilot projects contribute to making the case?

# References

American Friends Service Committee. (n.d.). *California Healing Justice*. Retrieved from https://www.afsc.org/program/bay-area-healing-justice.
Brief for Prison Fellowship et al. (2010). *As Amici Curiae in Support of Appellees, Schwarzenegger et al. v. Plata and Coleman et al., No. 09-1233*. November 1, 2019. Retrieved from https://www.americanbar.org/content/dam/aba/publishing/preview/publiced_preview_briefs_pdfs_09_10_09_1233_AppelleeAmCuPrisonFellowship.pdf.

Brudney, J. L., & England, R. E. (1983). Toward a definition of the coproduction concept. *Public Administration Review, 43*(1), 59–65.

Bryson, J. M., & Anderson, S. R. (2000). Applying large-group interaction models in the planning and implementation of major change efforts. *Public Administration Review, 60*(2), 143–153.

California Youth Connection. (2012). *Waves of Opportunities: California Youth Connection Leadership & Policy Conference 2012.* San Francisco: California Youth Connection.

California Youth Connection. (n.d.). *Legislative Achievements.* Retrieved from https://calyouthconn.org/leadership-in-action/legislative-achievements/.

Courtney, M., Dworsky, A., & Napolitano, L. (2013). *Providing Foster Care for Young Adults: Early Implementation of California's Fostering Connections Act.* Chicago, IL: Chapin Hall at the University of Chicago.

Danielson, C., & Lee, H. (2010). *Foster Care in California: Achievements and Challenges.* San Francisco: Public Policy Institute of California. Retrieved from https://www.ppic.org/publication/foster-care-in-california-achievements-and-challenges/.

Foster, L. K. (2001). *Foster Care Fundamentals: An Overview of California's Foster Care System* (CRB-01-008). Sacramento: California Research Bureau. Retrieved from https://www.library.ca.gov/Content/pdf/crb/reports/01-008.pdf.

Gen, S., & Lugar, E. (2019). Does mode of public outreach matter? In R. Kerley, J. Liddle, & P. T. Dunning (Eds.), *The Routledge Handbook of International Local Government* (pp. 307–324). New York: Routledge.

Judicial Council of California. (2019). *California's Three Strikes Sentencing Law.* Retrieved from https://www.courts.ca.gov/20142.htm.

kidsdata.org. (2019). *Children in Foster Care.* Palo Alto, CA: Lucile Packard Foundation for Children's Health. Retrieved from https://www.kidsdata.org/topic/20/foster-in-care/trend#fmt=16&loc=2&tf=1,108.

Magnani, L., & Wray, H. L. (2006). *Beyond Prisons: A New Interfaith Paradigm for Our Failed Prison System.* Minneapolis, MN: Augsburg Fortress Publishers.

Myers, S. A., & Sun, J. (n.d.). *Schwarzenegger v. Plata (09-1233).* Ithaca, NY: Legal Information Institute. Retrieved from https://www.law.cornell.edu/supct/cert/09-1233.

Needell, B., Cuccaro-Alamin, S., Brookhard, A., Jackman, W., & Shlonsky, A. (2002). *Youth Emancipation from Foster Care in California: Findings Using Linked Administrative Data.* Berkeley: Center for Social Science Research, University of California at Berkeley. Retrieved from http://cssr.berkeley.edu/childwelfare/pdfs/youth/ffy_report.pdf.

Nobel Media. (2019). *The Nobel Peace Prize 1947.* Retrieved from https://www.nobelprize.org/prizes/peace/1947/summary/.

Partnership for Children & Youth. (n.d.). *About PCY.* Retrieved from https://www.partnerforchildren.org/about-pcy-1.

Partnership for Children & Youth. (n.d.). *History.* Retrieved from https://www.partnerforchildren.org/history.

Partnership for Children & Youth. (n.d.). *Summer Learning.* Retrieved from https://www.partnerforchildren.org/summer-matters.

Perry, M., Khalilnaji-Otto, N., & Brackenridge, K. (2018, January). *Summer Learning—A Smart Investment for California School Districts.* Stanford: Policy Analysis for California Education. Retrieved from http://www.summermatters.net/wp-content/uploads/2018/02/summer-learning.pdf.

Roberts, N. (Ed.). (2008). *The Age of Direct Citizen Participation*. Armonk, NY: M. E. Sharpe.

Rosen Bien Galvan & Grunfeld LLP. (2019). *Coleman/Plata in the Supreme Court*. Retrieved from https://rbgg.com/news/coleman-plata-supreme-court/#AmicusBriefs.

Salley-Gray, J. (2009, May 20). *Bill Analysis: AB 12 (Beall and Bass)—As Amended April 29, 2009*. Sacramento: California Assembly Committee on Appropriations. Retrieved from http://www.leginfo.ca.gov/pub/09-10/bill/asm/ab_0001-0050/ab_12_cfa_20090519_170540_asm_comm.html.

Smith, G. E., & Huntsman, C. A. (1997). Reframing the metaphor of citizen-government relationship: A value-centered perspective. *Public Administration Review, 57*(4), 309–318.

Weber, M. (2016). Bureaucracy. In J. M. Shafritz & A. C. Hyde (Eds.), *Classics of Public Administration* (8th ed., pp. 63–68). Boston: Cengage Learning.

Weiss, G. (2013). *The Fourth Wave: Juvenile Justice Reforms for the Twenty-First Century*. Washington, DC: National Campaign to Reform State Juvenile Justice Systems. Retrieved from https://nicic.gov/fourth-wave-juvenile-justice-reforms-twenty-first-century.

Youth Law Center. (2016). *Overview of the Foster Care System in California*. San Francisco, CA: Youth Law Center. Retrieved from https://ylc.org/wp-content/uploads/2018/11/Foster-Care-Overview-FACT-SHEET-040116.pdf.

# Inside-Outside

# 5

In successful advocacy campaigns…you need a champion inside, and you need a champion outside.
—Ted Lempert, Children Now

For decades leading to 2013, California's system for financing primary and secondary education was the twisted outcome of lawsuits, ballot initiatives, and legislative fixes that started in the 1970s with the landmark *Serrano v. Priest* cases. Those cases rightfully concluded that the quality of public education in California's districts may not be based upon local property values, but instead must be substantially equal across the state. When the state began redistributing property tax revenues based primarily upon pupil attendance among its over 1000 school districts, a property tax revolt ensued. Proposition 13 gashed local government budgets, and a series of ad hoc interventions were adopted to shore up funding for specific educational concerns.

The result was a convoluted method for funding public schools that was 40 years in the making. School funding was still fundamentally based upon pupil attendance: The more students attending a school, the more funding the school received from the state. But that foundation was supplemented by about 60 "categorical" sources earmarked for specific needs (Herdt 2013). Reflecting on this convoluted funding system, one state senator compared it to the Winchester Mystery House, the California tourist trap of mazes, doors, and dead-ends (Schrag 2013).

Enter Children Now, a nonpartisan nonprofit advocacy organization, focused on advancing the health, education, and welfare of children in California. They pursue their mission primarily through public policy advocacy, and they claim a long history of achievements, going back to 1998, that include numerous legislative victories, online county scorecards that track child well-being, and even *Dora*

© The Author(s) 2020
S. Gen and A. C. Wright, *Nonprofits in Policy Advocacy*,
https://doi.org/10.1007/978-3-030-43696-4_5

*the Explorer*, who—they claim—resulted from Children Now's advocacy for more diverse children's shows. Children Now is led by Ted Lempert, a long-time legislative champion of children's issues (Children Now, n.d.). He served eight years as a member of the California State Assembly, when he earned numerous awards for his advocacy for education and children's issues. He also served on the San Mateo County (California) Board of Supervisors, where he founded that county's Youth Commission.

Since 2005, Lempert and Children Now had targeted educational funding reform as one of their top priorities. That year, a research project organized by Stanford University identified the state's educational funding system as a major contributor to the underperformance of schools (Center for Education Policy Analysis, n.d.). The system was "inequitable, incomprehensible, illogical, and bore no relationship to who the children were," said Lempert. So much so that his organization decided not to pursue incremental reform, as they would with other issues. Instead, they sought comprehensive reform. "If you have an irrational finance system, sometimes the only way to fix it is by blowing it up, and not take just a piece of it and make it more irrational."

The proposed reform developed in the following years, and its essence was distilled into two parts. First, the existing menu of ad hoc categorical grants would be mostly replaced by a "weighted funding formula" that was based on the assumption that different students required different amounts of resources to get the same education. English language learners and students from low-income households, for example, require more resources than their peers to achieve the same educational standards. School budgets, under this proposal, would be weighted to account for such socioeconomic characteristics of their students. Second, local districts and schools would decide how to spend their budgets to best meet the needs of their students, rather than having those expenditures dictated by categorical funds. Together, the reforms were referred to as the "local control funding formula" (LCFF), and Children Now would be a leader in its adoption.

Children Now tried to advance this proposal during Arnold Schwarzenegger's governorship, but the Great Recession gave Schwarzenegger a $20 billion state budget deficit to close, and his own policy priorities focused on environmental protection (Frank 2010). But when Jerry Brown succeeded Schwarzenegger as governor, Lempert saw a "historic opportunity" to push through this education reform (Lempert 2013). Brown had already prioritized increased funding for public education, and this reform could help that funding be more effective. To capitalize this opportunity, Children Now worked with the Brown's staff to get LCFF on the governor's legislative agenda. They did not lobby state legislators directly, like advocates using the public lobbying strategy would (Chapter 3). Instead, the

Democratic Governor would work on getting support from the legislature controlled by Democrats. Children Now would back the governor with research, information, and demonstrated public support for the proposal. They were well positioned to play that supporting role, because they had already spent years as the clearinghouse of information on education finance. According to Lempert, Children Now's website was "ground zero on information and communications" on LCFF.

Media coverage of the proposal largely attributed it to the governor, with one calling it "Gov. Brown's sweeping plan for changing how schools are funded" (Fensterwald 2013). "It's the governor's proposal," said Lempert, and it was his public victory when the proposal was adopted in 2013, even though Children Now and other advocates had been working on the idea for years before the governor arrived. They understood that their work would be mostly behind the scenes, and this was part of their strategy for getting the reform passed.

Still, not every part of their strategy could be planned. They had to wait for the opportunity to work with an ally on the inside of the legislative process, but few could have guessed that it would be Brown. "Jerry Brown as governor? What are you talking about?" Lempert mocked. Brown had already served two terms as governor starting in 1975, following Ronald Reagan. He returned to the office in 2011, succeeding another Republican actor, Arnold Schwarzenegger. "Part of successful advocacy is being nimble" and adapting to the circumstances, Lempert reflected.

They also could not plan how long it would take for the proposal to be adopted. Lempert only knew that substantive change takes time. "If you hear this story, you might ask, 'From 2005 to 2013, what have these guys done? We didn't want incremental change. Sometimes you do… but we wanted to get the big win, which is why it took so long."

## The Inside-Outside Strategy

Organizations that use the inside-outside strategy view two separate and complementary tactics necessary for successful advocacy of policy change: a champion on the inside of the policymaking body, who leads the proposed changes through the insider politics and processes of the institution, and demonstrated outside support from the public, to apply pressure for change. Advocates using this strategy develop and support both the inside champion and the outside pressure, in order to open an opportunity for policy change, what Ted Lempert called a "policy window."

More specifically, advocates focus on establishing and nurturing relationships with one insider—such as a key legislator or an executive, or sometimes a small group of key decision makers—who can navigate the policy process and lead the decision-making body toward their position (02:+2). (Table 5.1 summarizes the factor array for this strategy.) The advocates do this in lieu of directly lobbying a majority of legislators (such as in the public lobbying strategy), which they view as an ineffective or inefficient tactic. They assume that the inside champions have a better understanding of the competing interests of their peers, so they are in better positions than the advocacy organizations to negotiate for support. As one advocacy director put it, they do not broadly lobby the legislator because "we want to get things done!" Instead, it's more effective to find an allied champion within the decision-making body whom they can support.

On the outside, advocates build public support through information campaigns and media work (01:+3, 06:+3, 05:+1). This may include tactics such as framing and labeling issues, briefings and presentations, earned and paid media advocacy, and research dissemination. Such work often requires staff with specialized skills in research and public relations. The research can be original or others', but in this strategy the policy preferences are substantiated by evidence, in order to garner support from the public and media editorial boards, and to provide support to the inside champion. To translate such evidence to the public, these policy advocates develop messages and frame the issues in ways with broad appeal. One policy director using this strategy said her job is to "dewonkify" complex problems and solutions to messages that anyone can understand.

Unlike other strategies that engage the public, however, the purpose of the outside component of this strategy is to apply political pressure on the decision-making body (10:+2), not to enhance democracy (11:−3, 12:−2, 21:−2). Indeed, the political view of this strategy recognizes the power in legislative and administrative processes and chooses to work within that power structure rather than bypassing it through direct reforms (17:−3, 13:−2). Together, the inside and outside tactics lead to the advocates' ultimate objective, which is a favorable policy change (16:+2) (Fig. 5.1).

In the Children Now example, Lempert positioned his organization to be the outside champion of reforming the state's process of financing public schools. They gathered and analyzed data, synthesized relevant research, and developed and disseminated arguments for their proposed policy change. Children Now became "ground zero" on the issue, according to Lempert. In other campaigns, however, the advocacy organization might organize a broader outside champion, such as a coalition of groups or the public itself. In one campaign we studied, for example, the advocacy organization sought stricter standards on car emissions,

**Table 5.1** Factor array for inside-outside strategy

| Tactic (advocacy activity and its expected outcome) | Factor array | Relative extreme |
|---|---|---|
| 01: Developing messages, framing issues, labeling, and other strategies of rhetoric can change policymakers' views | +3 | High |
| 06: Using the media to disseminate information can change policymakers' views | +3 | High |
| 02: Lobbying and building relationships with policymakers can change their views | +2 | |
| 10: Building coalitions and networks with like-minded organizations and individuals can change policymakers' views | +2 | |
| 16: Using the media to disseminate information can hasten policy change | +2 | High |
| 05: Rebutting opposing views can change policymakers' views | +1 | High |
| 08: Policies can change social and physical conditions | +1 | |
| 15: Research and analyses can change policymakers' views | +1 | |
| 20: Developing messages, framing issues, labeling, and other strategies of rhetoric can change the public's views | +1 | |
| 04: Building coalitions and networks with like-minded organizations and individuals can change the public's views | 0 | |
| 09: Using the media to disseminate information can change the public's view | 0 | |
| 14: Public mobilizations (e.g., protests, letter writing campaigns, rallies) can set the policy agenda | 0 | |
| 19: Changes in the public's views can change policymakers' view | 0 | Low |
| 22: Changes in policymakers' views can change policies | 0 | Low |
| 23: Research and analyses can change the public's views | 0 | High |
| 03: Monitoring and evaluating existing policy can change how it is implemented | −1 | |
| 07: Monitoring and evaluating existing policy can set the policy agenda | −1 | |
| 18: Rebutting opposing views can change the public's views | −1 | |

(continued)

**Table 5.1**  (continued)

| Tactic (advocacy activity and its expected outcome) | Factor array | Relative extreme |
|---|---|---|
| 24: Policy advocacy in general produces more effective policies | −1 | |
| 12: Policy advocacy in general makes policymaking more people-centered | −2 | |
| 13: Pilot programs and demonstration projects can lead to policy change | −2 | Low |
| 21: Public mobilizations (e.g., protests, letter writing campaigns, voter registration) can build democracy | −2 | Low |
| 11: Policy advocacy in general builds legitimacy in a democracy | −3 | Low |
| 17: Litigation can change policy | −3 | Low |

*Note* See Chapter 2 for an explanation of the factor array scores

(information campaigns, media work, rebuttals) + (lobbying, coalitions) → policymakers' views → policy change

**Fig. 5.1**   Inside-outside strategy

but their effort was heavily opposed and outspent by representatives of major oil companies. Rather than standing alone to face that opposition, the advocacy organization built a coalition of organizations and garnered broad public support through their research and media work. The policy director explained that it was actually *helpful* to have a "big bad opponent" that already suffers from a negative public image. It made it easier for the advocacy organization to consolidate public interest and support for their campaign.

## Theoretical Foundations

The inside-outside strategy echoes Jack Walker's (1991) broad taxonomy of interest group tactics, but it combines them into one. He wrote, "…in order to bring pressure upon government officials most groups concentrate *either* on an 'inside' [tactic] of conventional lobbying *or* an 'outside' [tactic] meant to shape and mobilize public opinion" (p. 103, italics added). We observed organizations adopting both into a coherent strategy. The inside component here, however, is not as general as Walker's. For his inside strategy, Walker described broad-based lobbying of "political and administrative leaders" usually applying leverages including financial resources, substantive expertise, and constituency pressure. In the inside-outside strategy, however, we observed focused lobbying and recruitment of an identified political partner, such as a single legislator or executive. Here, the strategy is aligned with John Kingdon's (1984) conception of a *policy entrepreneur*: a key legislator or executive who can usher the issue through the decision-making process.

The strategy also mirrors other key aspects of Kingdon's (1984) streams theory, which states that the window of opportunity for policy change opens with the confluence of multiple streams of events. The problem stream represents the public's and decision makers' broad recognition of a social problem that warrants policy intervention. That recognition can be affected by media coverage, trends in social indicators, research reports, etc. The policy stream represents the varied policy alternatives that might mitigate or solve the social problem. This stream is fed by all the sources of policy ideas, such as think tanks, special interest groups, agencies, legislators, and others. The politics stream represents the political will to address the social problem. It ebbs and flows with election cycles, focusing events, changes in political leadership, and other social forces that build and deplete political capital among decision makers. According to Kingdon, these three streams exist and evolve independently, but their convergence in time marks a window of opportunity for policy change. In the inside-outside strategy, the policy advocates induce the streams' convergence by actively engaging them. In the problem and policy streams, advocacy organizations articulate the social problems needing policy intervention and develop proposed solutions to them, providing the evidence and arguments supporting them. In the politics stream, the advocates develop political will among decision makers by demonstrating strong public support and pressuring decision makers to act. While Kingdon's streams identify the *conditions* necessary for policy change, the inside-outside strategy identifies *assignments to key players* inside and outside the decision-making process, to facilitate policy change.

## Current Usage

Engaging policy decision makers, through lobbying and building relationships, is a key tactic of this strategy because it is how advocates usually develop the "inside" component. In contrast, the "outside" component can be developed through varied tactics including coalition building, public education, issue

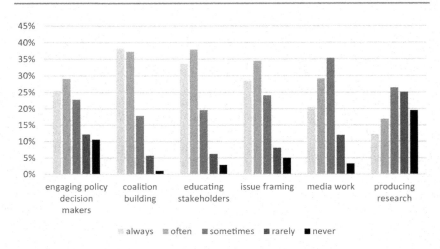

**Fig. 5.2**  Advocates' usage of key tactics in the inside-outside strategy

framing, media work, and producing and disseminating research. The popularity of these individual tactics is summarized in Fig. 5.2. Of the 685 organizations that responded to these tactics, engaging policy decision makers always or often is used by 55% while only 23% rarely or never used it. Among the tactics that can constitute the outside component, coalition building is the most popular, with 75% of respondents using it always or often. Educating stakeholders is a close second, with 72%, followed by issue framing at 62%, media work at 49%, and producing research at 29%.

We cross-tabulated the tactic of engaging policy decision makers with each of the other five tactics to estimate the proportion of advocacy organizations who appear to employ this strategy. We found that 54% (370) of our respondents use some variation of this strategy often or always in the policy work. We focused on these 370 respondents to describe the types of organizations that use the inside-outside strategy often or always.

Compared to the other organizations in our dataset, those employing the inside-outside strategy view policy advocacy as a much more important part of their mission. Over 60% of inside-outside strategists view policy advocacy as extremely important to their mission, with another 32% viewing it as very important. Clearly, this is an important advocacy strategy for those organizations that are more centered on policy advocacy ($\chi^2_{(4)} = 102.3$, $p = 0.00$). In contrast, only 30% of all other organizations view policy advocacy as extremely important

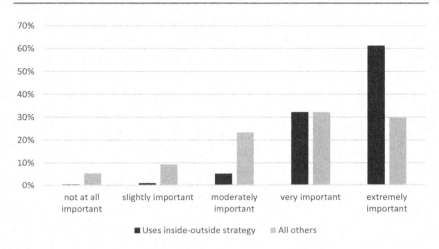

**Fig. 5.3** Importance of policy advocacy to mission of inside-outside strategists (*Note* $\chi^2_{(4)} = 102.3, p = 0.00$)

**Table 5.2** Resources devoted to policy advocacy by inside-outside strategists

|  | Staff devoted to policy-advocacy (%) | Financial resources devoted to policy advocacy (%) |
| --- | --- | --- |
| Uses inside-outside often or always | Mean = 51<br>S.D. = 30 | Mean = 43<br>S.D. = 32 |
| All others | Mean = 38<br>S.D. = 33 | Mean = 36<br>S.D. = 34 |

to their mission. This relative importance of policy advocacy to these organizations is reflected in the resources they devote to advocacy. Those using the inside-outside strategy devote about 13% more of their staff's time to advocacy (51% versus 38%, $t_{(565)} = 5.00, p = 0.00$) and about 7% more of their budget (43% versus 36%, $t_{(553)} = 2.70, p = 0.01$) (Fig. 5.3 and Table 5.2).

Next, we checked for any relationships between using the inside-outside strategy and particular advocacy issues. Respondents were asked to check the categories of public issues in which they are engaged, using a list of 20 established by NTEE. As shown in Fig. 5.4, no one issue category accounted for a majority of the organizations using the inside-outside strategy. Education and health/

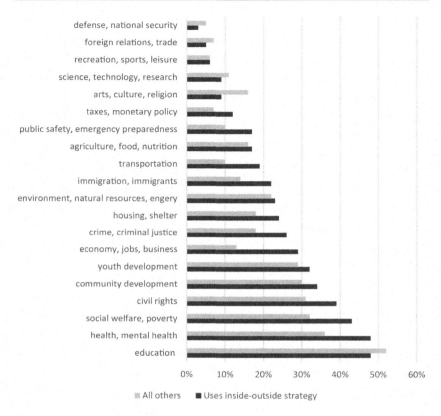

**Fig. 5.4**  Public issues engaged by inside-outside strategists

mental health came the closest with 48% working in each of those issues, closely followed by social welfare/poverty (43%) and civil rights (39%). (Note that respondents were asked to mark all the issues in which their organizations advocate.) In several issue areas, inside-outside strategists were significantly more involved than advocates using other strategies: health/mental health ($\chi^2_{(1)} = 9.24$, $p = 0.00$), social welfare/poverty ($\chi^2_{(1)} = 9.91$, $p = 0.00$), civil rights ($\chi^2_{(1)} = 5.12$, $p = 0.02$), economy/jobs/business ($\chi^2_{(1)} = 23.37$, $p = 0.00$), crime/criminal justice ($\chi^2_{(1)} = 6.33$, $p = 0.01$), housing/shelter ($\chi^2_{(1)} = 4.71$, $p = 0.03$), immigration/immigrants ($\chi^2_{(1)} = 8.63$, $p = 0.00$), transportation ($\chi^2_{(1)} = 10.48$, $p = 0.00$), public

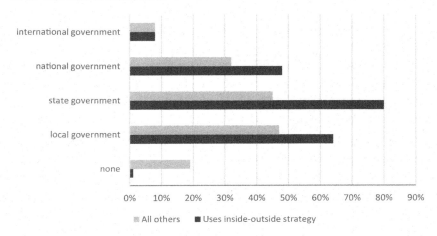

**Fig. 5.5** Levels of government targeted by inside-outside strategists

safety/emergency preparedness ($\chi^2_{(1)} = 7.57$, $p = 0.01$), and taxes/monetary policy ($\chi^2_{(1)} = 4.21$, $p = 0.04$). In only two issues do inside-outside strategists engage at a significantly lower level than other advocacy organizations: arts/culture/religion ($\chi^2_{(1)} = 8.46$, $p = 0.00$) and defense/national security ($\chi^2_{(1)} = 3.29$, $p = 0.07$). Among all these policy issue categories, the largest difference in engagement was for economy/jobs/business. Inside-outside strategists engage these issues at a rate that is over double that of other organizations (29% versus 13%).

Advocates using this strategy also distinguish themselves by the breadth of government entities with which they engage. As Figs. 5.5 and 5.6 show, inside-outside strategists work in local ($\chi^2_{(1)} = 19.93$, $p = 0.00$), state ($\chi^2_{(1)} = 90.61$, $p = 0.00$), and national ($\chi^2_{(1)} = 18.18$, $p = 0.00$) levels of government more than all other strategists combined. They also work with bureaucratic ($\chi^2_{(1)} = 57.01$, $p = 0.00$), judicial ($\chi^2_{(1)} = 14.13$, $p = 0.00$), legislative ($\chi^2_{(1)} = 108.95$, $p = 0.00$), and executive ($\chi^2_{(1)} = 74.56$, $p = 0.00$) branches of government significantly more than all other strategists in our data. Given government decision makers' key role in this strategy, this wide application across government is not surprising. However, its apparent application in the judicial branch of government is not obvious. The difference for that branch was the least significant, and we did not encounter a case specifically exemplifying this application.

Organizations using the inside-outside strategy also tend to be membership organizations with larger incomes than all other advocacy organizations.

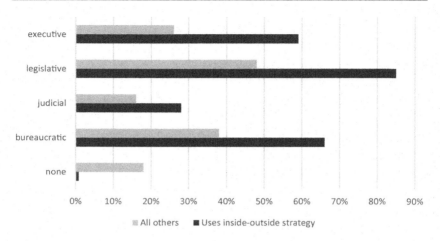

**Fig. 5.6**  Branches of government targeted by inside-outside strategists

They are more likely to have individual ($\chi^2_{(1)}=6.97$, $p=0.01$) and organizational ($\chi^2_{(1)}=7.29$, $p=0.01$) memberships, and less likely to have no memberships ($\chi^2_{(1)}=4.91$, $p=0.03$). And compared to all other advocacy organizations, they disproportionately occupy the upper strata of the income distribution ($\chi^2_{(8)}=69.80$, $p=0.00$) (Figs. 5.7 and 5.8).

The following three cases exemplify how the inside-outside strategy has been applied to local and state policy issues. The first briefly describes how a nonprofit applied the strategy to effect a local ban on plastic bags, which quickly led to the policy's spread across their region. Another case describes how the educational advocacy organization StudentsFirst used the strategy to influence a state legislature to reform their teacher evaluation system. The third case looks at a targeted effort by the American Lung Association to raise the tobacco tax in California. Although the ballot initiative did not pass, the advocates' reflection of their effort provides helpful insights into the strategy's implementation.

## Banning Plastic Bags

Single-use plastic bags were first introduced to shoppers in 1977, and their popularity rose out of consumers' concerns over deforestation from paper bag usage (Romer 2010). By 2007, the city of San Francisco alone was using about 180

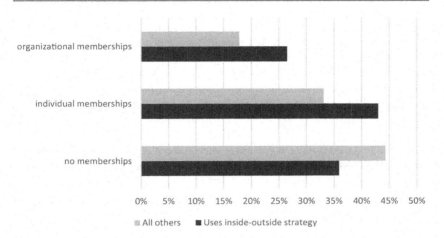

**Fig. 5.7** Memberships of inside-outside strategists

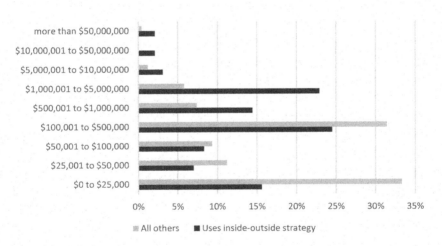

**Fig. 5.8** 2013 Income distribution of inside-outside strategists

million plastic bags per year. The problem was that the bags often became litter. Plastic bags are not recyclable by most curbside programs. Furthermore, when they are disposed as garbage, their lightweight makes them easily carried by the wind out of the waste stream and into the environment. In the San Francisco Bay, for example, plastic bags became a primary source of plastic pollution (Save the Bay, n.d., Stopped Pollution).

As early as 2005, San Francisco considered reducing plastic bag usage by imposing a 17-cent fee per bag fee. Stiff opposition from the plastic bag industry curtailed that plan, so instead the city sought to work with the city's grocers to voluntarily reduce plastic bag usage by 10 million per year (Romer 2010). This might have been achieved through more efficient bagging of groceries and the promotion of reusable bags, but the agreement did not substantially reduce plastic bag usage. In 2007, then-Mayor Gavin Newsom signed the Plastic Bag Reduction Ordinance, making San Francisco the first US city to significantly regulate plastic bag usage. The ordinance banned single-use plastic bags by large grocery stores, while requiring the use of reusable, recyclable, or compostable bags.

Behind the scenes of that ordinance, and several similar ones that would soon come throughout the San Francisco Bay Area, was Save the Bay (Save the Bay, n.d., Stopped Pollution). Save the Bay is a California nonprofit founded in 1961 to "protect, restore, and celebrate" the San Francisco Bay (Save the Bay, n.d., Our Mission), before the Environmental Protection Agency and today's major environmental statutes were established. Much of their work is in preventing pollution from entering the bay, and a key target was plastics. Stephen Knight was Save the Bay's political director, in charge of the organization's policy advocacy, and he described his organization's advocacy strategy for the local plastic bag bans.

He called it a "triangle of engagement." On the top point of the triangle, Save the Bay lobbied specific city council members, the inside component of the strategy. "We need a champion there in order to pass a plastic bag ban," he said. On the second point, they mobilized their membership and the public to demonstrate their substantial concern over the issue. Knight made it clear that this outside tactic supported the inside champions, consistent with the inside-outside strategy, rather than drove policy change itself. "We have about 12 thousand members and donors. That's a pretty large number to cite in a city council meeting. But I wouldn't call it 'key'," said Knight. "They are a useful tool, but they do not set or lead policy... we activate them when we need them" to support our initiatives. The third point of Save the Bay's triangle was specific city staff to gather information and prepare reports on the issue. Translated into the inside-outside strategy, the city staff straddled both tactics by being inside the formal decision-making body but providing informational support to the actual decision makers.

Knight summarized their campaigns as a confluence of "scientific facts" and "political judgement," and Save the Bay supported both ends. They wrote fact sheets on the amounts of trash generated, the proportions that are plastic, and their disposal in the bay. And they built local coalitions of interest groups, students, and neighborhood associations.

Save the Bay campaigned for plastic bag bans city-by-city around the San Francisco Bay Area. There are over 100 cities in the 9-county Bay Area. By 2013, Save the Bay had worked on bans that covered over 80 cities and 65% of the Bay Area's population.

In 2016, California voters passed Proposition 67, becoming the first state in the country to effectively ban all single-use plastic bags (Ballotpedia, n.d., California Proposition 67). Save the Bay was one of many nonprofit sponsors of the proposition.

## Evaluating Teacher Performance

StudentsFirst was a national policy advocacy organization established in 2010 when its founder, former Washington DC chancellor of schools Michelle Rhee, appeared on The Oprah Winfrey Show to kick off her "movement to transform public education" ("Michelle Rhee's Big Announcement" 2010). "Somebody needs to fix it!" exclaimed Oprah, referring to a public education system that Rhee claimed lacked qualified teachers, had bloated bureaucracies, and didn't give parents choices for their children. "You can do it! I am behind you!" That day, Rhee declared her organization's goals of gaining one million members and raising one billion dollars to organize communities and reform education policies.

Away from the glaring spotlight of Oprah's show, StudentsFirst had detailed plans for the most important policy changes they sought and the ways they would effect them. We met with Eric Lerum, their former Vice President of National Policy who oversaw the organization's legislative analyses and policy agenda, to discuss these plans. He told us their organization works primarily with state legislatures, rather than national or local stakeholders, because states have primary policy authority over K-12 public education. They organized their policy agenda around three basic "pillars" of education reform. The first was focused on elevating the teaching profession through reforms such as raising standards for teacher quality and changing the methods of evaluating teacher performance. The second focused on parents' access to school information and greater school choice, so they are empowered to select schools that best meet their children's needs. The third focused on enhancing the governance of schools, such that they are more accountable for their uses of resources and their students' educational outcomes.

When we spoke with Lerum, these three pillars were manifest as 37 specific policy campaigns in 18 states.

One was a bill in Georgia's legislature aimed at changing how that state's teachers and principals are evaluated. House Bill 244 in 2013 modified Georgia's professional standards for elementary and secondary education teachers and school leaders (Official Code of Georgia, Title 20, Chapter 2). Under the old code, a teacher's performance was evaluated against seven criteria: student achievement, classroom observations, participation in professional development, interpersonal skills, timeliness and attendance, adherence to school procedures, and personal conduct. But the code was mostly silent on how these criteria were measured and weighted in the evaluations, leaving those processes to the discretion of the schools or counties. Lerum said the loose policy, like those of many other states, resulted in "perfunctory" evaluations in which nearly all teachers received "satisfactory" ratings. Meanwhile, the students at those schools were not meeting learning standards at the same high rates. This had real ramifications for both students and teachers, Lerum claimed. Teachers weren't getting meaningful feedback to improve their classroom practice, which perpetuated a stagnant level of student underperformance.

StudentsFirst aimed to reform this system by tying teachers' evaluations more explicitly to students' performance and refining the formative feedback that teachers receive in their evaluations. Under House Bill 244, teachers would be evaluated by multiple measures that "prioritize growth in student achievement" and includes students' perceptions. The proposal prescribed student growth to account for at least 50% of the evaluation. Furthermore, the evaluations would be the primary basis for decisions regarding a teacher's retention, promotion, compensation, or dismissal. The bill identified four rating levels of teacher performance—"exemplary," "proficient," "needs development," and "ineffective"—and detailed the circumstances that warrant specific personnel actions. To enhance families' information about their schools, the bill also allowed Georgia's Department of Education to publish schools' teacher-performance data without identifying individual teachers. Lerum summarily explained that of all the school-based factors that affect student achievement, the quality of the teacher is the most influential, and a meaningful performance evaluation system can help improve the quality of teachers.

In Georgia, StudentsFirst had a chapter that consisted of a state director who managed the state team, an outreach director who coordinated the local membership, and contract lobbyists. The lobbyists worked within the statehouse, building relationships with legislators, educating them about how teachers should be evaluated, and backing them with information and a public support. This was their inside tactic, and they took a broader approach than Children Now did in California. StudentsFirst lobbied several Georgia legislators, rather than a single inside champion, to build broader support from the beginning. This may have been a practical adaptation of the tactic to a part-time legislature that is only in session for forty days per year. The limited time legislators spent together may require a heavier inside effort by the policy advocate.

On the outside, the outreach director employed several tactics to demonstrate the broad support for this reform. At that time, StudentsFirst had 30,000 members in Georgia, who were individuals who had "signed-up" with the organization, as Rhee had implored on The Oprah Show. The members' engagement with StudentsFirst varied widely, but their ideal member supported their advocacy by writing letters to the editors of local newspapers, testifying at legislative hearings, attending lobby days or rallies at statehouses, and networking and recruiting new members. Many did none of these things, but their membership still signaled their support for StudentsFirst's agenda.

Lerum explained the influence that the membership brought to their campaigns. "Bringing members to the capitol and getting them to the hearings, for us, was key," he said. "People see this happening at school board meetings, but statehouses are farther removed sometimes, even though they're the ones setting education policy. They really don't hear from the public a lot, and for years I think they only heard from one side... and that's from anybody in the establishment: associations, unions, systems people. For us to be able to get parents there, teachers there, students, and community members... to get a physical presence in a hearing room in the statehouse, for legislators to have people they can ask questions to and put a face to the testimony, it always makes a huge difference." Lerum further explained, "Teachers are particularly important, because everybody listens to teachers. They know what's going on. They're from the front lines."

Supporting the stateside operations was StudentsFirst's headquarters in Sacramento, California. There, a communications team organized earned and paid media for Georgia's campaign and coordinated editorial board meetings, to develop public support for their proposals. A policy team at the headquarters also provided legislative analysis that shaped the specific contents of the bill in Georgia, and helped promote it in Georgia's legislative process.

Their campaign for House Bill 244 took two years, partly because of the short forty-day legislative session in Georgia. StudentsFirst had expected that they would not be able to both introduce and pass the bill in one session, so they planned for a "long game" and got the bill passed in its second session.

In 2016, StudentsFirst merged with 50Can, another education advocacy nonprofit, to complement 50Can's advocacy resources with StudentsFirst's lobbying leverage (Resmovits 2016). Michelle Rhee had already stepped down as its chief executive officer in 2014, and the organization had downsized considerably.

## Raising the Tobacco Tax

In this advocacy strategy, the inside champion is a typically a few members of the formal decision-making body, who can lead the policy proposal through its adoption process. For example, it could be a caucus of elected representatives in a state assembly, a town council member, or key administrators in a government agency. In these examples, the nonprofit advocate supports the inside champion with information and public outreach. But who could the inside champion be for a citizens' initiative process,[1] in which the formal decision-making body is the voting public? For the American Lung Association in California (ALA), it was themselves in the case of the 2012 Proposition 29 campaign.

ALA in California bluntly claims their purpose is "to save lives" through education, advocacy, and research on lung health and disease (ALA 2019, Mission Impact & History). The national organization was originally founded in 1904 to prevent, detect, and treat a single disease, tuberculosis. That fight produced their groundbreaking Christmas Seals fund-raising campaign, which continues as an annual tradition for the organization and many American households. Since that founding, the organization has broadened its scope to general air quality and lung health. In California, ALA focuses on air pollution, climate change, indoor air quality, and smoking.

Kimberly Amazeen was their Vice President of Program and Advocacy in 2012, and oversaw all of their work on tobacco control. Her staff occupied seven offices throughout the state, from which they lobbied at the state capital and worked on policy development with local governments. "As we say, it all starts local and then trickles up," she told us. "When there's enough momentum [from local efforts], we will get a sponsor to support legislation [at the state level]."

Proposition 29 proposed to raise the state's excise tax on cigarettes by $1 per pack to $1.87 (Ballotpedia, n.d., California Proposition 29). The revenue from the increase would have increased funding for the state's tobacco control initiatives and cancer research. The necessity for the tax increase, according to Amazeen, was the success of the state's Tobacco Control Program, which was the result of the state's $0.25 per pack tax passed by voters in 1988 (California Department of Public Health 2017). The program is credited with dramatic reductions in the rates of smoking and cancer, four times faster than the rest of the country, according to Amazeen. But the decline in smoking also reduced tax revenues for

---

[1]Currently, 27 US states have a citizens' initiative or referendum process.

the program. Furthermore, California's tobacco tax was among the lowest in the country and had not been raised since 1998 (Boonn 2014). Proposition 29 aimed to shore up the program's revenues so it could continue its activities with the growing population.

It made sense for ALA to be the inside champion on a citizens' initiative. At that time, it already had over 20 years of experience with voter propositions in the state, so it was well able to usher the idea through the process. They managed the petition process, from drafting the proposition's language, to collecting voters' signatures to meet ballot qualifications, to submitting required documentation with the Attorney General of California. "Just in order to get the signatures to qualify for the ballot was almost a year-long effort," Amazeen said. "Our staff and volunteers went out on weekends and nights and lunchtime to go get the signatures needed."

The outside champion was a coalition calling themselves Californians for a Cure, led by three prominent voluntary health organizations: ALA, the American Heart Association, and the American Cancer Society California Division. They raised $12.3 million for the campaign, primarily from the coalition itself as well as the Lance Armstrong Foundation and Michael Bloomberg (Ballotpedia, n.d., California Proposition 29). As the outside champion, the coalition aimed to show broad public support for the proposition while increasing it. They did so through many tactics, including coalition building with local organizations, engaging editorial boards of newspapers, writing letters to the editor, presenting at local events, buying media, and using their grassroots action network to disseminate information. They had 2 or 3 people dedicated to meeting with editorial boards, from the *SF Chronicle*, to the *LA Times*, to the Bakersfield Californian, to build the show of support for the proposition. ALA's staff at all their offices gave presentations in all their communities. The campaign's leaders engaged in public debates against former legislators, and even physicians, who opposed the proposition. Through all these activities, the coalition focused their messages on the health improvements they expected from the tax. Supporters estimated that the tax would raise $600 million per year for cancer research, prevent 228,000 children from smoking, and save the lives of 104,000 people who quit smoking, "sparing [them] the pain and cost of battling cancer, emphysema or heart disease" (Eke et al. 2012).

There was broad public support for the proposal, but the coalition was fighting a mobilized and experienced tobacco industry that spent millions of dollars to sway people through media. The coalition's campaign was outspent by the tobacco industry by about 4 to 1. The opposition also formed a coalition, called Californians Against Out-of-Control Taxes & Spending. Their $46.8 million war chest was funded primarily by tobacco companies, the most prominent being Altria/Philip Morris and R. J. Reynolds (Ballotpedia, n.d., California Proposition 29). Not surprisingly, their messaging focused not on the pleasures of tobacco, but instead on the potential waste from the tax. Teresa Casazza of the California Taxpayers Association said, "...like high-speed rail, stem-cell research and other ballot-box budget initiatives before it, Proposition 29's good intentions are overshadowed by the fact that California simply cannot afford another billion-dollar government boondoggle to create another wasteful spending program" (Ballotpedia, n.d., California Proposition 29).

In June 2012, Proposition 29 ultimately failed by a slim margin of 0.2%, or 24,076 voters (Ballotpedia, n.d., California Proposition 29). Still, Amazeen chose to share this campaign with us, because she felt her organization had come very close to victory, and the campaign's executive committee felt that victory could be had in a future election with a couple adjustments in their tactics. "Losing, by definition, means that we fell short," she said. "It wasn't successful and we had to rethink our [tactic] moving forward." The first adjustment was clearer messages about how the tax revenues would be spent. They had been attacked hard by opponents on what the tax would specifically fund and how taxpayers would know if it were successful. The second was to put the proposition on a November general election ballot, rather than on a June primary election ballot. ALA's polling regularly showed 60% support for tobacco taxes, but they failed to get enough supporters to the polls in the primary election. President Barack Obama was the presumed Democratic nominee, favored by those who also supported Proposition 29, so they had less incentive to go to the polls. Meanwhile, Mitt Romney had not yet wrapped up the Republican nomination, spurring voting by those who tended to oppose Proposition 29 (Gerston 2012). These tactical adjustments appeared to make the difference. Four years later, during the November 2016 presidential election, Californians overwhelmingly passed Proposition 56, which increased the tobacco tax by $2 per pack to focus on youth prevention programs (California Department of Public Health 2017). ALA led the coalition in the campaign, this time fending off a $71 million effort by the tobacco industry to defeat the measure (ALA 2016).

It's important to consider how the ALA's *tactics* in this case might be similar to those of another organization using the public power strategy (Chapter 8). Indeed, both rely on a few similar tactics—coalition building, media work, building public support—so their advocacy activities might make them hard to distinguish. But two important distinctions separate their *strategies*: context and viewpoint. The tactics would be similar in this case *because it was a citizen's ballot initiative*, where the decision-making body is the voting public. Had the tobacco tax been proposed in the context of the state's legislative assembly, the ALA's tactics would have expanded to include a partnership with an inside legislative champion that they could support from the outside.[2] Meanwhile, the other organization employing the popular power strategy would see no changes in its tactics because it focuses on building public support without engaging elected officials directly. The second distinction would be the two organizations' viewpoints. The strategies presented in this book are primarily distinct in their underlying beliefs about how policy change happens, and less so in the tactics they employ. The inside-outside strategy recognizes the critical independent role that formal decision makers play in policy change. The public power strategy, on the other hand, views the actions of formal decision makers as dependent upon public preferences. These different viewpoints are important because they influence the tactics used in different contexts. In this case of Proposition 29, we know ALA employed the inside-outside strategy—and not the popular power strategy— because of our analysis using Q-methodology. We also confirmed it in a second campaign we discussed with ALA. In 2012, they also led a campaign to support the Advanced Clean Cars Regulation, which aimed to raise California standards on tailpipe emissions. In that case, the formal decision-making body was the California State Air Resources Board, and ALA's tactics included supporting specific champions inside the air board.

### Discussions

5a. One policy advocate said her work in developing outside support is to *dewonkify* complex policy problems and solutions into messages and arguments that can be easily understood by the public. Identify a complex policy problem or solution important to you. How would you translate it into a message with broad appeal?

5b. Children Now partnered with California's governor as their inside champion on educational finance reform. Think of a policy issue important to you or an organization with which you are affiliated, and identify potential inside champions in an appropriate government body.

---

[2]Interestingly, ALA had also tried to pass tobacco taxes through the legislature—over 30 attempts according to Amazeen—but found that the tobacco industry's heavy contributions to legislators' campaigns made their fight there too difficult. So they opted for a voter initiative to bypass the legislature.

Why did you select them, and what strengths and weaknesses would they bring to your campaign?

5c. Save the Bay and StudentsFirst leaned heavily on their memberships to provide outside support for their campaigns, while the American Lung Association and Children Now mobilized coalitions and the general public for support. What factors might lead policy advocacy organizations to choose different sources of outside support? How would a membership base versus general public be mobilized in a campaign?

5d. California Governor Jerry Brown is widely credited for the reforms in education finance that Children Now had championed for years before Brown was governor. How important is it for a nonprofit to get credit for its advocacy? What recognition, if any, do nonprofits need for policy advocacy? How might crediting an elected official with a policy win provide benefit to an advocacy campaign?

5e. The American Lung Association of California set itself up as the inside champion on a citizens' ballot initiative. If your state has a referendum or initiative process, find recent proposals that are important to you and research the organizations that led the process. If not, consider the benefits and drawbacks that a citizen initiative process could bring to your state.

5f. Californians for the Cure fought a campaign against a tobacco and taxpayer coalition that was far better funded, but perhaps not as positively regarded by the public. Indeed, the American Lung Association's Senior Director of Policy and Advocacy, Bonnie Holmes-Gen, said, "It is always helpful when you have a big, bad opponent... to generate a lot more public interest and support." To mitigate this handicap, the tobacco industry sent physicians and former legislators to represent their interests in media engagements. How does the public's perception of an interest group affect who should represent it? Consider a current policy cause, describe who should represent it, and explain why this messenger enhances the campaign.

# References

American Lung Association. (2016). *Mission Moment November—2016*. Retrieved from https://www.lung.org/about-us/media/mission-moment-november.html.
American Lung Association. (2019). *Mission Impact & History*. Retrieved from https://www.lung.org/about-us/mission-impact-and-history/.

Ballotpedia. (n.d.). *California Proposition 29, Tobacco Tax for Cancer Research Act (June 2012)*. Retrieved from https://ballotpedia.org/California_Proposition_29,_Tobacco_Tax_for_Cancer_Research_Act_(June_2012).

Ballotpedia. (n.d.). *California Proposition 67, Plastic Bag Ban Veto Referendum (2016)*. Retrieved from https://ballotpedia.org/California_Proposition_67,_Plastic_Bag_Ban_Veto_Referendum_(2016).

Boonn, A. (2014). *State Cigarette Tax Rates & Rankings*. Retrieved from https://www.tobaccofreekids.org/assets/factsheets/0097.pdf.

California Department of Public Health. (2017). *California Tobacco Control Program Overview*. Retrieved from https://www.cdph.ca.gov/Programs/CCDPHP/DCDIC/CTCB/CDPH%20Document%20Library/AboutUS/ProgramOverview/AboutUsProgramOverview081216.pdf.

Center for Education Policy Analysis. (n.d.). *Getting Down to Facts*. Stanford University. Retrieved from https://cepa.stanford.edu/gdtf/overview.

Children Now. (n.d.). *Our Team*. Retrieved from https://www.childrennow.org/about/team/.

Eke, C. C., Warner, J., & Gray, R. J. (2012). *Prop 29 Imposes Additional Tax on Cigarettes for Cancer Research*. Retrieved from http://voterguide.sos.ca.gov/past/2012/primary/propositions/29/arguments-rebuttals.htm.

Fensterwald, J. (2013). *Democratic Senators Offer Alternative to Brown's Funding Formula*. EdSource. Retrieved from https://edsource.org/2013/democratic-senators-offer-alternative-to-browns-funding-formula/30860.

Frank, R. M. (2010). The legacy of Arnold Schwarzenegger. *Daily Journal*. Retrieved from https://law.ucdavis.edu/centers/environmental/files/The-Legacy-of-Arnold-Schwarzenegger.pdf.

Gerston, L. (2012). *Prop. 29, the GOP Primary and Big Tobacco*. Retrieved from https://www.nbcsandiego.com/blogs/prop-zero/Prop-29-Tobaxcco-Tax-GOP-Primary-146331215.html.

Herdt, T. (2013). Facing California's top challenge. *Ventura County Star*. Retrieved from https://www.vcstar.com/news/2013/jan/29/herdt-facing-californias-top-challenge.

Kingdon, J. W. (1984). *Agendas, Alternatives and Public Policies*. New York: Longman.

Lempert, T. (2013). *Resolving to Transform Our School Finance System*. EdSource. Retrieved from https://edsource.org/2013/resolving-to-transform-our-school-finance-system/24887.

Michelle Rhee's Big Announcement. (2010, December 6). *The Oprah Winfrey Show*. Retrieved from http://www.oprah.com/own-oprahshow/michelle-rhees-big-annoucement-video.

Resmovits, J. (2016). Michelle Rhee's StudentsFirst will merge with education advocacy group 50Can. *Los Angeles Times*. Retrieved from https://www.latimes.com/local/education/la-me-edu-michelle-rhee-studentsfirst-50can-20160329-story.html.

Romer, J. R. (2010). The evolution of San Francisco's plastic-bag ban. *Golden Gate University Environmental Law Journal, 1*(2), 439–465.

Save the Bay. (n.d.). *Our Mission*. Retrieved from https://savesfbay.org/who-we-are/our-mission.

Save the Bay. (n.d.). *Stopped Pollution*. Retrieved from https://savesfbay.org/impact/stopped-pollution.

Schrag, P. (2013). Fixing the schools: The dream lives on. *Sacramento Bee*. Retrieved from https://www.sacbee.com/2013/01/11/v-print/5106586/fixing-the-schools-the-dream-lives-on.

Walker, J. (1991). *Mobilizing Interest Groups in America: Patrons, Professions, and Social Movements*. Ann Arbor: University of Michigan Press.

# Direct Reform

# 6

It's litigation. It's education. And it's prompting public action.
   —CEO of a foundation focused on social equity, describing their policy
advocacy strategy (name withheld)

The Lawyers' Committee for Civil Rights (LCCR) of the San Francisco Bay
Area "...advances, protects and promotes the rights of communities of color,
immigrants and refugees - with a specific focus on low income communities and
a long-standing commitment to African-Americans - by leveraging the power
of the private bar to support direct service, impact litigation and policy advocacy legal strategies" (LCCR, n.d., Mission & Values). It is a regional affiliate
of the national organization that was founded at the request of President John F.
Kennedy to support the civil rights movement in the 1960s. Since its founding
in 1968, the regional affiliate has successfully litigated major cases with broad
impact on social justice issues, including the racial integration of school districts,
the inclusion of women and minorities in public employment and in receiving public services, and the employment and educational rights of immigrants
(LCCR, n.d., History & Timeline).

   An important issue they recently advocated for was greater inclusion of
women- and minority-owned businesses in the awarding of service and construction contracts by the California Department of Transportation (Caltrans).
LCCR, staffed by employed and volunteer private-practice attorneys, represented
an association of businesses that included the Coalition for Economic Equity
and the San Diego chapter of the National Association for the Advancement of
Colored People (NAACP). Beginning in 2008, LCCR worked with their clients
and Caltrans officials to reform administrative processes that would more broadly
open up the competition for contracts to traditionally disadvantaged businesses.

© The Author(s) 2020
S. Gen and A. C. Wright, *Nonprofits in Policy Advocacy*,
https://doi.org/10.1007/978-3-030-43696-4_6

The effort fit within a wider national public policy framework supported by the US Department of Transportation's Disadvantaged Business Enterprise (DBE) program. The program aims to counter effects of discrimination by creating a level playing field for women- and minority-owned businesses competing for transportation-related contracts. Under the program, at least 10% of federal funds going to States and localities should be expended through DBEs (Associated General Contractors of America 2012). Each state establishes overall goals for DBE contracting empirically, based on the level of participation one would expect in the absence of discrimination. Under this federal policy, LCCR worked with Caltrans to improve access to transportation contracts by businesses led by disadvantaged groups.

In 2005, however, a non-minority-owned contractor challenged and won a lawsuit against the Washington State Department of Transportation's implementation of the DBE program, claiming that the state did not show sufficient evidence of ongoing discrimination to justify the DBE program there. Four years later, when Caltrans announced its plans—developed with LCCR—to reinstate a race-conscious DBE program based on recent evidence of disparities in contracting, the San Diego Chapter of Associated General Contractors of America sued in federal court, alleging Caltrans' violations of Title VI of the Civil Rights Act and the Equal Protection Clause of the Fourteenth Amendment. As a vested partner in the issue, LCCR filed a motion to intervene and formally represent the Coalition for Economic Equity and the NAACP in the case.

Oren Sellstrom was LCCR's Legal Director at the time. (In 2015, he became the Litigation Director at the Boston affiliate.) A graduate of Harvard Law School and former law clerk, Sellstrom had extensive experience in litigating civil rights cases in state and federal courts. He led LCCR's efforts from administrative advocacy with Caltrans to legal defense in court. There was no legislative advocacy with the case.

In 2011, a US District Court judge ruled in favor of Caltrans' DBE program (American Civil Liberties Union of Northern California 2011), but the plaintiffs appealed. In 2013, the Ninth Circuit Court of Appeals ruled in the case, also affirming Caltrans race-conscious DBE program. The decisions were based upon Caltrans' demonstrated underrepresentation of minority-owned businesses in their contracting activities. Said Sellstrom in a press release about the case, "Small businesses owned by women and minorities are a vital part of our state, employing thousands of Californians and strengthening the communities where they are located. It is essential that these businesses be allowed to compete on an equal basis for federally-funded contracts."

The case is typical of how LCCR advocates for civil rights and social justice in policy and government practices. The organization pushes government entities to do more to advance its causes, the government often gets sued in response, and LCCR intervenes to defend the reform against litigation. As Sellstrom described to us, "We are always representing our clients, in terms of letting government entities know that there are folks out here that [they] need to pay attention to and that have legal rights... At the same time, it is often that there are very specific asks or demands, that we want these specific reforms."

Although this case involved individual organizations, it affected businesses throughout California and beyond. Indeed, the outcome of this case is easily measured. The case was won in a federal court, with the decision applying to areas in the entire western US. According to Sellstrom, the number of minority-owned businesses that are doing contract work with Caltrans has since risen from less than 2% to nearly 10%. Even so, the larger war is ongoing. "Like a lot of our work, it is an ongoing struggle and you can't really take your eye off the ball, or things backslide or get worse. It just requires constant vigilance." The mission of trying to achieve equality will hopefully end, but not in the foreseeable future. LCCR tries to be proactive when they can, and set a next benchmark, but there is also a certain amount of work that is reactive, where they try to hold the line to prevent backsliding.

## The Direct Reform Strategy

When we think about public policy, our focus often narrows to the outputs of legislative bodies, such as statutes and ordinances of Congress, state legislatures, or city councils. A broader perspective of the concept, however, recognizes that how policies are implemented and evaluated are just as impactful as getting them adopted.

The direct reform strategy of policy advocacy distinguishes itself from others by the use of tactics that bypass legislative processes. Instead, it focuses on monitoring and influencing policy implementation in the executive and bureaucratic branches of government, and litigation in the judicial branch (07:+1, 17:+3). In the Caltrans case, LCCR worked with the state agency to develop contracting practices that leveled the competitive playing field for women- and minority-owned businesses. Later, when the practices were challenged in a lawsuit, LCCR defended the program in court.

Advocates employing the direct reform strategy supplement their efforts in government agencies and the courts with information campaigns aimed at building public awareness and support for their causes (06:+2, 16:+2, 20:+2). This can include messaging through paid and earned media, and research dissemination. Their underlying assumption is that bureaucratic and legal systems are influenced by public pressure, just as is often assumed about the legislative system. The inclusion of this tactic is somewhat surprising, given the common perception of the bureaucracy and judiciary being staffed by apolitical career professionals. Legislatures consist of elected representatives of the public, so we would expect public pressure to influence them. But agencies and courts consisting of non-elected specialists are assumed to resist public pressures. Not so, according to these policy advocates. Building public awareness of issues, and their stakes in it, is a critical component of this strategy.

Even so, these advocates' aim is not a more democratic or responsive political system (12:−3, 18:−2, 21:−2), nor is it to *mobilize* the public or create coalitions around their causes (10:−2, 14:−3). Instead, this strategy focuses on specific policy changes to improve social or physical conditions of their represented interests (08:+3) (Fig. 6.1, Table 6.1).

Like the Caltrans case, advocates using this strategy are often litigants using the judicial system to seek policy relief for those they represent. Sellstrom called this "impact litigation," the pursuit of policy change through the court system for large numbers of people, such as through class action lawsuits. Of course, this approach to direct reform requires specialized training in the legal system. Even so, the sizes and the sophistication of these organizations vary widely in our data, though the basic components of this strategy are common among them.

## Theoretical Foundations

The direct reform strategy includes tactics that target judicial or administrative processes, in lieu of legislative processes, to affect specific reforms in policies or administrative practices. In the litigation tactic, advocates in our dataset were plaintiffs or legal counsel to plaintiffs in lawsuits or threats of lawsuits. Their policy preferences are thus directly advanced through *adversarial legalism* (Kagan 1991, 1998), the theory of policy change that leverages the judicial process to advance causes, engage in political bargaining to reach compromises, and invoke

(litigation, monitoring) + information campaign → policy change → social/physical conditions

**Fig. 6.1**   Direct reform strategy

**Table 6.1** Factor array for direct reform strategy

| Tactic (advocacy activity and its desired outcome) | Factor array | Relative extreme |
|---|---|---|
| 08: Policies can change social and physical conditions | +3 | High |
| 17: Litigation can change policy | +3 | High |
| 06: Using the media to disseminate information can change policymakers' views | +2 | |
| 16: Using the media to disseminate information can hasten policy change | +2 | High |
| 20: Developing messages, framing issues, labeling and other strategies of rhetoric can change the public's views | +2 | High |
| 07: Monitoring and evaluating existing policy can set the policy agenda. | +1 | High |
| 03: Monitoring and evaluating existing policy can change how it is implemented | +1 | High |
| 09: Using the media to disseminate information can change the public's views | +1 | |
| 19: Changes in the public's views can change policy-makers' views | +1 | |
| 01: Developing messages, framing issues, labeling and other strategies of rhetoric can change policymakers' views | 0 | |
| 02: Lobbying and building relationships with policymak-ers can change their views | 0 | Low |
| 04: Building coalitions and networks with like-minded organizations and individuals can change the public's views | 0 | |
| 05: Rebutting opposing views can change policymakers' views | 0 | |
| 22: Changes in policymakers' views can change policies | 0 | Low |
| 24: Policy advocacy in general produces more effective policies | 0 | |
| 11: Policy advocacy in general builds legitimacy in a democracy | −1 | |
| 13: Pilot programs and demonstration projects can lead to policy change | −1 | |
| 15: Research and analyses can change policymakers' views | −1 | |

(continued)

**Table 6.1**  (continued)

| Tactic (advocacy activity and its desired outcome) | Factor array | Relative extreme |
|---|---|---|
| 23: Research and analyses can change the public's views | −1 | |
| 10: Building coalitions and networks with like-minded organizations and individuals can change policymakers' views | −2 | Low |
| 18: Rebutting opposing views can change the public's views | −2 | |
| 21: Public mobilizations (e.g., protests, letter writing campaigns, voter registration) can build democracy | −2 | Low |
| 12: Policy advocacy in general makes policymaking more people-centered | −3 | Low |
| 14: Public mobilizations (e.g., protests, letter writing campaigns, rallies) can set the policy agenda | −3 | Low |

*Note* See Chapter 2 for an explanation of the factor array scores

legal rights, duties, and procedural requirements related to policy. As the theory's name suggests, the tactic takes an adversarial approach, rather than a more congenial approach like lobbying.

The litigation tactic can fit organizations that have staff attorneys, emphasize issues such as civic rights or good governance, challenge ideological opponents, and earn media coverage of their issue (Epstein et al. 1995). Kagan (1991) cautions that adversarial legalism has drawbacks as well as benefits: while the courts can enable the politically weak to demand their rights from the government, as in the case of the civil rights movement, the unpredictable and costly nature of litigation makes this a potentially risky tactic. Group mobilization of the law, when people or organizations come together to form class action lawsuits, can spread risk and work together with other strategies, such as when a group of organizations form a coalition to file an amicus brief with the courts (Wasby 1983).

In the influencing policy implementation tactic, advocates monitor administrative processes and outcomes, or demonstrate successful reforms on small scales to agencies and the public, with the aim of inducing broad-based reform. In effect, these advocates lower the risk of systemic change by demonstrating success on a smaller scale first. Their tactic adapts incremental decision making to break down systemic change into a sequence of lower-risk decisions. While Lindblom (1959) formulated incrementalism as a descriptive theory of sub-optimal decision making, advocates take advantage of incrementalism's low-risk outcomes to promote their proposed changes.

In the direct reform strategy, advocates complement the above tactics with information campaigns to build public awareness of the issue. This often involves media work to disseminate information and viewpoints, particularly on issues that may be unfamiliar to the general public. Using the media in this way has been shown to raise public awareness of issues, increase political pressure for policy change, and speed the process of policy change (Linsky 1988).

## Current Usage

The direct reform strategy combines advocacy tactics with widely varying individual usages. On one hand are the core activities of reform: litigation and monitoring. Neither of these are commonly used by our survey respondents (see Chapter 2 for a description of the national survey). Only 13% use litigation always or often, with 73% using it rarely or never. Policy monitoring is a little more popular, with 37% using it always or often, and 36% using it rarely or never. On the other hand are the tactics aimed at building public support, which are widely used across strategies. Media work is employed by 49% of our respondents often or always, with just 15% using it rarely or never. Issue framing is used by 62% of respondents often or always, and just 13% use it rarely or never (Fig. 6.2).

We cross-tabulated the organizations to identify those that use combinations of these tactics—litigation or monitoring with media work or issue framing—which constitute the strategy. To describe organizations employing this strategy, we focused on those using it at least "often." Even though substantial numbers of the organizations use these tactics "sometimes," limiting the analysis to those on the more frequent end provides more assurance that the following descriptions are indeed characteristic of organizations focusing on this advocacy strategy. Of the 671 organizations in our dataset that responded to the questions on all these tactics, 249 organizations met this criterion and the following descriptions focus on them.

Frequent users of the direct reform strategy generally see policy advocacy as a central activity of their organization. When asked, "How important are your organization's advocacy activities to achieve your organization's mission?" 96% responded "very important" or "extremely important," compared with 70% of policy advocacy organizations focusing on other strategies (Fig. 6.3). Organizations often using this strategy devote about half of their staff time and financial resources to policy advocacy, about 12% more than the other policy advocacy organizations (Table 6.2).

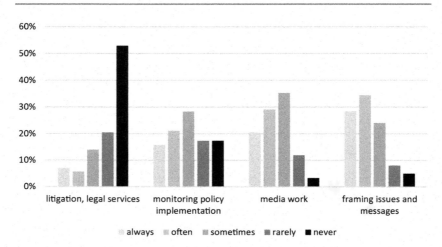

**Fig. 6.2** Advocates' usage of key tactics in the direct reform strategy

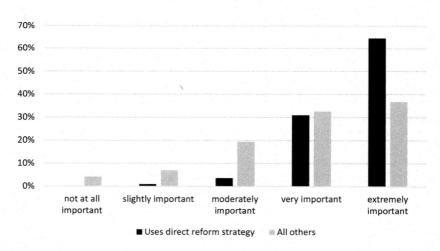

**Fig. 6.3** Importance of policy advocacy to mission of direct reform strategists (*Note* $\chi^2_{(4)} = 67.94$, $p = 0.00$)

**Table 6.2** Resources devoted to policy advocacy by direct reform strategists

|  | Staff devoted to policy advocacy (%) | Financial resources devoted to policy advocacy (%) |
| --- | --- | --- |
| Uses direct reform often or always | Mean = 53<br>S.D. = 29 | Mean = 47<br>S.D. = 33 |
| All others | Mean = 40<br>S.D. = 32 | Mean = 35<br>S.D. = 32 |

Next we analyzed the issues and venues associated with the direct reform strategy. We asked respondents to identify the public issues in which their organizations are engaged, using the categories of issues established by NTEE. As Fig. 6.4 shows, those using the direct reform strategy generally focus on the same issues as other policy advocates, but there are some noteworthy exceptions. They are more likely to focus on social welfare and poverty ($\chi^2_{(1)}= 6.93$, $p = 0.01$); civil rights ($\chi^2_{(1)}= 2.96$, $p = 0.09$); economy, jobs, and business ($\chi^2_{(1)}= 3.62$, $p = 0.06$); and public safety and emergency preparedness ($\chi^2_{(1)}= 5.07$, $p = 0.02$). They are more likely to target the national government ($\chi^2_{(1)}= 17.47$, $p = 0.00$), and state ($\chi^2_{(1)}= 31.65$, $p = 0.00$) and local governments ($\chi^2_{(1)}= 4.27$, $p = 0.04$), with a majority of them targeting each (Fig. 6.5). Consistent with this finding, direct reform strategists are less likely to target no level of government ($\chi^2_{(1)}= 20.14$, $p = 0.00$).

Our analysis of the branches of government targeted did reveal an important distinction to understand in this strategy (Fig. 6.6). Direct reform strategists are far more likely to target *each* branch of government—including the legislative branch—than other policy advocates ($\chi^2_{(1)}> 24$ and $p = 0.00$ for each branch). This seems to contradict the tenant that claims they *bypass* legislative processes in lieu of judicial and administrative processes, but it actually highlights the distinction between tactics and strategy. The primary tactics of the direct reform do indeed bypass legislatures in lieu of judicial and administrative venues, but the targets of their strategy may include legislatures who may be compelled to provide statutory responses to court cases or administrative monitoring. One of the following cases (Banning trans fats) illustrates this distinction when lawsuits brought by a policy advocate were ultimately followed by legislative action supporting the advocate's cause.

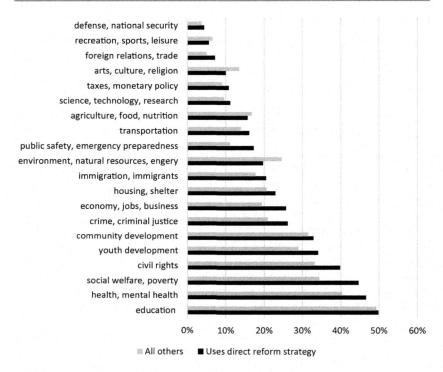

**Fig. 6.4** Public issues engaged by direct reform strategists

In our sample, those using this strategy often or always are slightly older than the others—mean year of founding is 1987 (S.D. = 23 years) compared to 1993 (S.D. = 56 years)—but the difference is not statistically significant. There are also insignificant differences, and very wide variances, in their numbers of employees and volunteers. For organizations using direct reform, their mean full-time-equivalent (FTE) employees is 13 (S.D. = 30), compared with 46 (S.D. = 678). Their FTE volunteers is 41 (S.D. = 118) compared to 26 (S.D. = 92).

However, nonprofits using direct reform do tend to be membership organizations (Fig. 6.7). This is true for both individual memberships ($\chi^2_{(1)}$= 5.67, $p = 0.02$) and organizational memberships ($\chi^2_{(1)}$= 7.56, $p = 0.01$). Furthermore, the direct reformers with memberships tend to have more members than their counterparts. The average individual memberships is 7637 (S.D. = 28,844) compared to 568 (S.D. = 1697). For organizational memberships, direct reform-

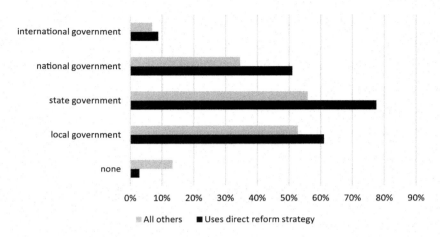

**Fig. 6.5** Levels of government targeted by direct reform strategists

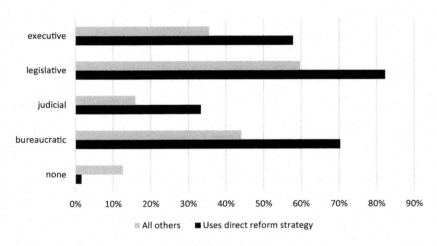

**Fig. 6.6** Branches of government targeted by direct reform strategists

ers average 191 (S.D. = 518) compared to 64 (S.D. = 138). Having memberships may provide these organizations a comparative advantage in their information campaign tactics, as their members can help promote the information. Nonprofits employing the direct reform strategy also tend to be better-funded organizations

$(\chi^2_{(8)} = 48.8, p = 0.00)$, perhaps reflecting a relatively higher expense of litigation as a tactic (Fig. 6.8).

Two cases illustrate diverse settings in which this strategy has been used. The first describes a one-person advocacy organization called Ban Trans Fats, with a

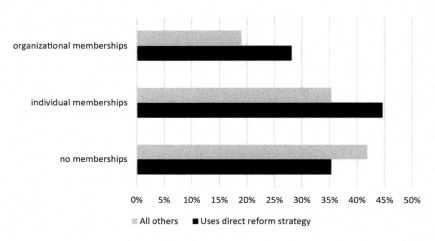

**Fig. 6.7**   Memberships of direct reform strategists

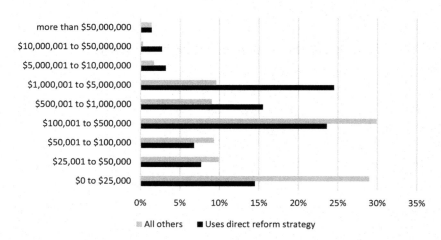

**Fig. 6.8**   2013 Income distribution of direct reform strategists

mission that is encapsulated in its name. This organization was founded by an advocate who was personally affected by the link between trans fats and health, and it catalyzed local and national policy changes using tactics including litigation and earned media. The second case study highlights efforts by two large environmental advocacy organizations, Environmental Integrity Project and Sierra Club, to ultimately shut down coal-fired power plants in the United States through policy monitoring and lawsuits, coupled with an ingenious campaign to make the issue personal to the general public.

## Banning Trans Fats

Trans fats found their way into our diets through partially hydrogenated oils (American Heart Association, n.d.), artificial oils first developed over a century ago. The first of these was a "crystallized cottonseed oil," which went to market under the acronym Crisco (Hallock 2013). The ingredient became popular because of its low cost and long shelf-life, as well as fluctuations in the supplies and demand for butter and animal lard.

On June 16, 2015, however, the Food and Drug Administration (FDA) adopted a new regulation that effectively eliminated trans fats from food products by 2018. Food companies had until June of that year to either remove the ingredient from their products, or petition to use small quantities of it for specific purposes. The FDA based their decision on evidence that trans fats are not safe for use in foods because of its link to heart disease. The Center for Science in the Public Interest had estimated that trans fats have caused about 50,000 fatal heart attacks per year (Leonard 2015). Furthermore, healthier oils are readily available for food companies, though at a higher cost. The move appears to be a death knell for an ingredient that was once ubiquitous in cookies, pastries, popcorn, fried foods, and other processed foods. But the decline in usage has been gradual, beginning in 2003 (Leonard 2015), following studies from the 1990s that linked it to heart disease (Hallock 2013), and advanced by a lawyer who believed his stepfather died from eating trans fats laden margarine.

Stephen Joseph is a public interest lawyer who fought to ban trans fats for a very personal reason. His stepfather was a health-conscious eater, always following popular literature on diet and health. Through the 1980s, margarine was espoused as a healthier alternative to butter, and Joseph's stepfather ate it every day. A few years after his stepfather's death, in 2002, Joseph read a *San Francisco Chronicle* editorial (Put trans fat on label 2002) calling for the labeling of trans fat in processed foods, such as margarine. The article immediately followed the defeat of a bill in the California state legislature that would have required such labeling. It was the first time Joseph had heard of trans fat, and he saw a connection between his stepfather's eating habits and his death. Joseph shared the article with his mother, who believed that if her husband had known the dangers and prevalence of trans fat, he would have made better dietary choices. Joseph's mother wrote letters about her husband's fate to the Department of Health and the parliament in her native Britain, but got no meaningful responses. That is when Joseph decided to take the issue up himself, where he lived in California. The *Chronicle* editorial claimed that the FDA had been studying the health risks of trans fats since 1994, "But this guardian agency has done nothing to curb its use or require labels to note its existence. The reasons are plain. Trans fat is so widely used that it can't easily be banned." Joseph did not resign himself to this conclusion. Instead, he took it as a personal challenge, and in 2003, he founded Bantransfats.com, Incorporated.

## Lawsuits as Direct Reform

Joseph's initial target for his campaign was a giant: Nabisco's Oreo cookies. Besides being a popular and iconic packaged cookie that used trans fats, Oreo presented Joseph with other qualities important to Joseph's tactic. First, trans fat was not labeled on the package, and trans fat was not well understood by the public. This allowed Joseph to use as a basis for a suit a California law that shields companies from liability for unhealthy products when it is well-known that the product is unsafe. "But this product, trans fat, is not commonly known to be unsafe," he said. "That's why trans fats is a far stronger case than tobacco or McDonald's because people know those are dangerous" (Severson 2003). (Earlier that same year, a class action lawsuit filed against McDonalds by an obese customer was thrown out of court.)

Second, the cookie was directly marketed to children. A Nabisco Web site for Oreos, he claimed, included games for children, such as school contests for stacking Oreo cookies. This allowed Joseph to steer away from the choices of adult consumers and focus on a more vulnerable population. Lastly, there were direct market competitors of Oreo cookies that did not use trans fats. That allowed Joseph to test for himself whether the ingredient was necessary for a good-tasting affordable cookie. He emphasized that his objective was not to take down Oreo cookies or promote healthy diets. "I wasn't going to file the lawsuit if taking out the trans fats would make Oreos inedible," he said. Instead, he was focused on removing from food products an *unnecessary* ingredient that the National Academy of Science's Institute of Medicine had concluded was not safe for consumption (Severson 2003). He bought a package of Newman-O's and was satisfied. "I like Oreos, but I really like the Paul Newman ones more. I ate the whole packet. They were really good!"

On May 1, 2003, Joseph filed a lawsuit in Marin County Superior Court, California, to prevent Kraft Foods from selling Nabisco Oreo cookies to children in California because the cookies are made with trans fats. The relatively narrow focus and jurisdiction of the suit belied the broad reach it potentially had, and Joseph understood this from the beginning. Any changes that Nabisco would make to keep the California market—whether from a ruling on the lawsuit or, more likely, the intense publicity he expected to get from the case—could practically affect food products for the country. The objective of this first suit, to Joseph, was to draw intense public attention to the harmful ingredient. The suit was a tactic within a larger strategy to ban trans fats.

Joseph issued a press release on his Web site, Bantransfats.com, about his lawsuit, and he waited. Journalist Kim Severson of the *San Francisco Chronicle* was the first to contact him, on May 9th, and cover the story. Her article appeared on the 12th (Severson 2003), and claimed Joseph's suit was the first of its kind in the United States. The Associated Press released an article the same day, reaching 1400 daily newspapers including *USA Today* which published it under the title "California suit seeks ban on Oreos." Both of these printed stories took a positive tone with the suit, each citing earlier research linking trans fats to health problems. However, that evening, CNN aired an interview with Joseph by anchor Anderson Cooper, which took a more negative view of the suit. Cooper compared the suit to prior ones against fast food restaurants, which were declared frivolous and thrown of out court. Despite these opposing perspectives—or perhaps because of it—the story quickly gained national attention and a media frenzy was on. Joseph claimed that two servers supporting his email and Internet accounts crashed with the onslaught of attention. He was also hit with a deluge of interview requests, and he replied to several—including *The View*, *NBC*, and *Fox News*—to maximize national coverage. He believed the media was key to raising public awareness of the dangers of trans fats.

On May 13th, Joseph appeared on *Good Morning America*, when host Robin Roberts continued the public critique of his suit. "Isn't it up to the consumer, as well, just not to buy these products if you know that they're bad?" she asked. Joseph emphasized with Roberts, as he did with Cooper the day before, that trans fats were largely unknown to the public yet harmful. In fact, part of his tactic in giving these interviews was to keep repeating the words "trans fats" to raise public awareness. The tactic worked. He claimed that in the 15 minutes he was on the show his Web site received 80,000 hits. That same day, *The Wall Street Journal* published an editorial calling Joseph "San Francisco's Cookie Monster." The next day *The Denver Post* published its own editorial, "Let them eat tofu," which named Joseph the recipient of their "Doofus Award." Still, a minority of other articles were more supportive, including some published in *The New York Times, CBS.com, MSNBC.com,* and *US News and World Reports.* Reflecting on those few days, Joseph admitted the opposing media was doing more to publicize the issue than the supporting media. He estimated that during this initial media coverage, he received over 100 phone calls, over 10,000 emails, and was covered on television "nonstop."

The national coverage did come with some personal cost to Joseph. His email account was inundated with opinions on his suit, most of them of the trolling variety. Joseph estimated that "95% of the emails I received were hostile. I mean *really* hostile." Here is a sampling:

YOU SHOULD BE ASHAMED OF YOURSELF! TRYING TO BAN OREOS. DON'T YOU HAVE ANYTHING BETTER TO DO? With everything that is going on in the world, can't you find a better cause? Can't you think of anything else that should be banned, that you can put your efforts into? There are starving children in the world, abused children, molested children, illiterate children, orphaned children and you are focusing your pathetic little life on OREOS? Common sense tells people that Oreos are high in sugar and in fat and if people choose to give their children Oreos then that is their decision. That is why we live in AMERICA, LAND OF THE FREE, WHERE WE CAN EAT WHATEVER THE HELL WE WANT!!! IF YOU DON'T LIKE IT MOVE TO AFGHANISTAN, YOU DAMN TERRORIST!

"STOP suing and CLOGGING up the courts with these ridiculous lawsuits!"

"I hope you choke to death on an Oreo cookie full of trans fats."

I made Oreo cookies at my job which now I am a baker at. You need to understand if you win we can be out of job. You wouldn't care cause your job gets more money than us poor people.

There were a few supporting emails too, such as these:

I read the lawsuit over the Oreo cookies and I thought 'Hey these are my cookies and he has no right to ban them.' Instead, I decided to look into this a bit further and what I saw I was shocked... I have been putting trans fats into my family and grandkids. Oreos are our favorite cookies and it is nothing for me to buy a bag or two a week, not knowing that I have been poisoning my family and myself. Thanks for bringing this into the light...

I am so glad that someone has finally taken the lead in getting this issue into the media. THANK YOU for standing up for us!

Despite the mostly personal attacks, Joseph saw the silver lining. Trans fat had entered the space of public discourse and had become a "main event." After the first several days of intense media coverage, Joseph felt his campaign would be successful.

Joseph had actually quietly dropped the suit shortly after media coverage began. Joseph claimed he had a private conversation with Kraft representatives who agreed to remove trans fats from Oreo cookies if he dropped the lawsuit without prejudice. Joseph agreed, and was even surprised when Kraft announced a few months later that they would work to remove trans fats from all their products. Despite the end of the suit, the story continued for several days, with dozens more articles and editorials published throughout the United States and internationally in the UK, Canada, Australia, and Singapore. And for Joseph, the campaign continued. For him, the Oreo cookies suit was a means to build public pressure to at least require the labeling of trans fats on food products, or at most to ban the ingredient all together.

About one week later, on May 22nd, Joseph filed a petition to the US Food and Drug Administration (FDA) on behalf of BanTransfats.com to protect consumers by forcing the FDA to regulate the labeling of trans fats. By this point, there had already been failed legislative attempts to require the labeling of trans fat, but now public awareness of trans fat, and public pressure to label it, was rising. By the end of that summer, the Bush administration instructed the FDA to issue a rule to put trans fats on nutrition labels of food products. That rule went into effect in 2006 (Center for Food Safety and Applied Nutrition 2003).

And just as the labeling rule went into effect, Kraft quietly manufactured its reformulated Oreos without trans fats. They weren't marketed as such, but their nutrition label indicated it. To Joseph, this was the tipping point for the whole issue. He even cited the *domino theory* when describing this event. Oreos are black and white, like dominos, and when the first falls, others would too. "Everyone had to follow because you could not be out there and not be trans fats free. You just couldn't survive."

Joseph knew that he was not solely responsible for the eventual ban on trans fats, and his telling of his story was peppered with the many researchers, politicians, journalists, and other activists that applied pressures in their own ways. Indeed, he acknowledged that his own awareness of trans fats was through others' work. Still, he didn't downplay the catalyzing influence of his lawsuit. "If it was going to happen anyway, it wouldn't have happened at that speed… When I got involved, it wasn't moving." The California state legislature had failed to pass a bill to label trans fats, despite growing scientific evidence of its health effects. And consumers were mostly unaware of the issue. His strategy was to draw high public attention, which would compel some government action. The lawsuit—against a private company—was his tactic to get both. He summarized, "If you want to get action, you've got to file a lawsuit," and "… you've got to get the media with you. If you don't get the media, forget it."

## Demonstration Projects as Direct Reform

While the trans fats dominos began falling among the packaged food industries, restaurants lagged behind. They continued to be major users of trans fats, and foods prepared in restaurants would not be subject to the labeling requirements of packaged foods. So Joseph next set his sights on restaurants.

McDonald's picked themselves to be Joseph's first restaurant target. In 2002, before Joseph got involved in trans fats, McDonald's announced their independent initiative to reduce trans fats in their menu. It was part of larger effort to respond to evolving consumer tastes by making their products healthier, and they publicly claimed they would reduce trans fats by 48% in their French fries by early 2003. In late 2003, after he filed suit against Kraft, Joseph inquired with McDonald's on their progress in reducing trans fats. He discovered that little had been done. Ralph Alvarez, McDonald's US Chief Operating Officer at the time said in a statement, "While speedy implementation is an admirable goal, we are most focused on the satisfaction of our customers and the quality of our products" (McDonald's hit with fat lawsuit 2004). In 2004, Joseph filed a federal lawsuit against McDonald's for false advertising.

As with his experience with Oreos, Joseph took a lot of public anger for suing McDonald's. As one person wrote to him,

> If I want to eat McDonald's Fries or their nuggets etc. THAT IS MY CHOICE and I'LL SUFFER THE CONSEQUENCES! … If the taste changes because of your frivolous lawsuit then you should pay for their losses in profits.

The case was eventually settled in 2005, with McDonald's agreeing to publicize the status of their efforts to remove trans fats from their menu, and pay $7 million to the American Heart Association to finance a consumer education campaign on trans fats (McDonald's settles trans fats lawsuits 2005). But for Joseph, the question remained whether the change from a trans fat frying oil would make the food taste bad.

Restaurants remained heavy users of trans fats, particularly to fry foods, claiming that trans fats last longer and make fried food tastes better than zero trans fat oils. Joseph searched for evidence supporting the claim but could not find any, so he decided to test it himself. As in the case of Oreos, Joseph didn't want to ban trans fats from French fries if doing so would make them taste bad. But this time, a personal comparison test would not do. He wanted to scientifically compare the performance of trans fats against zero trans fats oils, to convince restaurants to make the change. Joseph admits that it was a gamble, because "I really did not know" if trans fat free oils were better. He had heard anecdotal evidence, but restaurants did not have the capacities or will to do the testing themselves.

In 2006, Joseph contracted with Texas A&M University's Food Protein R&D Center (now the Process Engineering R&D Center) to hold an independent test of frying oils. Joseph invited several producers of cooking oils to have their products compared against a leading partially hydrogenated oil in a frying contest. Seven companies responded with nine zero trans fat oils.

They were AAK-FryChef, ACH, Bunge, Cargill, ConAgra, Loders Croklaan, and Whole Harvest (FryTest.com 2007).

Their oils would be compared to the trans fat oil on several criteria, including: fatty acid profile (trans, saturated, monounsaturated, and polyunsaturated fatty acids); food to oil ratio, the weight of oil used to cook the unit weight of food; fry life, as measured by the mass concentration of "total polar materials" (a standard of 24% TPM was applied); sensory changes determined by trained panelists; and consumer preferences determined by at least 40 tasters (FryTest.com 2006). The test tasters judged the food fried in different oils on appearance, color, flavor, crispiness, greasiness, and overall liking. The identities of the oils were coded to facilitate blind testing.

French fries were selected as the test food, because they represent the "overwhelming majority of deep fried food" (FryTest.com 2006, p. 2). They are also more uniform in physical qualities than other popularly fried foods such as chicken and fish. The Lamb Weston 3/8" Straight Cut Fry, with no coatings or seasonings, was selected for the contest.

The testing was conducted from November 2006 to February 2007. Each oil was used to cook French fries 300 times in 13 frying days. Reflecting on the work required to plan and implement the test, Joseph said, "I've never done anything more difficult in my life. This was the most difficult thing, and my biggest achievement!"

To Joseph's relief, the test results looked great for the trans fat free oils (FryTest.com 2007). They all demonstrated "excellent" fry lives that were equivalent to or better than that of the partially hydrogenated oil. They also found that the price difference for using zero trans fat oils was "totally insignificant." Most impressively, all nine zero trans fat oils were preferred over the partially hydro-genated oil by the consumer panelists. (The test, including full details of the pro-cedures and results, are kept online at FryTest.com.) "The oil companies went touting themselves afterwards. We're the best for this! We're the best for that!" said Joseph. And the restaurants paid attention. "We had a tremendous response from the restaurants afterwards… They used the results to make the switch," said Joseph. After the frying oil test, owners and governments across the country were considering options for removing trans fats from their restaurants. "The moral of the story is you can't just say it. You got to prove it," Joseph said.

He later testified at a New York City hearing on a proposed ban on trans fats in that city's restaurants, and in 2007, the city became the first in the country to phase out trans fats (Radcliffe, n.d.). "The doughnuts did not disappear from New York City," Joseph said. "They are just healthier." A subsequent study, published in *JAMA Cardiology*, confirmed this conclusion, attributing a 6.2% drop in hospi-tal admissions for heart attacks and strokes to bans of trans fats (Bakalar 2017). After New York, other cities and states took steps to reduce or eliminate trans fats, and by the end of 2007, Bantransfats.com went dormant because Joseph felt it had catalyzed and set in motion the eventual end of trans fats.

Stephen Joseph's case illustrates three key tactics of the direct reform strat-egy: litigation, media work, and demonstration projects. His application of these tactics is not necessarily typical, however. He chose to sue and lobby private cor-porations—and targeted iconic products in Oreos and McDonald's French fries—with the expectation that the public awareness it would generate might influence public policy indirectly. His case is also unusual in that he was essentially a one-person advocate. As such, his case demonstrates how the media and the judi-cial system can help under-resourced policy advocates get a more level playing field with large institutions.

## Closing Coal-Fired Power Plants

A second case of the direct reform strategy contrasts advocates in larger, better-resourced organizations, fighting a national war with battle fronts in mul-tiple states. It sounds like a quixotic quest, but instead of allegorical windmills in Spain, it's literal coal-fired power plants in the United States. The giant-slayer in this story is Eric Schaeffer, a dedicated and top-ranking Environmental Protection Agency official who ultimately left his job in order to influence the agency's reg-ulation of energy plants from the outside.

## The Outside Advantage in Direct Reform

The Environmental Integrity Project (EIP) is a nonprofit organization established in 2002 after Schaeffer, its founder and executive director, publicly resigned from the EPA to bring light to the George W. Bush administration's efforts to weaken standards established under the Clean Air Act. At the time of his resignation, Schaeffer was EPA's director of the Office of Regulatory Enforcement, the part of the agency charged with ensuring that industries, governments, and other pollution-generating entities comply with environmental regulations governing air and water quality, and toxics and waste management (Office of Regulatory Enforcement 1994). While under the Clinton administration, Schaeffer's office brought lawsuits against some of the largest power companies in the country, forcing them to comply with air quality standards and reduce their emissions of nitrogen oxide, sulfur dioxide, and other pollutants. But the Bush administration worked with lobbyists representing those same companies to loosen regulations on pollutants. "In a matter of weeks, the Bush administration was able to undo the environmental progress we had worked years to secure… It became clear that Bush had little regard for the environment—and even less for enforcing the laws that protect it. So… I resigned, stating my reasons in a very public letter to [EPA] Administrator [Christine] Whitman" (Schaeffer 2002, p. 1). Loosening regulations, and being selective in enforcing them, happens "behind the scenes, in complicated ways that attract less media attention (and therefore may be politically safer)" (p. 2). Whitman herself later confirmed the administration's efforts when she published her memoir in 2005, describing "…how obsessed so many of those in the energy industry, and in the Republican Party, have become with doing away with environmental regulation" (quoted in Little 2005, p. 1). Rather than facilitate those policy changes, Schaeffer chose to fight them, from outside the agency. He secured funding, particularly from the Rockefeller Family Fund, which allowed him to leave the agency and found EIP.

The organization's goal is to "help local communities… obtain the protection of environmental laws" (Who we are 2017a). They do this by holding "federal and state agencies, as well as individual corporations, accountable for failing to enforce or comply with environmental laws," and by providing "objective analysis of how the failure to enforce or implement environmental laws increases pollution and affects public health."

Their core tactic to advancing their mission consists primarily of lawsuits against permits to emit pollutants, citizen suits against polluters, and suits against the EPA itself and other government agencies for failing to implement and enforce environmental laws and regulations. Schaeffer brought to EIP his inside understanding of EPA's enforcement processes to advocate from the outside for better enforcement. Schaeffer understood that being on the outside of the EPA allowed him to advocate for policy change in ways he was not able to from within. When describing his public resignation letter criticizing the Bush administration, he admitted "This is the kind of thing you can't say when you're in government, and it is something I really feel needs to be said," and they "reflect the views of just about all the civil servants working in enforcement" (EPA resignation prompts hearings 2002). He later reflected that while at the EPA, "I never saw many environmentalists in my office pushing on enforcement issues. It's just not an area where they interact much," though he saw the potential influence that could come from it. "They count on [EPA] to do the right thing, and we generally got support from them. They cheered us on, but I didn't interact with them." When EPA's enforcement with coal-fired plants was being held back by the Bush administration, Schaeffer saw how the coal industry influenced that action, and he saw the need for "pressure from the outside" from environmental interests.

EIP represents the plaintiffs in their suits, who are usually local communities and environmental groups like the Sierra Club. EIP looks for winnable cases, and then finds the clients that will work with them to bring the suits to court. They complement this tactic with scientific research and policy analysis to support their suit's cases, and media outreach to build public awareness and support of their battles. Today EIP has about 24 attorneys on payroll, along with key staff to manage research and communications.

EIP's docket mostly focuses on three specific sources of pollution: coal-fired power plants, petroleum refineries, and concentrated animal feeding operations. These targets stemmed directly from EPA's own foci when Schaeffer worked there, and they represented the pollution sources that offered the greatest potential cuts in pollutants.

## Making Pollution Unprofitable

During EIP's first years, a wave of permit applications for new coal plants came to the EPA. By that time, EIP had convened a few national meetings of interest groups focused on climate change, greenhouse gases, and coal's contributions to them. The group rallied to challenge these new permits in court, as well as current permits for existing plants, with EIP representing the plaintiffs.

Their suits generally do not seek to directly prevent the construction of plants, or directly close down existing ones, by court order. Rather, they often seek to raise the emission standards in the permits, based on effects on environmental quality and public health, to levels that make it unprofitable for the plant to continue. Removing pollution from plant emissions bears operational costs, and removing more pollution bears more operational costs, which can cut into the power companies' profits. Schaeffer called this tactic a "grind-it-out permit challenge," that required them to "know the law and work hard with experts" in emissions from power plants.

They target permit applications for new plants, as well as permit renewals for existing plants, and they have been instrumental in the eventual closure of several plants. "I don't think because we were so brilliant and so terrifying that we stopped a $2 billion coal plant," Schaeffer explained. Instead, the EIP lawsuits meant that the power companies "were going to have to spend more on [emissions] controls" than they had planned, and the increased costs of production made them unworthy of their investments. "We were two or three years into it [and] the price of gas starting dropping. Those plants just had nowhere to go," in terms of profitability.

## EIP Case of the Fayette Power Project

<u>Summary</u>: EIP sued the Lower Colorado River Authority (LCRA) for violations of the Clean Air Act at the Fayette Power Project, a coal-fired power plant located between Houston and Austin and serving over 1,000,000 customers in central Texas. The federal complaint was filed jointly with the Texas Campaign for the Environment and Environment Texas, alleging violations "in 20 different rolling 12- month periods during a five-year span," in which, "particulate matter emissions exceeded the cap of 5155 tons per year…" (Ankrum 2012). The case was ultimately settled out of court, with LCRA agreeing to reduce mercury emissions at the plant, use clean fuels for start-ups (either distillate oil or natural gas), and continuously monitor emissions (Texas Campaign for the Environment 2013).

Within a few years of the settlement, and after Austin passed a law that would source at least 55% of its energy from renewable sources by 2025, LCRA planned to retire the plant in 2022 (Cameron 2014).

<u>Timeline of key events</u>:

- July 15, 2010: EIP, Texas Campaign for the Environment, and Environment Texas send a letter of intent to sue to LCRA, claiming the plant violated the federal Clean Air Act.

- March 7, 2011: The three organizations formally sue LCRA, filing the complaint with the Southern District of Texas, Houston division. The complaint asks the court to "assess a civil penalty against LCRA" for the maximum amounts, ranging from $32,500 to $37,500 per day, for each violation (Ryser 2011).
- June 8, 2012: EIP and Texas Campaign for the Environment send a second letter of intent to sue to LCRA, this time focusing on particulate matter emissions from the power plant (Ankrum 2012). The letter of intent is filed as the first suit is expected to go to trial in February of 2013.
- June 15, 2012: LCRA issues a press release rebutting the claims of the letter, stating, "This notice of intent to file yet another lawsuit with similar allegations as in a previous suit is completely unwarranted and harassing... FPP is one of the cleanest and most efficiently operated coal plants in Texas" (Lower Colorado River Authority 2012).
- February 19, 2013: A settlement is reached in the lawsuit, requiring LCRA to reduce mercury emissions and provide monitoring of the plant. LCRA also agrees to publish its emissions data online.
  December 22, 2014: Austin, Texas commits to 55% of its energy to be generated from renewable sources by 2025. "The plan is the result of months of negotiations between the City Council, Austin Energy, faith leaders, the Sierra Club, and seven other environmental organizations, and is expected to result in a 75-80% reduction in carbon emissions in the city's electricity generation..." (Roselund 2014).

In other cases, EIP seeks to force government agencies to regulate polluters more effectively. For example, emissions permits issued by the EPA had focused on regulating coal-fired plants during normal operations, but "...a lot of emissions of particulates from power plants happen during start up and shut down" phases, Schaeffer explained. "It's actually a significant loophole for some of these plants. So, we're trying to close them." In another example, EIP and Environment Texas found that the State of Texas penalized illegal pollution releases so infrequently, that it incentivizes power plants to pay the fines—when imposed—rather than reduce emissions (Clark-Leach and Metzger 2017). "The penalties assessed by Texas for this illegal pollution amounted to the equivalent of only three pennies per pound [of pollutant]. The small size and infrequency of these fines is a major problem, because operators are less likely to spend the money required to fix known plant issues when fines for illegal pollution are not severe enough to offset the economic benefit of delaying investment in plant repairs and upgrades" (p. 1). Closing regulatory loopholes in technical processes like power production doesn't usually attract a lot of public attention, but "it feels good, because it feels like you're getting a broader effect" than just closing specific plants.

In all their cases, EIP relies on sound scientific research to support their efforts in court and with the public. These can be highly technical topics that are not easily understood in court arguments or dining room discussions. Emphasizing the critical role of research and information dissemination in supporting these suits, Schaeffer said, "At the EPA I learned pretty fast that your engineers can make your case," Schaeffer said. "If you've got a good engineer, the industry will respect your position." The technical information they bring, in turn, makes their case stronger with the public. "When you can take the right set of numbers to the public, it can make a difference" by building their support.

## A Partner to Build Public Awareness

To raise public awareness of coal-fired power plants, and build support for their campaign to close them, EIP relied on partners with expertise in public communications. When EIP first formed, they sought to coordinate with other environmental groups already focused on coal-fired plants. Schaeffer organized these "gatherings of the tribes," as he called them, to raise money, develop strategies, share resources, divide labor, and generally coordinate their collective action aimed at their common goal. The Sierra Club sponsored these national meetings and would become a key partner with EIP in the campaign against coal-fired plants, particularly in developing and implementing a public information campaign.

The Sierra Club, of course, is the century-old organization founded by John Muir, that is now "… the nation's largest and most influential grassroots environmental organization – with three million members and supporters" (Who we are 2017b). Bruce Hamilton is their Deputy Executive Director and has been with the Sierra Club since 1977, when he was the regional organizer for Wyoming, Montana, the Dakotas, and Nebraska. He now leads the development of the Club's advocacy strategies on complex issues, including Beyond Coal, their campaign against coal-fired power plants.

The Club's general approach to environmental protection and promotion is though public policy. Hamilton explained, "We very much focus on public policy as the solution. We recognize that while it's important to have everybody live the right sort of lifestyle that would fit within a sustainable earth, that if you don't really operate through government institutions, you're never going to get the kinds of changes that are necessary to address the great problems that face the world. Those big problems are produced by institutional decisions that lead to the threats, so institutional decisions need to lead to the solutions."

In 2005, the Sierra Club held a summit of delegates from their chapters throughout the United States to prioritize the Club's policy advocacy issues. They overwhelmingly identified climate change as the most important issue for the Club to address. "It was the biggest threat to the planet," reflected Hamilton, "and the Sierra Club was the organization that if we didn't show up... we were never going to get the kind of change that was needed." The Club eventually developed the "Climate Recovery Partnership" as an umbrella program that had four focused campaigns. One was Beyond Coal, the Club's "flagship campaign" to shut down all coal-fired power plants in the country. Like EIP, the Sierra Club identified coal-fired plants as a policy advocacy target with the largest potential returns on investment, especially during the George W. Bush administration, which pushed for the construction of 200–300 new coal-fired plants to promote the nation's energy independence. In 2011, the Club received a $50 million grant from Bloomberg Philanthropies to support the Beyond Coal campaign.

The Sierra Club employed the direct reform strategy in this campaign with two key tactics. First, like EIP, they sought stricter emissions standards for the plants in order flip the cost-benefit balance to a net loss for the power companies. Indeed, Sierra Club was sometimes the plaintiffs in the lawsuits filed by EIP against coal-fired plants. Second, they sought to build public support for their efforts to further restrict pollution emissions from these plants. This second tactic tapped a key comparative advantage of the Sierra Club over EIP, as well as the coal industry: a large and mobilized membership. "We have a grassroots army," said Hamilton.

"Boots on the ground... [millions of] members and supporters that are joining the Sierra Club and committed to working on policy change." They are "the best lobbyists that money *can't* buy... We are never going to be able to match [the coal industry's] money, so we invest heavily on the people side of the equation so that can hopefully overcome the power of money."

One way they built public support was to create awareness of individual's personal exposure to pollutants from coal-fired plants. This was during the George W. Bush administration, when the Sierra Club didn't feel that directly lobbying legislators would be successful. Instead, they focused on building public support through creative communications and media work. In this effort, the Sierra Club sponsored an ongoing event that invited everyone to clip off small samples of their hair and send them to a lab that analyzed them for mercury contamination.

Coal-fired power plants are the largest single source of mercury pollution, which accumulates up the food chain into people near and far from the power plants (Toxic mercury 2017). The lab sent reports back to sample donors who were generally surprised to find the toxin in their bodies. By the time the Obama administration arrived, Hamilton concluded, advocacy activities like these helped the Sierra Club build enough public pressure to support stricter limits on mercury emissions from power plants.

## Measuring Progress

While EIP and the Sierra Club would like to see all coal-fired power plants closed, they mark their successes by calculating averted pollution, and that metric allows them some slack in desired outcomes. "We can't tell you—for the kind of money that is available to NGOs, and given the ways our laws work—that we can flat out keep this [power] plant from being built," explained Schaeffer. "But we can tell you one of two things: either that plant will not happen, or it will be a cleaner plant." And their returns on these efforts are very positive, according to EIP's analysis. "If you got two to three hundred tons of fine particles out of the air—let's say from a 25-to-30-thousand-dollar investment, [and] a ton of fine particles is $1500 in health damages—your rate of return is like a hedge fund." Reflecting on the work of EIP in its first dozen years, Schaeffer proudly concluded, "I think we help to catalyze the national effort [to close coal-fired power plants], and I feel really good about that."

### Discussions

6a. Find a class action lawsuit in the news that could have public policy implications. Describe the litigant, the defendant, the suit, and its potential to shape public policy.

6b. The direct reform strategy pairs judicial or administrative action with educational outreach to the public. What are the potential benefits of pairing these two tactics? Do you think that public outreach influences the judicial or administrative processes? How, or why not?

6c. Stephen Joseph of Ban Trans fats sued private companies (e.g., Kraft, McDonalds) and held a cooking oil demonstration project for restaurants. How did such advocacy activities catalyze public policy change?

6d. During his campaign to ban trans fats, Stephen Joseph was ridiculed by some media outlets and ruthlessly trolled online. How should a policy advocate manage and react to intense criticism?

6e. EIP's suit against the Lower Colorado River Authority's Fayette Power Project was settled out of court with the coal plant remaining in operation, but with further restrictions on pollution emissions and monitoring. Now the plant is scheduled to be retired by 2022, because a significant portion of the plant's customers are committing to renewable energy sources. To what extent can EIP's campaign be credited with the eventual elimination of pollutants from that plant when it closes? Do you think the plant would be scheduled for shut down without the EIP's suit? Why or why not?

6f. Ban Trans Fats was essentially a one-person show, while the campaign against coal-fired power plants was a partnership among larger and better-funded organizations. What are the commonalities and differences in how these diverse campaigns used the direct reform strategy?

# References

American Civil Liberties Union of Northern California. (2011, March 24). *Equal Opportunity Victory for Minority and Women-Owned Businesses in Caltrans Contracting Lawsuit* [Press release]. American Civil Liberties Union of Northern California. Retrieved from https://www.aclunc.org/news/equal-opportunity-victory-minority-and-women-owned-businesses-caltrans-contracting-lawsuit.

American Heart Association. (n.d.). *Trans Fats*. Retrieved from http://www.heart.org/HEARTORG/HealthyLiving/HealthyEating/Nutrition/Trans-Fats_UCM_301120_Article.jsp#.V58FY_krKM9.

Ankrum, N. (2012, June 29). Clear as smoke: LCRA may face lawsuit over Fayette emissions. *Austin Chronicle*. Retrieved from http://www.austinchronicle.com/news/2012-06-29/clear-as-smoke-lcra-may-face-lawsuit-over-fayette-emissions/.

Associated General Contractors of America, San Diego Chapter, Inc., v. California Department of Transportation et al., Coalition for Economic Equity, and National Association for the Advancement of Colored People (United States Court of Appeals for the Ninth Circuit February 9, 2012). Brief for the United States as Amicus Curiae Supporting Appellees.

Associated Press. (2003, May 12). California suit seeks ban on Oreos. *USA Today*. Retrieved from http://usatoday30.usatoday.com/news/nation/2003-05-12-oreo-suit_x.htm.

Bakalar, N. (2017, April 12). Trans fat bans tied to fewer heart attacks and strokes. *New York Times*. Retrieved from https://www.nytimes.com/2017/04/12/well/eat/trans-fat-bans-tied-to-fewer-heart-attacks-and-strokes.html.

Cameron, C. (2014, December 22). *Austin to get 55% of its power from renewables by 2025*. Inhabitat.com. Retrieved from http://inhabitat.com/austin-to-get-55-of-its-power-from-renewables-by-2025/.

Center for Food Safety and Applied Nutrition. (2003, August). *Guidance for Industry: Trans Fatty Acids in Nutrition Labeling, Nutrient Content Claims, Health Claims; Small Entity Compliance Guide*. U.S. Food and Drug Administration. Retrieved from http://www.fda.gov/food/guidanceregulation/guidancedocumentsregulatoryinformation/labelingnutrition/ucm053479.htm.

Clarl-Leach, G., & Metzger, L. (2017). *Breakdowns in Enforcement: Texas Rarely Penalizes Industry for Illegal Air Pollution Released During Malfunctions and Maintenance*. The Environmental Integrity Project and Environment Texas. Retrieved from https://www.environmentalintegrity.org/reports/breakdowns-in-enforcement/.

Cooper, A. (2003, May 12). Interview with Stephen Joseph. *CNN.com*. Retrieved from http://www.cnn.com/TRANSCRIPTS/0305/12/se.15.html.

EPA resignation prompts hearings. (2002, March 1). *Deseret News*. Retrieved from www.deseretnews.com/article/print/898971/EPA-resignation-prompts-hearings.html.

Epstein, L., Kobylka, J. F., & Stewart, J. F. (1995). A theory of interest groups and litigation. In S. Nagel (Ed.), *Research in Law and Policy Studies*. Greenwich, CT: JAI Press.

FryTest.com. (2006). *FryTest.com Oil Contest: Final Testing Protocol*. FryTest.com LLC. Retrieved from http://www.frytest.com/images/FRYTEST%20FINAL%20TESTING%20PROTOCOL%2012-15-06.pdf.

FryTest.com. (2007). *The Zero Trans Fat Cooking Oil Contest: Announcement of Results*. FryTest.com LLC. Retrieved from http://www.frytest.com/images/Media%20release%20-%20zero%20trans%20oil%20contest%20results.pdf.

Hallock, B. (2013, November 7). Rise and fall of trans fat: A history of partially hydrogenated oil. *Los Angeles Times*. Retrieved from http://www.latimes.com/food/dailydish/la-dd-rise-and-fall-of-trans-fat-20131107-story.html.

Joseph, S. (2003, May 22). *Citizen Petition Regarding Trans Fat Labeling. Petition Filed with the U.S. Food and Drug Administration*. Retrieved from http://www.fda.gov/ohrms/dockets/dailys/03/Jun03/060303/94p-0036-cp00002-01-vol1.pdf.

Kagan, R. A. (1991). Adversarial legalism and American government. *Journal of Policy Analysis and Management, 10*(3), 369–406.

Kagan, R. A. (1998). Adversarial legalism: Tamed or still wild? *New York University Journal of Legislation and Public Policy, 2*(2), 217–245.

Lawyers Committee for Civil Rights (LCCR). (n.d.). *History & Timeline*. Retrieved from http://www.lccr.com/who-we-are/history-timeline/.

Lawyers Committee for Civil Rights (LCCR). (n.d.). *Mission & Values*. Retrieved from http://www.lccr.com/who-we-are/mission-values/.

Leonard, K. (2015, June 15). FDA bans trans fat in move that will alter US food landscape. *U.S. News & World Report*. Retrieved from http://www.usnews.com/news/articles/2015/06/16/fda-bans-trans-fats-in-move-that-will-alter-us-food-landscape.

Let them eat tofu. (2003, May 14). *Denver Post*, p. B-06.

Lindblom, C. (1959). The science of muddling through. *Public Administration Review, 19*(Spring), 79–88.

Linsky, M. (1988). *Impact: How the Press Affects Federal Policy Making*. New York: W. W. Norton.

Little, A. G. (2005, February 7). *Ex-EPA chief's book assails GOP right*. NBCNews. com. Retrieved from http://www.nbcnews.com/id/6880585/ns/us_news-environment/t/ex-epa-chiefs-book-assails-gop-right/#.UlrRjVCfi3Q.

Lower Colorado River Authority. (2012, June 15). *LCRA General Manager Becky Motal Responds to Claims Against Fayette Power Project*. Retrieved from http://www.lcra.org/about/newsroom/news-releases/2012/pages/lcra-general-manager-becky-motal-responds-to-claims-against-fayette-power-project.aspx.

McDonald's hit with fat lawsuit. (2004, July 9). *CNN/Money*. Retrieved from http://money.cnn.com/2004/07/09/news/fortune500/mcdonalds_lawsuit/.

McDonald's settles trans fats lawsuits. (2005, February 12). *New York Times*. Retrieved from http://www.nytimes.com/2005/02/12/business/mcdonalds-settles-trans-fats-lawsuits.html.

Office of Regulatory Enforcement. (1994). *Office of Regulatory Enforcement: An Organizational Overview* (Report # EPA 300-K-94-001). U.S. Environmental Protection Agency.

Put trans fat on label. (2002, July 13). *SFGate*. Retrieved from http://www.sfgate.com/opinion/editorials/article/Put-trans-fat-on-label-2823660.php.

Radcliffe, S. (n.d.). NYC's trans fat ban leads to better eating. *Men's Fitness*. Retrieved from http://www.mensfitness.com/nutrition/what-to-eat/nycs-trans-fat-ban-leads-better-eating.

Roselund, C. (2014, December 12). *Austin, Texas plans for at least 950 MW of solar PV by 2025*. PV-Magazine.com. Retrieved from http://www.pv-magazine.com/news/details/beitrag/austin–texas-plans-for-at-least-950-mw-of-solar-pv-by-2025_100017500/#ixzz4 18iL7ipe.

Ryser, J. (2011, March 14). Groups sue LCRA charging violations of CAA at 1,645-MW, 30-year- old Texas coal plant. *Electric Utility Week*.

San Francisco's Cookie Monster. (2003, May 13). *Wall Street Journal*. Retrieved from http://www.wsj.com/articles/SB105279000281512700.

Schaeffer, E. (2002, July–August). Clearing the air: Why I quit Bush's E.P.A. *Washington Monthly*. Retrieved from http://www.washingtonmontly.com/features/2001/0207.schaeffer.html.

Severson, K. (2003, May 12). Lawsuit seeks to ban sale of Oreos to children in California / Nabisco taken to task over trans fat's effects. *SFGate*. Retrieved from http://www.sfgate.com/health/article/Lawsuit-seeks-to-ban-sale-of-Oreos-to-children-in-2617337.php.

Texas Campaign for the Environment. (2013, February 22). *Utility Agrees to Reduce Coal Plan Emissions*. Retrieved from https://www.texasenvironment.org/courthouse-news-utility-agrees-to-reduce-coal-plant-emissions/.

Toxic mercury. (2017). *Sierra Club*. Retrieved from content.sierraclub.org/coal/burning-toxic-mercury.

Wasby, S. L. (1983). Interest groups and litigation. *Policy Studies Journal, 11*(4), 657–670.

Who we are. (2017a). *Environmental Integrity Project*. Retrieved from https://www.environmentalintegrity.org/who-we-are/#mission.

Who we are. (2017b). *Sierra Club*. Retrieved from http://www.sierraclub.org/about.

# Indirect Pressure

7

To enforce US federal, state, and local environmental statutes through citizen supervision.
—Tiffany Schauer, Executive Director of Our Children's Earth Foundation, on her organization's goal in policy advocacy

We want people to step up where government can't.
—Meredith Hendricks, former Executive Director of the Neighborhood Parks Council

Tiffany Schauer was an environmental attorney for over ten years, including five with the US Environmental Protection Agency, through the mid-1990s. During those early years of her career, she discovered that "the attacks on environmental regulatory standards and enforcement program funding decisions are not occurring in statehouses and legislative sessions, where the glare of public attention would be too great. Instead, the attacks most often occur in bureaucratic back rooms, out of the public eye, in obscure government departments where polluting industries can influence the decision-making process without risking the wrath of public opposition" (Our Children's Earth Foundation 2019a, About OCE). The results of this are that "our environmental laws simply are not being enforced adequately to ensure public safety and basic environmental protections." To counteract this dynamic, Schauer founded Our Children's Earth Foundation (OCE) in 1998, with the mission of enforcing environmental laws through "citizen supervision." Schauer's choice of words reflects her view of power in the processes of policy change. Formal government policymakers are needed to carry out laws, but they respond to the demands of citizens. So OCE's job is to mobilize citizens to apply pressure on the policymakers. OCE achieves this by promoting "public awareness of domestic and international human rights issues and environmental impacts through information dissemination, artistic expression, education projects, and private enforcement of environmental protection statutes" (Our Children's Earth Foundation 2019a, About OCE).

That last tactic—private enforcement of environmental protection statutes—is a key one for OCE. Annie Beaman, OCE's Director of Advocacy and Outreach and Co-Executive Director, calls their legal work "citizen suits," emphasizing OCE's role in mobilizing the affected communities whom they would represent in cases. Her job, she explained, is to find people needing help with specific environmental problems, but unsure about how to proceed. She collects witness statements that demonstrate the problems' impacts on the public, and bring these people into the policy change process. She "creates citizen advocates."

One example of OCE's approach was a 2004 lawsuit against the Tennessee Valley Authority (TVA)—the government corporation that provides electric power for parts of seven states surrounding Tennessee—for violations of the federal Clean Air Act at eleven sites where they were operating coal-fired power plants. Their suit claimed that TVA made major modifications to multiple power plants without first obtaining required permits and without installing pollution controls necessary under the Clean Air Act's "prevention of significant deterioration" (PSD) and "new source review" (NSR) provisions, which would normally require new emission sources to use best available control technologies (Salzman and Thompson 2003). The result, claimed the plaintiffs, was that TVA exceeded pollution emission limitations for sulfur dioxide and nitrogen oxides, two "criteria pollutants" used to judge overall air quality under the Clean Air Act.

OCE joined the suit as "citizen plaintiffs" on the case because TVA represented the single largest source of air pollution in the area at that time. It was the "biggest bang for our buck," explained Schauer, so if they were successful in their suit, they would be able to reduce emissions from the largest polluter in the area.

The case was drawn out over years, but eventually settled ten years after the original complaint. "Ten years means you can't give up," said Schauer. "You have to be relentless." And it required highly specialized skills and knowledge. Their team of lawyers who worked on this case had at least ten to twenty years of Clean Air Act litigation. They had to be "experienced" and "aggressive" to sue a large government corporation on their core work. Even so, as a small nonprofit, they were extremely disadvantaged. "This was a David and Goliath story," said Schauer. "We had nothing" compared to the resources of the TVA. But the courts made the TVA's resource-dominance less important, and provided OCE a more level opportunity to be heard. And they supplemented their suit with media work. They reached out to other nonprofits engaged in similar work to share a "loose web of awareness and resources and information," described Schauer.

Litigation is a key tactic in OCE's general strategy to get government agencies to uphold environmental statutes. Their case list boasts over sixty suits filed since 2001, with a local, state, or national government entity listed as defendants in at least two-thirds of them.

Public education and outreach are their other key tactics. They achieve this by "supporting films, planning and attending outreach events, forging strategic partnerships, and by creating and sharing resources with people and groups that are leading environmental advocacy efforts in their communities" (Our Children's Earth Foundation 2019c, Public Education). OCE describes their rationale for this tactic as a complement to their litigation (Our Children's Earth Foundation 2019c, Public Education):

> Information is power, but far too often the legal and regulatory systems that we depend on for environmental protection are effectively closed off to the people they are meant to serve. It is especially critical for people in communities impacted most heavily by pollution to be informed about environmental issues and how they can effectively engage with the legal and governmental systems that are in charge of protecting their local resources, ecosystems, and health. Working class people and people of color are by far the most impacted by pollution demographically, and children and seniors are the most vulnerable to suffer serious health problems related to pollution.

Besides empowering the public, education and outreach can also bring pressure on the courts hearing their cases. "Inherently the legal system is very political, and some of the decisions were inconsistent," explained Schauer. OCE had sued on similar issues in different courts, resulting in "inexplicable" differences in rulings. "So then we started looking into groups that may have been a little more plugged in politically, to try to figure out what was happening behind the scenes where the judges were being influenced in ways we were not aware of." In their view, judges are subject to "external influences" of the public.

The unusual way that OCE does public education and outreach is by supporting documentary filmmaking related to their advocacy issues. Such films are essential to the "ripple effects" of the educational work they do, said Beaman. The films help their issues get a much broader audience than the immediately affected areas of their lawsuits, and their sponsorship of the films helps the filmmakers get a broader viewership. "As a small organization, we can only bring so many lawsuits," said Beaman. "The films bring the issues to broader awareness." Not all of the films they support are related to their lawsuits, however, but they are certainly related to the environmental and social justice issues OCE works on.

**Our Children's Earth Foundation's Film Credits**

Overview: An unusual tactic of OCE's public outreach efforts is documentary filmmaking. As they explain on their film fund website, "We believe in the power of film to educate, create empathy, change perceptions, and inspire action on critical issues facing humanity and our planet" (Our Children's Earth Foundation 2019b, OCE Film Fund). In their view, the films develop indirect pressure from the viewers to government entities. OCE's sponsorship of documentaries has been prolific. Executive Director Tiffany Schauer even has an IMDb page as a producer with over ten film credits.

Example documentaries that OCE has sponsored:

- *Youth v Gov* (2020)—"Since 2015, twenty-one plaintiffs, now ages 12 to 23, have been suing the U.S. government for…creating the climate crisis they will inherit. But *Youth v Gov* is about more than just a lawsuit. It is the story of empowered youth finding their voices and fighting to protect their rights and our collective future. This is a revolution designed to hold those in power accountable for the past and responsible for the future. And many of the movement's leaders aren't even old enough to vote. (Yet.)" (youthvgovthefilm.com)
- *The Devil We Know* (2018)—"…the story of how corporate America – with the help of government – hid a global contamination of a known cancer-causing chemical… *The Devil We Know* reveals how two unlikely heroes – a gym teacher and a cattle farmer – took on one of the world's most powerful corporations while the government looked the other way" (thedevilweknow.com).
- *Death by Design* (2016)—"By 2020, four billion people will have a personal computer. Five billion will own a mobile phone. But this revolution has a dark side… the film tells a story of environmental degradation, of health tragedies, and the fast approaching tipping point between consumerism and sustainability" (deathbydesignfilm.com/about).
- *How to Change the World* (2015)—"In 1971 a small group of activists set sail from Vancouver, Canada in an old fishing boat. Their mission was to stop Nixon's atomic test bomb in Amchitka, Alaska. Chronicling this untold story at the birth of the modern environmental movement… the film centres on eco-hero Robert Hunter and his part in the creation of the global organization we now know as Greenpeace" (impactpartners.com/films/how-change-world).

In a few cases, OCE's lawsuits and filmmaking do come together. A recent example of this was their case against St. Petersburg, Florida, for violations of the Clean Water Act. OCE, along with two other organizations, sued the city in 2016 for chronic and willful discharges of raw or partially treated sewage into Tampa Bay, other surface waters, and aquifers. Their suit listed at least forty discharge violations in five years. Behind the suit was a dramatic story of a city hall cover-up and a city employee whistleblower, which was retold in a thirty-minute documentary by Caroline Smith called *St. Pete Unfiltered*. In this case, OCE's involvement with the film was not financial sponsorship, but rather as a character in the story as they sued the city.

In the film, Beaman explained that the public was confused about the sewage discharges in the bay, because of conflicting information from the city, the news, and other sources. "People felt that they couldn't trust the statements and the solutions being offered" by the city, she said. "One thing that you can trust in these kinds of situations, is a federal court to enforce the federal law." OCE's suit was aimed at bringing that certainty to St. Petersburg. In 2017, a state investigation concluded that 89 felonies and 103 misdemeanor violations of the Clean Water Act had been committed by St. Petersburg over the course of discharging one billion gallons of sewage into Tampa Bay and aquifers. In 2018, the city and OCE reached a settlement in the suit, which required the city to make specific sewer system improvements under federal oversight. In that same year, *St. Pete Unfiltered* was an audience selection winner at the Gasparilla International Film Festival.

## The Indirect Pressure Strategy

The strategies we have described so far have each viewed successful policy advocacy as specific combinations of advocacy activities that induce desired changes in policy or social conditions. Advocates using the indirect pressure strategy, however, are not united by the activities they use but rather by the pathway of change, from the public, to policymakers, to policy, and finally to social and physical conditions. Three of the top tactics in their factor array make this linkage clear (19:+3, 22:+2, 08:+3).

Advocates using this strategy still try to affect policy change by influencing formal policymakers, but they do so indirectly, rather than through lobbying or other direct tactics (01:−1). The activities that they used to trigger that chain reaction generally target the public, as a way to indirectly influence policymakers, and those activities are varied and scattered in the factor array. As Table 7.1

indicates, these advocates' tactics include conveying public opinion (19:+3), using the media (06:+2), implementing pilot programs (13:+2), monitoring policy implementation (03:+1), and conducting research and analysis (23:0) to apply pressure on the policymakers. These advocates believe that with these pressures, policymakers will affect their desired policy changes (22:+2) to improve social and physical conditions (08:+3). These advocacy goals are more specific and pragmatic than broader democratic conditions (12:−3, 24:−3, 11:−2) (Table 7.1 and Fig. 7.1).

OCE's key advocacy activities are quite similar to those of the Environmental Integrity Project, described in Chapter 6: litigation paired with media work (i.e., news, filmmaking) and public education. But their strategies differ on their views of how policies change. EIP sees their litigation as direct reform of policy, bypassing legislative actions by pursuing judicial remedies. OCE sees their litigation as a means of empowering citizens to force the government into action. The distinction is minor in the cases presented from these two organizations, but it is important to the broader ways that these two strategies are implemented. In the direct reform strategy, litigation is a common tactic, but the strategy also allows for other non-legislative tactics to induce policy change, such as demonstration projects. In the indirect pressure strategy, however, litigation is not a common tactic (17:−1). OCE was exceptional in this regard. But they do typify other tactics that are more common in indirect pressure, such as changing the public's views and media work. Indeed, while OCE Foundation did share with us litigation cases—and they have a long list of accompanying legal victories—their organization does have a strong independent arm of public education that includes public outreach, strategic partnerships, and filmmaking.

## Theoretical Foundations

At the heart of the indirect pressure strategy is an acknowledgment that government actors play a critical role in policy change, reflecting an institutional view of policymaking (Selznick 1996). *Institutionalism* is a view of policymaking that focuses on the formal players in the process, that is, those whose participation in policy change is required by constitution or law. These typically consist of elected officials, courts, and government agencies. Rather than engaging these formal players directly, however, indirect pressure strategists choose to influence them indirectly by raising concerns about issues among the public. Thus, their preferred tactics align with Jack Walker's (1991) "outside" approach, such as public education efforts, working with coalitions, and conducting public mobilizations.

**Table 7.1** Factor array for indirect pressure strategy

| Tactic (advocacy activity and its expected outcome) | Factor array | Relative extreme |
|---|---|---|
| 08 Policies can change social and physical conditions | +3 | High |
| 19 Changes in the public's views can change policymakers' views | +3 | High |
| 06 Using the media to disseminate information can change policymakers' views | +2 | |
| 13 Pilot programs and demonstration projects can lead to policy change | +2 | High |
| 22 Changes in policymakers' views can change policies | +2 | High |
| 02 Lobbying and building relationships with policymakers can change their views | +1 | |
| 03 Monitoring and evaluating existing policy can change how it is implemented | +1 | High |
| 09 Using the media to disseminate information can change the public's views | +1 | |
| 20 Developing messages, framing issues, labeling and other strategies of rhetoric can change the public's views | +1 | |
| 07 Monitoring and evaluating existing policy can set the policy agenda | 0 | |
| 10 Building coalitions and networks with like-minded organizations and individuals can change policymakers' views | 0 | |
| 14 Public mobilizations (e.g., protests, letter writing campaigns, rallies) can set the policy agenda | 0 | |
| 15 Research and analyses can change policymakers' views | 0 | |
| 16 Using the media to disseminate information can hasten policy change | 0 | Low |
| 23 Research and analyses can change the public's views | 0 | High |
| 01 Developing messages, framing issues, labeling and other strategies of rhetoric can change policymakers' views | −1 | low |
| 04 Building coalitions and networks with like-minded organizations and individuals can change the public's views | −1 | Low |
| 17 Litigation can change policy | −1 | |
| 21 Public mobilizations (e.g., protests, letter writing campaigns, voter registration) can build democracy | −1 | |
| 05 Rebutting opposing views can change policymakers' views | −2 | |
| 11 Policy advocacy in general builds legitimacy in a democracy | −2 | |

(continued)

**Table 7.1**   (continued)

| Tactic (advocacy activity and its expected outcome) | Factor array | Relative extreme |
|---|---|---|
| 18 Rebutting opposing views can change the public's views | −2 | |
| 12 Policy advocacy in general makes policymaking more people-centered | −3 | Low |
| 24 Policy advocacy in general produces more effective policies | −3 | Low |

*Note* See Chapter 2 for an explanation of the factor array scores

(public's view, media, pilot programs, etc.) → policymakers' views → policy change → social/physical conditions

**Fig. 7.1**   Indirect pressure strategy

Walker's own description of his outside approach even suggests this view of indirect influence. "Outside activities may sometimes be merely an indirect effort to exert influence upon the outcome of a specific policy decision," he explained, "but they are often intended to build support within the general public for an entirely new set of values that may eventually be manifested in public policy many years in the future" (p. 103).

Mosley (2011) observed that organizations sometimes favor indirect tactics when they appear to lack access or experience in insider tactics such as lobbying, or when they lack legal clarity on the permissible levels of lobbying. In our data, however, advocates preferred outside tactics as a means of establishing long-term public support to span many short-term tenures of elected officials. In essence, the outside tactics provide more temporal stability in their advocacy work.

## Current Usage

So far, in the strategies presented in Chapters 3–6, we matched nonprofits in our survey dataset to specific advocacy strategies based upon their use of favored advocacy activities in each strategy. For the indirect pressure strategy, however, the activities are quite diverse. Instead, the unifying element is their view of the pathway to policy change—from public, to decision makers, to policy, and finally to actual conditions. Figure 7.2 compares the importance of these intermediate

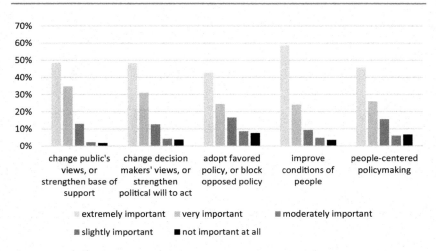

**Fig. 7.2**  Importance of key advocacy outcomes in the indirect pressure strategy

and final outcomes of this pathway among the organizations in our dataset. The four focused on the public's view, the decision makers' views, policy adoption, and conditions for people are all integral parts of the indirect pressure strategy. They also are each extremely important or very important among a majority of all respondents, across multiple advocacy strategies.

We therefore also examined the importance of people-centered policymaking as an advocacy outcome. To indirect pressure strategists, such outcomes focused on democratic systems are not important, and as Fig. 7.2 shows, relatively few organizations would agree with this view. Therefore, we screened our dataset for organizations that rated these first four outcomes very important or extremely important, while also rating "people-centered policy making" moderately important to not important at all. We found 37 organizations in our dataset meeting all these criteria. While we can reasonably assume that more organizations might adopt this strategy to lesser degrees, the 37 meeting these narrow criteria can represent the experiences of strict adherents to the strategy. The analyses that follow compare these organizations with all others in our dataset.

Figure 7.3 compares the importance of policy advocacy to the missions of nonprofits relying on the indirect pressure strategy versus those who do not. While the rates at the upper end of importance are higher for indirect pressure strategists, the differences are not statistically significant. Similarly, Table 7.2 summarizes the staff and financial resources devoted to advocacy, and no

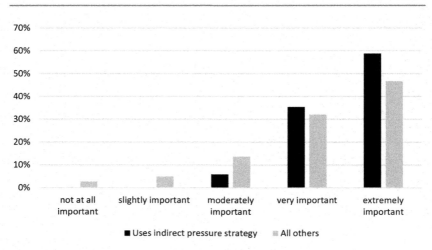

**Fig. 7.3** Importance of policy advocacy to mission of indirect pressure strategists (*Note* $\chi^2_{(4)}= 5.18, p = 0.27$)

**Table 7.2** Resources devoted to policy advocacy by indirect pressure strategists

|  | Staff devoted to policy advocacy (%) | Financial resources devoted to policy advocacy (%) |
|---|---|---|
| Uses indirect pressure strategy | Mean = 48<br>S.D. = 34 | Mean = 48<br>S.D. = 35 |
| All others | Mean = 45<br>S.D. = 32 | Mean = 40<br>S.D. = 33 |

significant differences were found between organizations that rely on the indirect pressure strategy and those who do not.

We begin to see some interesting distinctions starting with Fig. 7.4. It lists, in ascending order, the policy issues most engaged by indirect pressure strategists and compares those rates against all other advocacy organizations in our dataset. Overall, a majority of indirect pressure strategists (54%) use the strategy on education issues, and it is the only issue to garner more than half of these advocates. However, indirect pressure strategists advocate in five issues at significantly higher rates than other advocates do. Those issues are social welfare and poverty

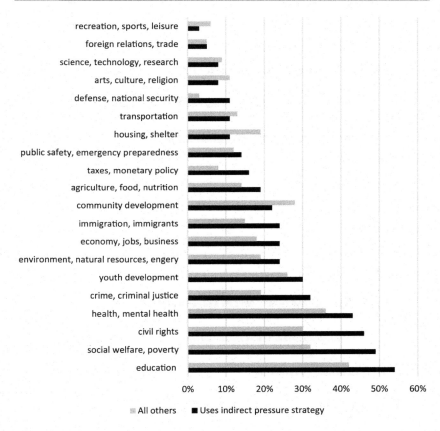

**Fig. 7.4** Public issues engaged by indirect pressure strategists

(49% versus 32%, $\chi^2_{(1)} = 4.58$, $p = 0.03$), civil rights (46% versus 30%, $\chi^2_{(1)} = 4.42$, $p = 0.04$), crime and criminal justice (32% versus 19%, $\chi^2_{(1)} = 4.27$, $p = 0.04$), taxes and monetary policy (16% versus 8%, $\chi^2_{(1)} = 3.43$, $p = 0.06$), and defense and national security (11% versus 3%, $\chi^2_{(1)} = 6.61$, $p = 0.01$). In no issue do indirect pressure strategists engage at a statistically significantly lower rate than other advocates.

Figures 7.5 and 7.6 display the rates at which advocates target the varied levels and branches of government. A majority of advocates using the indirect pressure strategy target state, local, and national governments at rates significantly higher

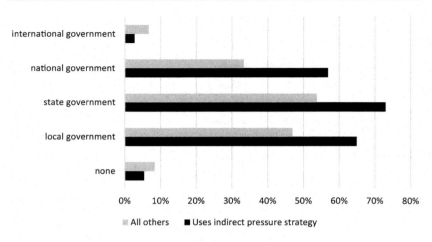

**Fig. 7.5** Levels of government targeted by indirect pressure strategists

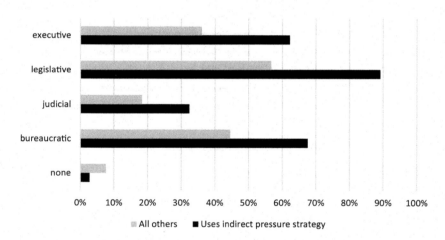

**Fig. 7.6** Branches of government targeted by indirect pressure strategists

than those of other advocates (73% versus 54% state government, $\chi^2_{(1)}=5.34$, $p=0.02$; 65% versus 47% local government, $\chi^2_{(1)}=4.55$, $p=0.03$; 57% versus 33% national government, $\chi^2_{(1)}=8.58$, $p=0.00$). On the branches of government, a vast majority of these advocates target legislative bodies (89% versus

57%, $\chi^2_{(1)}=15.29$, $p=0.00$), followed closely behind by bureaucracies (68% versus 45%, $\chi^2_{(1)}=7.52$, $p=0.01$) and executives (62% versus 36%, $\chi^2_{(1)}=10.27$, $p=0.00$). Nearly a third target the judicial branch (32% versus 18%, $\chi^2_{(1)}=4.59$, $p=0.03$). Their targeting formal decision makers across levels and branches of government is consistent with the strategy's view of the central role of government in the policy process, even if they tend not to directly engage them.

Over half of the nonprofits using the indirect pressure strategy have individual memberships, significantly more than the other advocacy organizations (54% versus 32%, $\chi^2_{(1)}=7.74$, $p=0.01$). See Fig. 7.7. Otherwise, their levels of organizational memberships and no memberships are indistinguishable from other advocates. This might reflect the strategy's reliance on affecting and mobilizing the public's views in order to trigger the chain reaction toward changes in social conditions (Fig. 7.1). Already having individual memberships facilitates that mobilization in campaigns.

Lastly, Fig. 7.8 displays the income distribution of nonprofits identified with the indirect pressure strategy, compared to all other advocacy nonprofits. Overall, they have higher representation among those with incomes above $1 million in 2013, though not in the wealthiest tier. Interesting, they also have high representation among the nonprofits in the lowest income level. This dichotomy suggests that this strategy can be deployed in ways that meet varied resource constraints. Mobilizing the public, for example, can be done through lower-cost grassroots networks or through higher-cost media engagement and information campaigns.

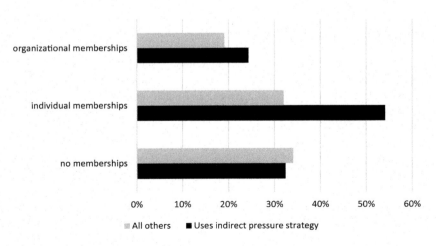

**Fig. 7.7** Memberships of indirect pressure strategists

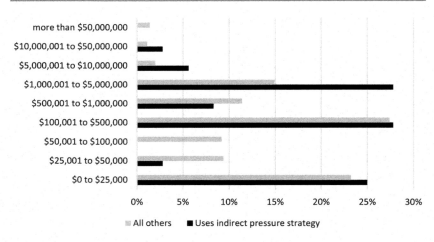

**Fig. 7.8**  2013 Income distribution of indirect pressure strategists

In the chapter's opening case, Our Children's Earth Foundation applied the indirect pressure strategy using public outreach and education with litigation. The following case illustrates other tactics used to mobilize the public and apply pressure on policymakers.

## Enhancing Local Parks

In 2007, Meredith Hendricks was the newly hired Deputy Director of the Neighborhood Parks Council (NPC) in San Francisco, when that city's parks were in desperate need of repair, maintenance, and enhancement. NPC's aim was to bring together advocacy, stewardship, philanthropy, and volunteers to ensure that San Francisco's parks and open spaces are accessible, clean, and safe places for healthy recreation and enjoyment. Its work complements that of the city's Recreation and Parks Department, by identifying needs and advocating for resources in ways that the city agency cannot do efficiently or effectively.

Hendricks brought to NPC a long history of engagement in environmental issues. It started when she was 12 years old and volunteered at the San Francisco Zoo, which evolved into over a decade of work there as an intern and eventually a zookeeper after she earned her degree in conservation biology. Over those years, she learned that the zoo was owned by the city, managed by its Recreation and

Parks Department, and existed in a complex and stifling political environment. She felt that more could be done to improve the zoo "if silos were broken down, if policies were different, and if political will was different."

She would later work for the Farallones Marine Sanctuary Association, a non-profit founded to support the 1200-square-mile marine sanctuary just outside of the Golden Gate. The association provided support in the form of public education, public outreach, and stewardship. Hendricks' experience there showed her how a nonprofit could sometimes initiate actions when the government cannot. Reflecting on these experiences, Hendricks said they served as her "social preparation... that allowed me to focus in on policy as a trigger-point for real change."

With this background, Hendricks joined the Neighborhood Parks Council, where she saw her fundamental charge as empowering communities to keep 220 local parks well maintained, and encouraging volunteers to take ownership of the city's open spaces. At the time, the city had been having a challenging time doing so by itself. The city's Recreation and Parks budget had fallen chronically behind costs of upkeep. With that deficit, the parks became worn over time, explained Hendricks. Irrigation, pathways, lighting, and other amenities deteriorated, and did so in disproportionate ways, making some neighborhoods "left behind." Parks that are not well maintained not only lose usage, but also devalue surrounding neighborhoods. They can also create inequities between neighborhoods that are able to invest their own resources in park upkeep and those that cannot.

Seven years earlier, in 2000, NPC had successfully advocated for the city's first bond measure in 50 years supporting parks. But according to SPUR, the San Francisco Bay Area Planning and Urban Research Association, the $110 million bond measure contained just "a single sentence" describing the purpose of the bond for construction and repair of facilities and acquisition of open space (SPUR 2008). The lack of specificity left many neighborhoods frustrated about where funds were actually spent. This time, Hendricks and NPC would need to do better to identify specific park improvements and to overcome public skepticism.

## Data and People

Their campaign revolved around two complementary tactics, both aimed at building public support for a new general obligation bond which would provide the city needed resources to address specific park improvement projects. The first tactic was to collect citywide data on the parks, to measure the parks' needs, which would become the basis of their argument for the bond. "We drive our movements with data," explained Hendricks. In this case, they developed a playground report card to assess the conditions of playgrounds, such as their safety, vandalism, lighting, cleanliness, and bathroom conditions. NPC organized volunteers to survey the conditions at 118 playgrounds (Examiner Staff 2008); then, they translated those conditions into the readily understood letter grades (i.e., A through F) in campaign materials. Twenty-five parks received grades of D or F. For example, some had warnings posted on the play structures that they may contain arsenic.

Besides the parks' conditions, they also collected data on elected officials' support for the parks. They didn't endorse any elected official, Hendricks explained, but they did rate each on how "park friendly" they were, to let the public know how each has acted on issues affecting the city's open spaces. These provided signals to voters on who to support in elections, creating pressure on the elected officials to act.

The second tactic was to develop a citywide coalition with their members and other nonprofits to raise public awareness through their communications network. That network was truly grassroots, in that volunteers carried the message and campaign throughout the city, rather than advertisements or other media work. They "needed neighborhood leaders in every part of the city that we could empower to be the messenger on our behalf," said Hendricks. "It all comes down to relationships" in the network. "We did it with almost no money." The wide span of relationships also "added a lot of credibility" to the campaign, reflect broad support for the issue.

Together, these two tactics provided the thrust of their campaign. "Our advocacy is about lining up data rigor with community relationships, and reinforcing what people *feel* with actual data," said Hendricks. The data turned regular people who supported parks into empowered advocates for them. With the data, they could speak "louder" to elected officials about how they are personally affected by the issue. The purpose of advocacy, to Hendricks, is to give people the information they need to be heard. No one can expect the city to uphold a vision of the parks without the people who enjoy them. Instead, the neighbors have to convey that vision to the city. Hendricks wants the neighbors to drive the vision for their parks and for those people to take that leadership role. "We want people to step up where government can't."

## Proposition A

In 2007, the city conducted its first third-party assessment of all its parks, which monetarily quantified what Hendricks had perceived through NPC's work. The report concluded that there was roughly $1.7 billion in unmet capital needs

(SPUR 2008), a tab that was orders of magnitude larger than the Recreation and Parks' annual budget. To begin addressing the parks' needs, the County Board of Supervisors voted to place Proposition A, the Clean and Safe Neighborhood Parks Bond, on the February 2008 ballot.

It proposed $185 million in bonds to fund numerous improvements of park and recreation facilities across the city. But unlike the 2000 bond that frustrated residents with its lack of specificity, the 2008 proposal named twelve parks to have improvement projects and included funds for citywide improvement of park restrooms, athletic fields, and nature trail (Department of Elections 2007). Hendricks explained that NPC worked closely with neighborhoods to "tailor the bond in a manner that was not only palatable to voters but would actually achieve what our most committed stakeholders wanted." Different neighborhoods in San Francisco required different things from their parks, so a successful bond had to make those differentiations. NPC's task was to "translate public opinion into discreet initiatives within the bond," said Hendricks.

The proposition also included $5 million for a Community Opportunity Fund that would finance neighborhood-nominated park projects that weren't already on the list. According to Hendricks, this opportunity fund derived directly from NPC's collection of neighborhood input on the parks' needs. Lastly, the proposition also set up "stronger accountability, reporting and transparency provisions than any other City bond measure," including a Citizen's General Obligation Bond Oversight Committee which would be funded by 0.1% of bond proceeds.

Organized opposition to the proposition was light, consisting mainly of a local taxpayers' association. But as a general obligation bond, passage required a two-thirds supermajority of voters to pass. The proposition passed with 71% of voters in support (Ballotpedia, n.d.).

## Raising the Public Radar

Hendricks explained NPC's rationale for focusing on the public rather than policymakers, saying that elected leadership changes frequently while the public's stakeholders in the issue do not. So, they choose to mobilize the public to be advocates of the issue no matter who is in public office. "Real people... speak louder" than legislators, she explained. So they organize people who know their neighborhoods, empower them with data, and let them advocate for the parks. Hendricks described her advocacy strategy as "raising the public radar" on the parks' conditions, maintenance, and enhancement. This closely aligns with the indirect pressure strategy. They worked with the public to induce action from government.

In 2011, as communities struggled to climb out of the Great Recession, the Neighborhood Parks Council merged with the other leading San Francisco parks advocacy organization to form the San Francisco Parks Alliance (Tucker 2011). Today, the Alliance continues the work of the Neighborhood Parks Council as the city's primary advocate for its parks.

**Discussions**

7a. An assumption of the indirect pressure strategy is that the public's interests have staying power, compared to those of ever-changing elected officials. For example, residents always want their public parks to be well maintained, while local elected officials place more attention on new and emerging issues. Do you think this is an accurate assumption? Is it more true for some policy issues than others? Compare, for example, the public's interests versus the elected official's interests in public education or gun rights. Explain your answers.

7b. Consider a policy issue that is important to you or an organization with which you are affiliated. Compare how could you advocate for the policy issue directly with policymakers, versus indirectly through the public.

7c. What are the advantages and disadvantages of advocating directly with policymakers (e.g., elected officials, bureaucrats) versus advocating indirectly through the public?

7d. Our Children's Earth Foundation uses filmmaking as a creative tactic to draw public attention to specific problems and to inspire or pressure people to act. Describe other creative ways to mobilize the public into action. What resources are required to implement them? What outcomes could you expect from them?

# References

Ballotpedia. (n.d.). *San Francisco Parks Bond, Proposition A (February 2008).* Retrieved from https://ballotpedia.org/San_Francisco_Park_Bonds,_Proposition_A_(February_2008).

Department of Elections. (2007, December 14). *Multiple Party Voter Information Pamphlet Consolidated Presidential Primary Election February 5, 2008.* City and County of San

Francisco. Retrieved from https://webbie1.sfpl.org/multimedia/pdf/elections/February5_2008.pdf.

Examiner Staff. (2008, April 26). Neighborhood parks are making the grade. *San Francisco Examiner*. Retrieved from https://www.sfexaminer.com/news/neighborhood-parks-are-making-the-grade/.

Mosley, J. (2011). Organizational resources and environmental incentives: Understanding the policy advocacy involvement of human service nonprofits. *Social Service Review, 84*(1), 57–76.

Our Children's Earth Foundation. (2019a). *About OCE*. Our Children's Earth Foundation. Retrieved from https://www.ocefoundation.org/about-us.

Our Children's Earth Foundation. (2019b). *OCE Film Fund*. Our Children's Earth Foundation. Retrieved from https://www.ocefoundation.org/programs/films.

Our Children's Earth Foundation. (2019c). *Public Education*. Our Children's Earth Foundation. Retrieved from https://www.ocefoundation.org/programs/education.

Salzman, J., & Thompson, B., Jr. (2003). *Environmental Law and Policy*. New York: Foundation Press.

Selznick, P. (1996). Institutionalism 'old' and 'new'. *Administrative Science Quarterly, 41*(2), 270–277.

SPUR. (2008, February 1). *Proposition A—Parks Bond*. SPUR, the San Francisco Bay Area Planning and Urban Research Association. Retrieved from https://www.spur.org/publications/voter-guide/2008-02-01/proposition-parks-bond.

Tucker, P. (2011). *Neighborhood Parks Council and San Francisco Parks Trust Join Forces to Create New Parks Support Group*. Business Wire. Retrieved from https://www.businesswire.com/news/home/20111005006595/en/Neighborhood-Parks-Council-San-Francisco-Parks-Trust.

Walker, J. (1991). *Mobilizing Interest Groups in America: Patrons, Professions, and Social Movements*. Ann Arbor: University of Michigan Press.

# Popular Power

8

We channel community grassroots democracy to where the power players are making (awful) decisions and make them listen… We know that change will not occur unless citizens demand it!
—Codepink (2019, Issues and Campaigns).

We're trying to create 'demand communities' all over Mississippi…
—Becky Glover, Parents for Public Schools. (Molnar 2013)

The strategies presented in this book (Chapters 3–8) are ordered by the advocates' levels of engagement with formal players in policymaking. They started in Chapter 3 with the public lobbying strategy, in which advocates lobby elected representatives and other government officials, with little to no public engagement. The final strategy defined in this chapter represents the opposite end of the spectrum.

## The Popular Power Strategy

Advocates using the popular power strategy are populists, in that they harness the power of the public to affect social change. They mostly avoid engagement with formal policymakers, because they expect the actions of those formal players to follow the public's will, and sometimes because they are fighting against the policy preferences of those formal players. To mobilize the public, popular power strategists use tactics that aim to influence the public's views of issues. Indeed, three of five statements rated +2 or +3 on the factor array are aimed at influencing the public's views (04:+3, 09:+3, 20:+2). See Table 8.1.

They employ a variety of activities to influence the public's views, including coalition building (04:+3), media and information campaigns (09:+3), framing

© The Author(s) 2020
S. Gen and A. C. Wright, *Nonprofits in Policy Advocacy*,
https://doi.org/10.1007/978-3-030-43696-4_8

**Table 8.1** Factor array for popular power strategy

| Tactic (advocacy activity and its expected outcome) | Factor array | Relative extreme |
|---|---|---|
| 04. Building coalitions and networks with like-minded organizations and individuals can change the public's views | +3 | High |
| 09. Using the media to disseminate information can change the public's views | +3 | High |
| 08. Policies can change social and physical conditions | +2 | |
| 20. Developing messages, framing issues, labeling and other strategies of rhetoric can change the public's views | +2 | High |
| 21. Public mobilizations (e.g., protests, letter writing campaigns, voter registration) can build democracy | +2 | High |
| 06. Using the media to disseminate information can change policymakers' views | +1 | |
| 10. Building coalitions and networks with like-minded organizations and individuals can change policymakers' views | +1 | |
| 14. Public mobilizations (e.g., protests, letter writing campaigns, rallies) can set the policy agenda | +1 | High |
| 22. Changes in policymakers' views can change policies | +1 | |
| 01. Developing messages, framing issues, labeling and other strategies of rhetoric can change policymakers' views | 0 | |
| 02. Lobbying and building relationships with policymakers can change their views | 0 | Low |
| 11. Policy advocacy in general builds legitimacy in a democracy | 0 | |
| 16. Using the media to disseminate information can hasten policy change | 0 | Low |
| 18. Rebutting opposing views can change the public's views | 0 | High |
| 19. Changes in the public's views can change policymakers' views | 0 | Low |
| 03. Monitoring and evaluating existing policy can change how it is implemented | −1 | |
| 12. Policy advocacy in general makes policymaking more people-centered | −1 | |
| 17. Litigation can change policy | −1 | |

(continued)

**Table 8.1** (continued)

| Tactic (advocacy activity and its expected outcome) | Factor array | Relative extreme |
|---|---|---|
| 24. Policy advocacy in general produces more effective policies | −1 | |
| 05. Rebutting opposing views can change policymakers' views | −2 | |
| 07. Monitoring and evaluating existing policy can set the policy agenda | −2 | Low |
| 13. Pilot programs and demonstration projects can lead to policy change | −2 | Low |
| 15. Research and analyses can change policymakers' views | −3 | Low |
| 23. Research and analyses can change the public's views | −3 | Low |

*Note* See Chapter 2 for an explanation of the factor array scores

and messaging (20:+2), public mobilizations (21:+2, 14:+1), and rebuttals or debate (18:0). These preferred tactics revolve around affecting broad public demand, rather than direct action or policymakers' views, in order to initiate policy changes and more responsive policymaking systems (14:+1, 21:+2). They do not engage in research (15:−3, 23:−3), pilot programs (13:−2), or monitoring and evaluation (07:−2, 03:−1), which assume a level of rationalism in policymaking, usually require significant resources to conduct, and tend to target narrow audiences. Instead, they prefer persuasion and argumentation to sway the public's views (20:+2, 18:0).

While the earlier strategies acknowledge some importance of formal players in the policy process, and often engages them, the popular power strategy ignores or eschews them (05:−2, 15:−3). In fact, their rating for lobbying matched the lowest among the strategies (02:0). Instead, organizations that apply the popular power strategy aim to sway the public's views in order to change policies (14:+1) and social conditions (08:+2), and build more responsive and democratic systems of policymaking (21:+2).

It's important to note that popular power strategists engage the public to affect policy directly, and not to change policymakers' views (19:0). This is a marked distinction in their view of policymaking, compared to the indirect pressure strategists (Chapter 7). While the latter engage the public to apply pressure on policymakers, popular power strategists view the public as having the ultimate power of policymaking themselves. Public officials follow public will. So they aim to mobilize that power to affect change (Fig. 8.1).

a) coalitions, media work, rebuttals/debate → public views→ policy agenda, change→
social/physical conditions
b) coalitions, media work, rebuttals/debate → responsive policies/democracy

**Fig. 8.1**  Popular power strategy

For example, one organization in our dataset facilitated a broad campaign on immigration reform. Their executive director explicitly discounted policymakers as their intended audience or policy change as their direct goal. "Others do that," she said. Instead, their measures of progress are the numbers of people and groups who are advancing the issue. By mobilizing people, they expect policy to follow. "We bring attention to issues… Instead of our audience being policymakers specifically, it's more all the people doing this work. And we say [to them] you should be thinking about this issue and this angle. Getting people to think in different ways, that is how we influence the debate." She called this kind of work the "infrastructure-building side of advocacy," focusing more directly on engagement and empowerment than policy outcome.

## Theoretical Foundations

Both the popular power strategy and the indirect pressure strategy (Chapter 7) engage the public as a key tactic. However, their purposes for public engagement are distinct. Thus, their theoretical affinities are too. Indirect pressure strategists' purpose in engaging the public is to affect the decisions of formal policymakers, recognizing their power in the process. Conversely, popular power strategists engage the public because that is where policymaking power primarily resides. The two may look alike in operation, but their views of power and policy change are different.

The popular power strategy embodies the stereotypical grassroots approach to policy advocacy and aligns with Walker's (1983) outside strategy and resource mobilization theory (McCarthy and Zald 2006). Advocates using the popular power strategy views elected officials and other government offices not as autonomous decision makers, but rather as reactive entities reflecting public will. Therefore, these advocates focus on building coalitions and mobilizing the public around its causes. Furthermore, by increasing public participation in policy processes, these advocates enhance democratic policymaking itself, in addition to affecting specific policy changes.

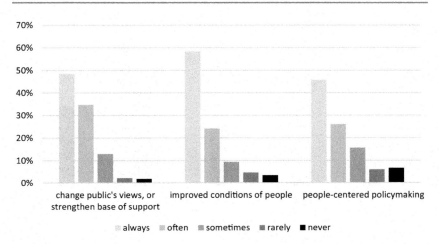

**Fig. 8.2** Advocates' usage of key tactics related to the popular power strategy

The strategy also invokes the Advocacy Coalition Framework (Sabatier 1988) in two ways. First, it views coalitions as the central actors in policymaking, so it devotes significant efforts to coalition building. Second, it recognizes the role of learning in the policy process, so information dissemination and media work constitute integral tactics in this strategy.

## Current Usage

The popular power strategy is defined not only by the advocacy activities they use, but also by the ones they don't use. To influence the public's views, they favor coalition building, public mobilization, framing and messaging, media work, or defensive activities (e.g., responding to opponents and reacting to the political climate). And they generally do not engage in research production, pilot studies or demonstration projects, litigation, and monitoring policy implementation. Figure 8.2 shows how frequently each of these advocacy activities is used by all the nonprofits in our survey. To isolate the organizations who use this strategy often, we screened for those who use any of the first five activities often or always, while using each of the last four rarely or never. We further screened these organizations by those that indicated that influencing the public's views,

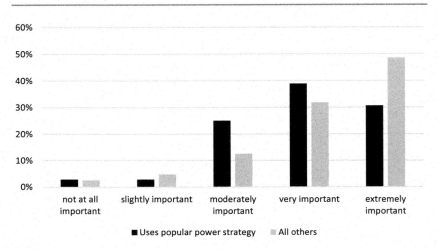

**Fig. 8.3** Importance of policy advocacy to mission of popular power strategists (*Note* $\chi_{(4)}^2 = 7.06, p = 0.13$)

strengthening democracy, and improving conditions of the public were very important or extremely important outcomes of their advocacy activities. This resulted in 42 nonprofits in our dataset that strongly adhere to the popular power strategy. The following analyses compare these advocacy organizations against all the others in our dataset.

Figure 8.3 shows that 31% of popular power strategists rated the importance of policy advocacy as extremely important to their organizations, 18% fewer than all the other organizations. But in the middle ratings of moderately important and very important, the popular power strategists make up the difference. Overall, the differences in importance of policy advocacy are statistically insignificant. Those using the popular power strategy hold policy advocacy as important as those who don't use the strategy.

Even so, those nonprofits using the popular power strategy devote significantly fewer resources toward policy advocacy than other nonprofits. See Table 8.2. Popular power strategists devote an average of 10% less staff time on policy advocacy than other advocates ($t_{(39.7)} = 2.01$, $p = 0.05$). They also spend about 14% less of their financial resources on policy advocacy ($t_{(39.3)} = 2.81$, $p = 0.01$). These differences may reflect the resource requirements of the favored tactics in the popular power strategy. Framing issues, developing messages, and media

**Table 8.2** Resources devoted to policy advocacy by popular power strategists

|  | Staff devoted to policy advocacy (%) | Financial resources devoted to policy advocacy (%) |
|---|---|---|
| Uses popular power often or always | Mean = 36 S.D. = 29 | Mean = 27 S.D. = 28 |
| All others | Mean = 46 S.D. = 32 | Mean = 41 S.D. = 33 |

work, for example, generally require fewer resources than litigation, pilot studies, and conducting research.

When comparing the public issues concerning advocates who use the popular power strategy against those who do not, a few clear distinctions are revealed. Popular power strategists are statistically more engaged in education (55% versus 42%, $\chi^2_{(1)} = 2.72$, $p = 0.10$), civil rights (45% versus 30%, $\chi^2_{(1)} = 4.60$, $p = 0.03$), and immigration issues (29% versus 15%, $\chi^2_{(1)} = 5.39$, $p = 0.02$). These are all issues in which broad swaths of the public often have strong opinions, giving nonprofits opportunities to mobilize them in this advocacy strategy. For all other issues we measured, advocates' engagement in them was not distinguishable by their use of the popular power strategy. Nonetheless, substantial proportions of nonprofits using the popular power strategy are engaged in health and mental health (41%), social welfare and poverty (33%), community development (29%), and youth development (26%) (Fig. 8.4).

When asked which levels and branches of government they primarily target in their policy advocacy, respondents using the popular power strategy were not significantly different from others. See Figs. 8.5 and 8.6. Regarding the levels of government, 60% target state government and 52% target local government. The higher levels of government attract a minority of popular power strategists. The only branch of government targeted by a majority of nonprofits using the popular power strategy is the legislative branch.

One surprising finding about these nonprofits that use the popular power strategy is that the proportion of them that have neither individual nor organizational memberships is significantly larger than that of other nonprofits (48% versus 33%, $\chi^2_{(1)} = 3.64$, $p = 0.06$). See Fig. 8.7. Since the strategy often mobilizes the public and creates coalitions, having memberships would seem to be advantageous. But this is not so for nearly half of these nonprofits in our data. Still, 26% of them have individual memberships and 21% have organizational memberships.

Finally, Fig. 8.8 charts the income levels of nonprofits often using the popular power strategy versus those who don't. Consistent with earlier observations

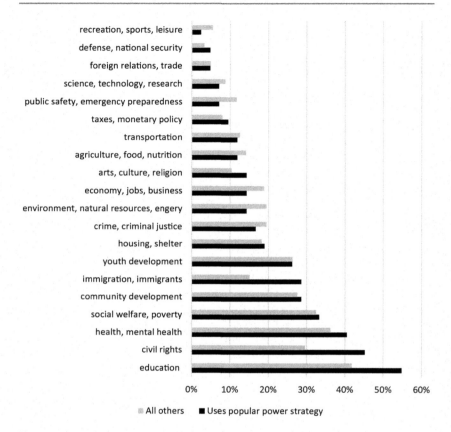

**Fig. 8.4**  Public issues engaged by popular power strategists

of their uses of resources in policy advocacy (Table 8.2), it shows that these nonprofits generally have greater representation in the lower levels of income. Organizations who earned less than $25,000 in 2013 represent 31% of the popular power strategists, compared to 23% of all others. A plurality of 42% earned between $100,000 and $500,000 compared to 26% of all others. No organizations using the popular power strategy were represented in the top two income levels.

Two cases that follow illustrate the variety of ways how the popular power strategy can be implemented in policy advocacy. The first recounts Codepink's

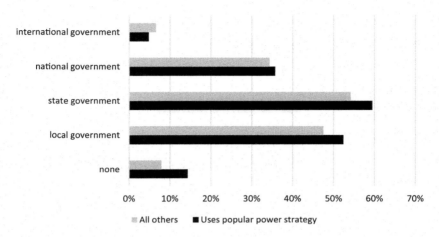

**Fig. 8.5** Levels of government targeted by popular power strategists

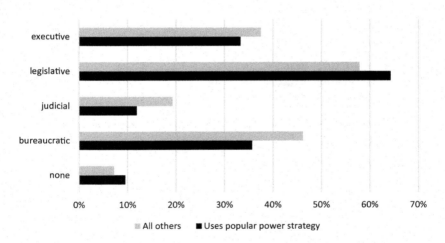

**Fig. 8.6** Branches of government targeted by popular power strategists

campaign to divert war expenditures toward domestic public services. The campaign focused on mobilizing two complementary groups and bringing voice to their stances on the issue. The second describes how Parents for Public Schools trains and empowers parents to take charge in their local schools and districts.

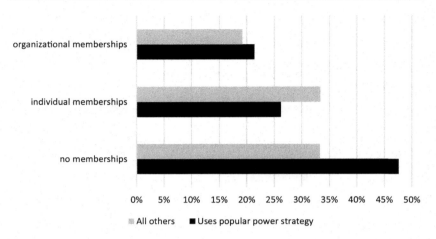

**Fig. 8.7**   Memberships of popular power strategists

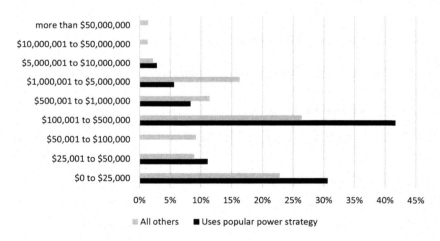

**Fig. 8.8**   2013 Income distribution of popular power strategists

## Bring Our War $$ Home

Codepink's founding was itself an act of protest and an example of the popular power strategy. It was a grassroots reaction to policies taken by political leaders. In their case, it was President George W. Bush's ramp up to war in Iraq, in the aftermath of September 11, 2001, terrorist attacks in the United States. To protest the move, a small group of women organized a vigil in front of the White House that began in November 2002. The vigil concluded four months later, on International Women's Day, after over 10,000 people had joined their effort (Codepink 2019, What is Codepink). Codepink emerged from that vigil, and continues its work today as a nonprofit focused on promoting peace and human rights, and ending wars and militarism.

Its name is a satirical play on the Bush administration's terror alert system (Codepink 2019, What is Codepink), which was implemented by the newly formed Department of Homeland Security in March of 2002 (Homeland Security 2017). The system was meant to alert the public about the current level of threat from terrorist attacks, conveyed through a five-color code: green = low risk, blue = guarded risk, yellow = elevated risk, orange = high risk, and red = severe risk (Jenkins 2004).[1] The founders of Codepink viewed the alert system as "based on fear" and "used to justify violence" (Codepink 2019, What is Codepink). So they offered an alternative color code, pink, "as a feisty call for people to 'wage peace.'"

"Feisty" is an appropriate adjective not only for the organization's beginnings, but also for its continuing approach to policy advocacy. According to their website, "with an emphasis on joy and humor, our tactics include satire, street theatre, creative visuals, civil resistance, and directly challenging powerful decision-makers in government and corporations. And of course, wearing pink!" (Codepink 2019, What is Codepink). Nancy Mancias, a campaign organizer for Codepink, was more blunt, describing their typical advocacy event as "in-your-face" and "radical," designed to be "theatric events" to draw public attention to issues. This is easily confirmed by viewing the Codepink channel on YouTube, where there are hundreds of videos from Codepink advocacy around the world and over the years.

---

[1]The advisory system was in place for less than ten years and was never in code blue or green during (Homeland Security 2017). During that span, it was derided as ineffective and "politically manipulated" (Shapiro and Cohen 2007). As one congressman said, the color codes "taught Americans to be scared, not prepared" (CNN Wire Staff 2011).

Mancias started volunteering with Codepink in 2003, shortly after the organization's founding. She was later hired by the nonprofit to organize advocacy campaigns, and she continues to do so on a national level. Fitting for Codepink's approach to policy advocacy, Mancias background is in theater, holding a bachelor's degree in drama from San Francisco State University (Codepink 2019, Nancy L. Mancias). The organization's approach to advocacy fit her style and skills, and she has played key roles in some of the organization's major campaigns over the years. She describes her work with Codepink as "a women's preemptive strike for peace."

Today, Codepink continues with many ongoing campaigns, focusing on varied issues in Iran, Palestine, Syria, Iraq, and Saudi Arabia, and on US issues of accountability for war actions, developing local economies, and drone warfare (Codepink 2019, Issues and Campaigns). Codepink also helps its supporters to travel abroad with them to learn more about international issues of conflict and peace, and to advocate overseas. Recent sponsored trips went to Palestine, Cuba, and Iran.

Codepink's advocacy tactics and strategy are exemplified in their Bring Our War $$ Home campaign. While the organization was founded in opposition to the military and war policies of the Bush administration, this campaign focused on the opportunity costs of those policies. In 2010, the US's war in Iraq was in its seventh year, as the country—and the world—was staggering from the Great Recession. Codepink leaders saw the disparity in the situation. "With record unemployment, home foreclosures, and budget cuts to education, health and other life supporting services," states an unpublished Codepink document, the United States "…dedicates 54% of our discretionary funds on military spending." Brown University's Watson Institute describes these opportunity costs succinctly:

> Spending on the wars has involved opportunity costs for the US economy. Although military spending does produce jobs, spending in other areas such as health care could produce more jobs. Additionally, while investment in military infrastructure grew, investment in other, nonmilitary, public infrastructure such as roads and schools did not grow at the same rate. (Watson Institute for International and Public Affairs 2018)

To address these costs, Codepink launched their campaign, aimed at diverting military and war expenditures toward domestic "life supporting" public services.

Their campaign aimed to raise public awareness of these costs of war and to increase demands for war expenditures to be diverted. The tactics they used consisted of two broad strands. The first was their more familiar activities of public events and protests to earn media attention and draw greater public support. The second was less familiar to Codepink. They sought to persuade city governments across the country to pass resolutions that support their call to bring the war dollars home. Because local government services were hard hit by the economic recession, and clearly felt by the public, mobilizing local government officials to make a common statement could influence change at the national level.

This second tactic was somewhat unfamiliar to Codepink, because it involved their nurturing relationships with mayors and councils, rather than protesting their actions. At the local level, "This was very much a behind-the-scenes advocacy [tactic] to work with individual mayors, rather than get in their faces with theatric events and protests," said Mancias.

Campaign documents produced by Codepink listed the five advocacy actions it encouraged its members to take: spread the message in their own communities, reach out to their elected representatives, pass a "Bring Our War $$ Home" resolution in their own cities, conduct "penny polls" in their communities, and use social media. For each of these activities, Codepink listed specific examples of what members could do, and for some they supplied materials for members to use. See Box 8.1.

---

### Box 8.1 Bring Our War $$ Home Tactics

Overview: The campaign sought to raise public demand to divert military expenditures toward domestic priorities such as education, housing, and healthcare. Codepink's approach was to mobilize support for it among two key groups: the public and local elected officials. They prescribed five advocacy activities for their members and provided support for these activities

Tactics prescribed by Codepink (edited for brevity and clarity):

| | |
|---|---|
| 1. Spread our message | • Communicate to your community how military spending leads to cuts in domestic programs |
| | • Download the [flyer] and pass it out at school board meetings, civic events… wherever people are considering where their tax dollars go, or should go |
| | • Build your own local group and listserv to support the campaign. Use our sign-up sheet and all-weather banners at rallies and events |
| | • Write letters to the editor of your local newspaper, linking news articles about city and state budget crises… |

| 2. Reach out | • Contact your senators and member of Congress with the Bring Our War $$ Home message |
|---|---|
| 3. Pass a resolution in your city | • Print out a flyer with key points about the effects of military spending on your local budget. Use the National Priorities Project website to find data outlining the costs of wars to your state, city, county, school district, or even zip code<br>• Download the Bring Our War $$ Home template resolution. Edit the template to include your city's specific information on war funding<br>• Gather signatures, hold public events to build support, and take it to your city council |
| 4. Conduct penny polls | This is a fun activity to do at a farmers' market, in front of the post office, or any popular community spot:<br>• Set up a table with a "penny poll" sign, and jars labeled "education," "environment," "health care," "housing," and "military"<br>• Give participants 10 pennies each, to distribute among the jars<br>• Invite the local media, and help them get pictures and interviews<br>• Afterward, inform the media or write a letter to the editor about the results of the penny poll |
| 5. Use social media | • Comment on online articles related to the federal budget, the "fiscal cliff," the costs of war, or related issues<br>• Follow @WarDollarsHome on Twitter<br>• Let your Facebook friends know your thoughts, and make suggestions about actions they can take |

Their strategy behind these activities revolves around mobilizing the public and building the public's voice in policy issues. This is best articulated in an older version of their organizational policy on resource sharing:

> Codepink does not require official affiliation or traditional 'membership' to speak, act, or protest with us. Anyone who is acting for peace can be Codepink! Our logos, photos, and the downloadable resources... are free for local groups to use. Central staff can help send email alerts and provide local contact info for local organizers.

The central website offers local webpages to groups. Our ideas and campaigns are freely available to any peace or justice group that wishes to adapt our tactics for their use. Local groups can endorse or cosponsor local events in the name of their local Codepink group without seeking permission from the central staff... We are a grassroots movement with a central organizing team. (Codepink, n.d.)

The viewpoint reflected in this policy and their advocacy tactics aligns closely with that of the popular power strategy. They aim to empower the public and amplify their voices to demand policy change.

Besides having local Codepink chapters lobby their own city councils to pass resolutions, the national organization sought to do the same with the United States Conference of Mayors, the nonpartisan association of mayors of US cities with at least 30,000 people. Codepink authored the resolution and lobbied the association to adopt it at their annual meeting.

In 2011, Codepink's campaign came to fruition when the US Conference of Mayors passed the resolution calling on the president to "bring these war dollars home to meet vital human needs, promote job creation, rebuild infrastructure, aid municipal and state governments, and develop a new economy based upon renewable, sustainable energy" (United State Conference of Mayors 2019).

## Parent Engagement in Public Schools

Deena Zacharin had her own private law practice in the late 1990s when she began exploring elementary schools in San Francisco for her soon-to-be school-age child. Her memory of the reputation of San Francisco schools from her own childhood was that people would line up to enroll their children in them. They were high quality and in high demand. So when her child was still a toddler, she went to her neighborhood public school to begin the enrollment process, expecting that she should be in the queue years in advance of kindergarten. She learned that there was no queue, and that the school was viewed as low performing. She could wait to enroll her child at the start of kindergarten. Still, Zacharin met the principal, observed some classes, and felt some "really great things were happening at the school." She remained optimistic that it was a good place for her child to attend.

Slightly before, Sandra Halladey had a preschool daughter preparing for kindergarten in another neighborhood of San Francisco. When she investigated her nearby school, she discovered two things. First, parents were confused about which schools were their assigned schools, and how to enroll their children in them. At that time, the school district was under a federal court consent decree that aimed to integrate what had been ethnically clustered neighborhood schools. To facilitate the desegregation, attendance areas of schools were essentially gerrymandered to increase diversity across the district's schools. "For example," a civil grand jury later reported, "the attendance area school for part of the Mission neighborhood was (and still is) on Nob Hill" (2007–2008 Civil Grand Jury 2008). The two neighborhoods are separated by other neighborhoods, as well as a major thoroughfare. Parents could request a different school than their assigned one, but their new assignment would be by lottery and would still be constrained by the consent decree's requirement of no more than 45% of any one race or ethnicity at any school in the district.

Second, Halladey found that the public schools were suffering from a negative reputation. She said her parental peers at her daughter's preschool had "terrible things to say" about the public schools, and many were opting for private schools. Local news appeared to feed this reputation, said Halladey. "The media portrayed a really bad impression of public schools, and the schools didn't know how to market themselves." For example, her first encounter with the neighborhood school that her daughter might attend was defeating. When she introduced herself to the office staff as a neighborhood parent who might enroll her daughter there, one staff member "scowled" and told her no one *wants* their child there. Halladey explored the school anyway, and, like Zacharin at her school, found a strong educational program there. The negative reputation of the school seemed to be unwarranted, and it disappointed Halladey because of her background in sales and marketing.

She eventually worked with the school's principal to help market the school to neighborhood parents, and she coached the principal in promoting the school. "Every event is a recruiting event," she recounted, from prospective parent visits, to PTA meetings, to school performances. Halladey later organized "enrollment fairs" with the district's student placement staff, to help parents through the process. Nothing like it had been done by the district. The events became so popular, that the school district contracted Halladey part-time to promote public schools around the city.

## Parents for Public Schools

In 1998, the principal at Zacharin's school introduced her to Halladey, because both seemed to see the hidden promise of the city's public schools, and both seemed eager to develop that promise. A year later, the two secured funding from the Zellerbach Family Foundation to help them incorporate a local chapter of Parents for Public Schools (PPS), a national nonprofit that works "to strengthen public schools by engaging, educating, and mobilizing parents" (Molnar 2013). Zacharin closed her private law practice and became the chapter's executive director, with Halladey as the associate director.

The national organization was founded in 1991 in Jackson, Mississippi, by a committed group of parents who chose not to follow the flight from public schools but instead demand higher standards and more resources for them. Today, it works to advance their vision that "parents are owners of their public schools," and it implements programs that "prepare parents for the responsibilities of ownership" (Parents for Public Schools, n.d., What we do). In their view, parents act as the owners when they move "beyond a reactive, help-only-when-asked mode, to identify problems and bring their talents and ideas to the policy table" (Parents for Public Schools, n.d., History). The national organization supports the local chapters with professional expertise and the network of chapters and parents across the country, but each chapter has the freedom to pursue their own agenda to address local issues.

Back in San Francisco, Zacharin and Halladey took the national organization's view to heart. Halladey reflected, "We brought the voice of parents, and real experiences of parents, to people at the school district who were very concerned—rightfully so—with the education component, but weren't really looking out...from a community engagement standpoint."

"At the time, educators had a real attitude that they knew what was best," said Zacharin. "They have the doctorate in education. So don't worry your little heads, just hand over your kids and everything will be fine. But things weren't fine." Enrollments were dropping, they said. Middle-class families were choosing private schools or leaving the city. Parents weren't getting their choice of schools for their children. Zacharin and Halladey acknowledged there was excellent education happening in the district, but parents were not always aware of them, or they faced barriers to get to them, like the school assignment system. "There was a real closed-door attitude" at the district, in which the schools operated outside of parental scrutiny. PPS sought to create a paradigm shift, in which the school district began having the parents shape policy and practices.

They organized training sessions for parents to be leaders in the school governance structure and to be partners with their schools' teachers and board. They also developed a media component to their operations, in which Halladey trained PPS members how to speak to the press. They even trained site staff in marketing skills, so they too could promote their schools. These activities mirrored the Parent Engagement Program developed by the national organization, which included several workshops aimed at developing parents into well-informed and proactive leaders of their schools. Topics in those workshops included parent engagement in schools, using data in accountability, common core curriculum, leadership styles, school comprehensive improvement planning, involving all parents, disaggregated data, community resources, and many others (Harper et al. 2013).

In all these advocacy activities, their purpose was to bring real stories of public education to life for policymakers. Halladey recalled, for example, that she was once in a meeting with then-San Francisco Mayor Gavin Newsom when the discussion turned to arts education. According to Halladey, "It was obviously going over his head, so afterwards I said 'you just need to come to see it.'" She took Newsom to her daughter's elementary school, where children were studying geometry with origami, and "his whole face lit up," said Halladey. "Then, every time he talked about arts education he related back to what he had seen... We brought stories to life for people, to inform policy."

PPS's focus on parent mobilization and empowerment is strategic. Turnover of district personnel is constant, said Zacharin, so parents can provide some stability and direction across a longer span of time. In her twelve years working in the district, reflected Zacharin, she worked with four superintendents and saw perhaps ten major initiatives started. In her view, this constant change contributed to the stunted progress of the district. This also made parent engagement more difficult, because of the changing personnel. But PPS provided a level of consistency, which allowed them to become the experts about the district's programs, even more so than the leaders of those programs, according to Zacharin.

Of course, parents turnover too, often when their children graduate from high school. So PPS trains parents not to just be advocates for their own children's education, but for public education in general, and to take a long-term, district-wide view of issues.

## Parent Leaders

Zacharin's and Halladey's pathways to PPS are themselves prime examples of what PPS aims to do: empower parents and community members to own their local public schools and shape local education policy. After two years at the helm of PPS-San Francisco, Zacharin was recruited by San Francisco's school district to lead their parent engagement programs. "It was an opportunity to bring that brand of parent engagement that we had [in PPS] to the school district," said

Zacharin, "to make change from within." She worked within the district for the next ten years. Halladey stayed with PPS for seven years, then was recruited into newly elected Mayor Gavin Newsom's transition team, to help develop his education agenda.

Reflecting on her time in PPS, Zacharin said some advocacy organizations operate from the outside of the policymaking bodies as a "thorn in the side." PPS, on the other hand, saw themselves as playing the role of the "friendly critic." Both shed light on the policy problems that need attention, but PPS works constructively with the government body to address them. The approach worked for PPS, in that it got them a seat at the table with decision makers. There were times when that seat had a "flavor of tokenism," said Zacharin, but PPS took advantage of it—regardless of the district's motive—to make parents' voices and demands count in policy.

### Discussions

8a. The popular power strategy aims to create social change and enhance democracy by mobilizing the public and empowering them to voice their views. Describe an example of this strategy that you have seen locally. What did they advocate for? Would you say they were successful? Why or why not?

8b. Identify a recent local protest. What were its objectives? Do you think it was successful? How might it contribute to changes in public policy?

8c. For the Bring Our War $$ Home campaign, Codepink's measure of success was the adoption of their resolution by city councils and the United States Conference of Mayors. It did not measure actual diversion of military spending toward domestic priorities. What are the advantages and disadvantages of this approach to measuring interim advocacy outcomes?

8d. Codepink described much of their policy advocacy as "in-your-face," while Parents for Public Schools viewed themselves as "friendly critics." Which do you feel is a better approach? Does it depend upon the policy issue? The level or branch of government? Explain. Also, which approach are you more comfortable with? Why?

# References

2007–2008 Civil Grand Jury. (2008). *San Francisco Kindergarten Admissions: Back to the Drawing Board*. San Francisco: City and County of San Francisco. Retrieved from http://civilgrandjury.sfgov.org/2007_2008/San_Francisco_Kindergarten_Admissions.pdf.

CNN Wire Staff. (2011, January 26). *Color-Coded Threat System to Be Replaced in April*. CNN. Retrieved from http://www.cnn.com/2011/POLITICS/01/26/threat.level.system.change/index.html.

Codepink. (n.d.). *Pink Action Principles*. Codepink. Retrieved from http://codepinkarchive.org/section.php@id=439.html.

Codepink. (2019). *Issues and Campaigns*. Codepink. Retrieved from https://www.codepink.org/issues_campaigns.

Codepink. (2019). *Nancy L. Mancias*. Codepink. Retrieved from https://www.codepink.org/nancy_mancias.

Codepink. (2019). *What Is Codepink*. Codepink. Retrieved from https://www.codepink.org/about.

Harper, M., Rutherford, J., & Bryant, M. (2013). *Evaluation Report for Parents for Public Schools*. Center for Educational Research and Evaluation, University of Mississippi.

Homeland Security. (2017). *Chronology of Changes to the Homeland Security Advisory System*. U.S. Department of Homeland Security. Retrieved from https://www.dhs.gov/homeland-security-advisory-system.

Jenkins, W. O. (2004). *Homeland Security Advisory System: Preliminary Observations Regarding Threat Level Increases from Yellow to Orange. Government Accountability Office* (Report GAO-04-453R). Retrieved from https://www.gao.gov/new.items/d04453r.pdf.

McCarthy, J. D., & Zald, M. N. (2006). Resource mobilization theory: Vigorous or outmoded? In J. H. Turner (Ed.), *Handbook of Sociological Theory*. New York: Springer Science & Business Media.

Molnar, M. (2013, June 18). Mississippi partnership contributes to higher student scores. *Education Week*. Retrieved from https://blogs.edweek.org/edweek/parentsandthepublic/2013/06/mississippi_partnership_contributes_to_higher_student_scores.html.

Parents for Public Schools. (n.d.). *History*. Parents for Public Schools, Inc. Retrieved from https://parents4publicschools.org/history/.

Parents for Public Schools. (n.d.). *What We Do*. Parents for Public Schools, Inc. Retrieved from https://parents4publicschools.org/what/.

Sabatier, P. A. (1988). An advocacy coalition framework of policy change and the role of policy-oriented learning therein. *Policy Sciences, 21*(2–3), 129–168.

Shapiro, J. N., & Cohen, D. K. (2007). Color blind: Lessons from the failed Homeland Security advisory system. *International Security, 32*(2), 121–154.

United States Conference of Mayors. (2019). *79th Annual Meeting: Calling on Congress to Redirect Military Spending to Domestic Priorities*. United States Conference of Mayors. Retrieved from https://www.usmayors.org/the-conference/resolutions/?category=c8869&meeting=79th%20Annual%20Meeting.

Walker, J. L. (1983). The origins and maintenance of interest groups in America. *American Political Science Review, 77*(2), 390–406.

Watson Institute for International and Public Affairs. (2018). *Costs of War*. Watson Institute, Brown University. Retrieved from https://watson.brown.edu/costsofwar/costs/economic.

# Considerations for Strategic Policy Advocacy

9

## Creative and Strategic Policy Advocacy

The preceding chapters have illustrated that a limited set of tactics can be utilized in a variety of ways, depending on the viewpoint of the advocates. The six strategies described in this book identify unique viewpoints of nonprofit organizations on the processes of policy change and how they seek to influence those processes. See Table 9.1 for a summary of views about their positions in the policy process. There is an association between selecting strategies and the focus issue and size of the nonprofit organization. This section recaps the six advocacy strategies and identifies associations between strategy selection and organizational profile (related to size, scope, issue area, and targeted level of government).

Lobbying is a popular tactic across the board, and most particularly in the *Public Lobbying* strategy for topics in the public interest, but where the issue is complex and/or those affected are not well mobilized. This tactic is most associated with membership organizations in our sample. While lobbying is used by organizations controlling the most resources, it is also used by those organizations with relatively fewer resources.

The combination of coalition building and research characteristic of *Institutional Partnership* strategy was used most frequently among advocates for health and mental health. While advocates using this strategy engage with all branches—legislative, bureaucratic, executive, and judicial—this strategy was most frequently applied at the state level. The use of pilot studies and demonstration projects as a form of evidence-building is characteristic of this approach, suggesting the need for resources, which aligns with the higher-income profile of organizations utilizing this approach.

© The Author(s) 2020
S. Gen and A. C. Wright, *Nonprofits in Policy Advocacy*,
https://doi.org/10.1007/978-3-030-43696-4_9

**Table 9.1**   Viewpoints associated with policy advocacy strategies

| Strategy | Viewpoints on process of policy change |
| --- | --- |
| Public lobbying (Chapter 3) | Advocates represent the public's interests, especially when the constituency does not, or cannot, act on its own behalf, due to lack of social capital or complexity of the issue (trustee perspective). Favorable policy change, improved physical and social conditions, and enhanced democracy result from advocates lobbying policymakers on the public's interests. |
| Institutional partnership (Chapter 4) | Advocates are partners with formal policymakers, bringing expertise, research, and messaging to the partnership. Policy change happens when they build collaborative and congenial relationships with policymakers to achieve mutual policy goals. |
| Inside-outside (Chapter 5) | Two champions are needed to create policy change: a champion on the inside of policymaking body, who lobby peers and can usher the issue through the approval process, and a champion on the outside who can support the inside champion with public messaging, media work, and defensive work. |
| Direct reform (Chapter 6) | Advocates can create policy change directly, through judicial and administrative processes, including litigation, demonstration projects, monitoring policy implementation, and evaluating policy outcomes. |
| Indirect pressure (Chapter 7) | The pathway to policy change leads from the public to policymakers, so these advocates engage the public and mobilize public opinion to put pressure on policymakers to act. |
| Popular power (Chapter 8) | Policy change happens when there is enough public demand for it. The public holds ultimate power in policymaking, so these advocates work to mobilize the public and communicate their demands. |

The *Inside-Outside* strategy relies on building targeted relationships with an inside champion while also building outside public support through coalitions, information campaigns, and media work. Our evidence suggests this is a particularly versatile strategy that organizations use across topic areas, levels of government, and branches of government. Yet it is also a strategy that may require significant resources, as it is most highly associated with organizations that have higher incomes as well as membership bases on which to draw.

*Direct Reform* strategy requires use of specialist skills in litigation or implementation monitoring, alongside media work or issue framing. While there is a focus on judicial and bureaucratic branches of government in this strategy, advocates target all branches of government as policy wins in the judiciary or administrative process may provoke action by the legislative or executive branches. Organizations that use this strategy are more likely to have higher funding and a membership base, though this varies as the case examples in Chapter 6 illustrate.

*Indirect Pressure* strategy is focused on the mechanism of change more than specific tactics—by working with the public to apply indirect pressure on policymakers, for policy change and ultimately improvements in social and physical conditions. This strategy is used at the local, state, and national levels, most frequently targeting the legislative branch, followed by the bureaucracy and judiciary. While having a membership appears to be an asset for this strategy, enabling advocates to mobilize their base, it is used by organizations with significant as well as with few resources, suggesting the strategy can be mobilized in the face of resource constraints.

Finally, the *Popular Power* strategy honors the authority of the people in a strong democracy, and views policy change as an output of what the public demands. These advocates therefore focus on tactics that mobilize the public and communicates their demands. Compared to other advocates in our sample, these advocates are more likely to be engaged in education policy, civil rights, and immigration issues, all issues that generally earn strong public opinions, thereby facilitating their mobilization. They devote significantly less staff and budget to policy advocacy, and tend to be among the lower-income nonprofits. This suggests that this is a popular strategy among leaner and start-up nonprofits.

It is important to remember that these six strategies do not define different categories of nonprofits, only different viewpoints on how policy changes and how advocates can affect those changes. Any individual nonprofit may use multiple strategies in a given campaign, and the same nonprofit might use different strategies for different campaigns. Articulating these strategies in this book only serves to clarify their views, tactics, expectations, and usage. Nonprofits are still left with deciding which strategy to employ for any given campaign.

That choice is particularly challenging within a political environment crowded with other interests and constantly in flux (Reid 2006). An advocacy effort may start with a particular plan or theory of change but remain open to modification as the situation requires. Mintzberg and Waters (1985) make distinctions between deliberate strategies—the articulation of intentions at the beginning of a plan—and emergent strategies—the adaptations that evolve in responses to the environment. While deliberate strategy focuses on direction and control, emergent strategic allows for strategic learning. Realized strategy becomes the combination of the deliberate strategy plus emergent strategy minus unrealized strategy that was left behind.

## The Challenges of Policy Advocacy

While policy advocacy can achieve important goals that are central to the missions of nonprofit organizations, including improving the lives of their target populations, there can be significant costs, and results are not guaranteed. As demonstrated in the case studies from previous chapters, engaging in policy advocacy generally requires professional staff with skills in advocacy-related competencies such as strategic communication, coalition building, policy monitoring, and even litigation. Yet while these costs are incurred by a nonprofit organization, the beneficial outcomes (if any) are delivered to the general population, rather than the members or specific constituencies of the nonprofit (Salamon 2002). In a time of contracting resources, nonprofit organizations may see advocacy as vital to promoting the well-being of vulnerable populations, as well as maintaining or expanding services that they themselves may deliver (Mosely 2011).

While the end goal for policy advocacy is often favorable policy change, it is not the sole measure of success. Advocates are often seeking goals other than simply changing one specific policy. This is practical in a pluralistic society, because few get exactly what they want in policies. Moreover, if favorable policy change was the only desired outcome, most advocacy efforts would be deemed failures. Policy advocates are competing against adversaries, who may oppose policy change due to preference for the status quo, dissent with the ideas proposed, or compete for limited resources (Teles and Schmitt 2016). As demonstrated in the six strategies, interim outcomes along the path to policy and social change are also significant. The goals may be to build a constituency around a policy issue, monitor how policy is implemented, or even prevent change to defend a policy, contributing to the goal of policy change.

There is growing interest in assessing the outcomes of advocacy work, not least by funders, who are interested in advocacy for its potential to create social change, but may be hesitant to fund policy advocacy because of their need to provide evidence of stewardship of funds and the challenges of evaluating advocacy (DeVita et al. 2004; Fagen et al. 2009). From the perspective of evaluating the outcomes of policy advocacy, there are several issues that cause difficulties, including complexity, time frames, changing dynamics and attribution (Guthrie et al. 2005). The time frames for short and long-term policy outcomes may vary, but the "arc of change" can span decades (Sabatier and Jenkins-Smith 1999). Funding cycles, by contrast, are generally for a year or two. While the policy goals may stay the same, the tactics may shift in response to the changing dynamics in the policy environment, and factors outside anyone's control including the political and economic environment may derail chances for success. Even with the big win, it is difficult, if not impossible, for a policy advocacy organization to claim attribution. Indeed, being perceived as trying to "own" a victory can undermine relations with allied organizations (Innovation Network Inc. 2008).

For a nonprofit organization to undertake a policy advocacy under these circumstances is challenging indeed. There will be times when funding tightens, the organization's supporters have doubts, and opposing sides increase their efforts. Because policy changes happen at such a slow pace, nonprofit organizations aiming to change policy need to be especially stable, with the ability to be nimble when a window of opportunity presents itself (Mandeville 2007). Advocates must be tolerant and patient, while maintaining their resolve. To chart their way and stay the course for the long-term, policy advocates need to measure their progress, in the short or medium term, along the path to ultimate policy change and social change. Having interim measures of success can maintain advocates' morale and sense that they are making progress (Innovation Network 2008). Advocacy organizations also need ways to measure their efforts, through an understanding of the proximal goals and pathways to change, to win funding, reassure supporters and share their advocacy successes.

Performance management and evaluation in policy advocacy is part of a larger global movement for accountability for nonprofit organizations. To some degree, lack of measurement of nonprofit advocacy may be self-protective, because it is likely that success is limited, and by limiting evaluation, organizations can maintain ambiguity and avoid criticism from funding sources and constituencies (Almog-Bar and Schmid 2014). While there is pressure to achieve visible performance outcomes relatively quickly, it is important for organizations to avoid "accountability myopia" by not just focusing on the short-term, but instead to consider the longer-term horizon and aim for organizational learning (Ebrahim 2005).

## Measuring and Evaluating Advocacy Performance

Measuring effectiveness of policy advocacy work is complex, but necessary to make informed decisions (Almog-Bar and Schmid 2014). In a survey of American nonprofit organizations conducting advocacy, respondents identified the most common benefit of evaluation as providing information to refine their strategy or next steps. The most common challenges were finding the time or money to conduct the evaluation and not having evaluation capacity within the organization, in terms of the requisite experience, knowledge, and skills (Innovation Network

2008). Performance monitoring that allows for assessing progress toward interim goals may be most helpful, because summative evaluation focused on the end goal contributes little to the advocacy campaign as it unfolds.

A starting point is to set benchmarks at the beginning of an advocacy campaign and revisit these at regular intervals, to prepare for eventually assessing outcomes (Holley et al. 2014). Benchmarks are reference points against which an organization's work can be compared. Guthrie et al. (2005) suggest the following considerations for benchmarks: aspirational and realistic goals; tolerance for risk; and flexibility. Determining benchmarks in and of itself can be challenging for different groups, as there may be varying perspectives and lack of consensus on the organizational goals and evaluation criteria. Multiple constituency framework recognizes that stakeholders may hold differing views. For example, paid staff and volunteers may hold distinct understandings around an organization's objectives and how these relate to their own preferences and priorities. Similarly, those working within an organization, and external stakeholders such as elected officials and bureaucrats, may perceive the goals of an organization quite differently (Jun and Shiau 2012). Moreover, when the object of evaluation is an advocacy coalition, the focus shifts from a single organization to the logic and influence of the network (Acosta 2012).

Given the nature of advocacy work and the need to adapt activities and expected outcomes as conditions shift, performance measurement and evaluation can aid organizations to plan their work and use continuous monitoring and evaluation to maintain flexibility and adapt as needed. Performance management in policy advocacy can provide value for making strategic decisions (LeRoux and Wright 2010), toward becoming a "learning organization." The concept of a learning organization positions an entity, such as a nonprofit, as having leadership and staff that share a vision and mental models of how to achieve goals that are adapted through experiences and dialogue (Senge 2006). This approach requires a mind-set toward evaluation that differs from typical program evaluation.

Evaluating advocacy efforts differs substantially from evaluating social service programs. Program evaluation assesses whether an intervention is designed in a way that delivers its intended outcomes and relies upon logic analysis to test a program's theory that connects actions to outcomes, using scientific knowledge about possible links and alternative explanations (Brousselle and Champagne 2011). However, evaluating the links between policy advocacy activities and intended outcomes is more nebulous and causality is difficult to establish (Glasrud 2001). There are also potentially many unpredictable and uncontrollable variables, related to shifts in policy windows (Kingdon and Thurber 1984). In a crowded political field, the aforementioned issues around whether a particular organization's efforts contributed to the end result are also difficult to establish. These constraints present the need for different approaches to monitoring and evaluating policy advocacy, using methodologies that are reflexive and adaptive, like successful advocacy efforts (Teles and Schmitt 2016). Like program evaluation in the 1980s, where social service evaluation was considered to be too hard, cumbersome, and expensive but gradually became the norm, advocacy evaluation may be going through a similar process, and may, over time, become more accepted (Carr and Holley 2013).

As an emerging field of practice, advocacy and policy change evaluation assess and analyze efforts by noting necessary inputs, use of tactics, and resultant outputs and outcomes and long-term impacts (Gardner and Brindis 2017). Like any evaluation, a critical first step is to clarify the advocacy initiative's goals, objectives, and activities and specify the evaluation's purpose, questions, and approach (Gardner and Brindis 2017). One of the key methods in organizing and designing advocacy and policy change, developed by Jim Coe and Juliette Majot (2013) of the Overseas Development Institute (ODI), outlines four dimensions of an advocacy initiative that evaluators must examine: (1) strategy, direction, and the strength of an initiative's program theory of change; (2) management and outputs, or monitoring and assessment of advocacy tactics; (3) outcomes and impact, and the extent to which change has occurred; and (4) understanding causes or why an advocacy initiative succeeded or failed (Coe and Majot 2013).

Developing a logic model to map out an advocacy campaign can guide strategic decision making as well as drive performance monitoring and evaluation. As discussed in Chapter 2, logic models are visual depictions of change efforts, diagramming the connections between inputs (resources and necessary conditions), the activities they enable (which we have called tactics in this book), the short and longer-term outcomes that may arise from these activities, as well as the ultimately desired impact (Knowlton and Phillips 2012). The *Advocacy Strategy Framework* tool, available through the Center for Evaluation Innovation, can be used to develop a logic model. It provides a set of questions and a diagram of potential audiences (public, influencers, and decision makers), outcomes (awareness, will, action), and tactics (Coffman and Beer 2015). While actions undertaken may be modified in response to changing conditions, the underlying logic may remain consistent (Holley et al. 2014). Moreover, logic models are increasingly expected by funders. However, the complex nature of policy advocacy should be kept in mind, with cause and effect between action and outcome poorly understood and subject to multiple factors (Ebrahim and Rangan 2010).

Evaluation focused on efficacy of an advocacy campaign specifies a theory of change and alternative causal hypotheses, and establishes causation through evidence that supports or refutes these hypotheses. The goal is to establish whether there is evidence in support of the causal chain anticipated by the advocates (Naeve et al. 2017). Since the planned activities may deviate from the actual in response to changing conditions, rigid "evaluation by timetable" (Teles and Schmitt 2016, p. 10) is to be avoided. Indeed, rather than retrospective evaluation of a completed advocacy campaign, prospective evaluation may be of more use, to enable immediate use of emerging findings for course correction. A realistic goal may be to "determine whether a *plausible and defensible case* can be made that an advocacy effort has had an impact on the policy process or *contributed* to a policy change, using means for establishing certainty and uniqueness of evidence" (Naeve et al. 2017, p. 14) (emphasis original).

Returning to the concept of logic model, which has framed the empirical research reported in this book, this section considers evaluation of inputs, actions, outputs, outcomes, and impacts. An important caveat is that a logic model for an advocacy campaign may be considered a heuristic to think through an initial strategy that will likely be adapted and modified, as policy advocates test their intended actions and modify them in response to opponents and changing political conditions.

## Inputs

In addition to the outcomes of advocacy, it is meaningful to consider the inputs, in terms of capacity and resources. Capacity is an important marker for potential long-term success: If an organization has increased its capacity, it will have more agility to respond to windows of opportunity when they arise (Guthrie et al. 2005). Being able to assess an organization's capacity to read the environment and adapt its strategy may be the most significant goal for initial evaluation, especially for outside funders (Teles and Schmitt 2016). Assessing capacity involves looking at an organization's resources and skills available through its leadership, staff, membership, and board of directors (Gardner and Brindis 2017).

Self-administered capacity assessment tools may be useful to assess readiness to engage in particular advocacy strategies, as well as identify areas for strengthening and necessary resources. The Alliance for Justice (2005) *Advocacy Capacity Tool for Organizational Assessment* assesses an organization's readiness to engage in four areas of advocacy: (1) advocacy goals and strategies; (2) conducting advocacy; (3) advocacy avenues or targets of influence; and (4) organizational operations to sustain advocacy. If measuring initiatives in an international arena, the *International Advocacy Capacity Tool* similarly measures groups around the world and their capacity to engage in advocacy. The *Advocacy Core Capacity Assessment Tool* (CCAT), which provides a glimpse into an organization's effectiveness in four areas: (1) leadership, (2) adaptability, (3) management, and (4) technical capacities, provides a general measure of whether or not an organization can meet the demands of advocacy (Gardner and Brindis 2017).

## Activities and Outputs

When evaluating policy advocacy, it is necessary to be prepared to assess the range of tactics that may be utilized, and also to recognize that tactics can change over the course of a campaign. A *Monitoring, Evaluation, and Learning* approach involves setting up a data collection system to monitor the implementation and results of advocacy tactics an *ongoing basis* (Gardner and Brindis 2017). Using this approach will allow evaluators to determine what tactics work and do not work, and also allow for tactics to be modified to fit the overall advocacy initiative goals.

By measuring outputs, a nonprofit can monitor implementation and performance, to assess whether or not an organization successfully planned, developed, and executed an advocacy strategy (Gardner and Brindis 2017). Outputs count things an organization has done—for example, meetings with decision makers, public rallies and publishing op-eds and policy documents (Carr and Holley 2013).

Organizations can use process indicators to measure their specific actions (Guthrie et al. 2005). Using the data collection method of record review, organizations can assess efforts to build constituencies through collecting data on the numbers of people attending events, signing petitions or participating in listservs (Harvard Family Research Project 2007). Tracking social media is also a way to measure outputs of an advocacy campaign (Guo and Saxton 2014). While process indicators are a useful tool for tracking activity for grant monitoring, they do not measure whether the advocacy campaign has achieved its goals; for that, assessing outcomes is critical.

## Outcomes

The outcomes for an advocacy campaign may be difficult to quantify and measure. For example, a civic organization's effort to increase community outreach can be measured through increased numbers of participants, compared to an effort to promote diverse community interests in policy processes, which may be more challenging to operationalize (Jun and Shiau 2012). Assessing the reach of a campaign is more straightforward than influence over policymakers (Gardner and Brindis 2017). Casey (2011) encourages thinking about whether an evaluation is assessing whether advocacy has effected profound change or simply whether the campaign left a "residue of reform" (p. 4).

Measuring progress toward interim goals may have greatest utility to an ongoing campaign, rather than waiting to evaluate end goals (Innovation Network 2008). Examples of interim outcomes indicators are provided in Table 9.2. Ebrahim and Rangan (2010) suggest influence is an intermediary outcome that can be assessed through "ecosystems" results. In terms of influence over a particular decision maker, Innovation Network (2008) recommends an approach that measures relationship building, through a stage model of winning over a champion: (1) demonstrates awareness; (2) promotes awareness and understanding; and (3) advocates for improved policy and practices (Devlin-Foltz and Molinaro 2010).

Using the policy process (see Chapter 1) as their guide, Andrews and Edwards (2004) recommend assessing the potential influence of advocacy organizations across six dimensions of the policy process: agenda setting, access to decision-making arenas, achieving favorable policies, monitoring, shaping implementation, and shifting the long-term priorities and resources of political institutions. Similarly, Casey (2011) proposes 6 possible levels of outcome advocacy: access, agenda, policy, output, impact, and structural. Media analysis can be a tool for assessing whether an issue is emerging on the public agenda, by measuring the level of media coverage, tone of coverage, and increase in interest after an event. Ways to do this include checking online media search engines for increase in media hits and types of coverage (Harvard Family Research Project 2007).

Outcomes mapping can be used as part of planning out a theory of change, as well as used as an approach to evaluating outcomes (Naeve et al. 2017). The focus is behavioral change in the individuals, groups, and organizations an initiative intends to influence, in collaboration with "boundary partners" that an organization is working with to effect change. Outcomes mapping involves developing a "performance story" to articulate what an organization has done to support outcomes within its sphere of influence, but without attempting to establish strict cause and effect, instead recognizing that multiple, nonlinear events lead to change (Earl et al. 2001). A project team identifies their intended outcomes and plans strategies; uses outcomes and performance monitoring to track the progress of key actors toward the expected goals; and plans evaluation based on priorities. Like outcomes mapping, outcomes harvesting also focuses on behavioral change in the intended targets of an initiative, but instead of identifying intended

**Table 9.2** Example indicators for interim outcomes of policy advocacy (Coffman and Beers 2015)

| Interim outcome | Definition | Example indicators |
|---|---|---|
| Changed attitudes and beliefs | Target audiences' feelings or affect about an issue or policy proposal | • Percentage of audience with favorable attitudes toward the issue or interest<br>• Percentage of audience members saying issue is important to them |
| Collaborative action among partners | Individuals or groups coordinating their work and acting together | • New organizations signing on as collaborators<br>• Policy agenda alignment among collaborators<br>• Collaborative actions taken among organizations (e.g., joint meetings) |
| Increased advocacy capacity | The ability of an organization or coalition to lead, adapt, manage, and technically implement an advocacy strategy | • Increased knowledge about advocacy, mobilizing or organizing tactics<br>• Improve media skills and contacts<br>• Increased ability to get and use data |
| Increased knowledge | Audience recognition that a problem exists or familiarity with a policy proposal | • Percentage of audience members with knowledge of an issue<br>• Web site activity for portions of Web site with advocacy-related information |
| Increased or improved media coverage | Quantity and/or quality of coverage generated in print, broadcast, or electronic media | • Number of media citations of advocate research or products<br>• Number of stories successfully placed in the media (e.g., op-eds)<br>• Number of advocates (or trained spokesperson) citations in the media<br>• Number of media articles reflecting preferred issue framing |

(continued)

**Table 9.2**  (continued)

| Interim outcome | Definition | Example indicators |
|---|---|---|
| Increased political will or support | Willingness of policymakers to act in support of an issue or policy proposal | • Number of citations of advocate products or ideas in policy deliberations/policies<br>• Number of elected officials who public support the advocacy effort<br>• Number of issue mentions in policymaker speeches (or debates)<br>• Number and party representation of bill sponsors and co-sponsors<br>• Number of votes for or against specific legislation |
| Increased public will or support | Willingness of a (non-policy-maker) audience to act in support of an issue or policy proposal | • Percentage of audience members willing to take action on behalf of a specific issue<br>• Attendance at advocacy events (e.g., public forums, marches, rallies) |
| New political champions | High-profile individuals who adopt an issue and publicly advocate for it | • New champions or stakeholders recruited<br>• New constituencies represented among champions<br>• Champion actions to support issue (e.g., speaking out, signing on) |
| Stronger coalitions | Mutually beneficial relationships with other organizations or individuals who support or participate in an advocacy strategy | • Number, type, and/or strength of organizational relationships developed<br>• Number, type, and/or strength of relationships with unlikely partners |
| Successful mobilization of public voices | Increase in the number of individuals who can be counted on for sustained advocacy or action on an issue | • New advocates recruited<br>• New constituencies represented among advocates<br>• New advocate actions to support issue |

outcomes in advance of a campaign, outcomes harvesting works backward from what has been achieved to how an organization's efforts may have contributed to these outcomes. Its developers suggest it is akin to forensic science, by using techniques to identify which events and factors led to an outcome (Wilson-Grau and Britt 2012). Arensman (2019) questions the assumption by outcomes mapping and outcomes harvesting proponents that advocacy outcomes are necessarily self-evident and measurable, cautioning that "outcomes become outcomes when they are interpreted as such by stakeholders making (strategic) decisions" (p. 13) and that the inherently political and contested nature of outcomes and outcome identification must be kept in mind.

## Impact

The literature is cautious about attempting to measure the impact of advocacy work (Ebrahim and Rangan 2010). The aforementioned issues of attribution and timescales suggest that nonprofit organizations will struggle to demonstrate causal links between their work and policy-related results. The framework composed by the Institute for Development Research (IDR) suggests only three impacts for which advocacy work should be measured: (1) policy changes that result from influencing decision-making structures; (2) civil society and the strengthening of civil organizations to continue to advocate and participate in decision making; and (3) democratic space or expanding civil society involvement in decision making (Chapman and Wameyo 2001, in Garnder and Brindis 2017).

In line with our ongoing analogy about tactics and strategies, it is possible to win advocacy battles but lose the war, as when legislation is passed but not sufficiently funded or a decision is not properly implemented (Casey 2011). Seeing the long-term impacts of policy change requires long time horizons. Teles and Schmitt (2016) note that "what really matters is whether a policy sinks deeply into society and political routines, not whether a piece of legislation passes" (p. 25).

## Advocacy Evaluation Methods

Developmental evaluation (Patton 1994, 2010) is particularly well-suited to evaluating advocacy, because it is an approach intended to measure and guide initiatives adapting to complex and dynamic environments. This approach contrasts to formative and summative evaluation. The purpose of formative evaluation is to assess implementation and emerging outcomes and inform refinements so that the model becomes standardized and stable. Summative evaluation assesses overall merit of mature program models, to determine if they "work" by meeting their intended goals and to inform decision making about whether a program should be continued, expanded, duplicated, or stopped (Patton et al. 2015). By contrast, developmental evaluation focuses on learning that can guide innovation and adaptation. Unlike traditional approaches to formative and summative evaluation that aim to control, predict, and bring order to chaos, developmental evaluation "adapts to the realities of complex, nonlinear dynamics rather than trying to impose order and certainty on a disorderly and uncertain world" (Patton 2010, p. 5). Applying a developmental evaluation approach becomes integrated into an initiative through a process of posing evaluative questions, applying evaluation logic and collecting real-time data that can be used to facilitate data-based reflection and decision making.

Developmental evaluation can involve any kind of methods, design, and data that can shed light on key questions (Patton 2010). Frequently used methods in advocacy evaluation are highlighted in Box 9.1. The remainder of this section describes innovative methods that have been utilized in advocacy evaluation to address the challenges described earlier in this chapter. Examples include bellwether methodology, policymaker ratings, intense period debriefs, contribution analysis, and process tracing. This list is not exhaustive—as the field of advocacy evaluation continues to evolve, new methods will be trialed and refined.

---

**Box 9.1 Commonly Used Advocacy Evaluation Methods (Coffman and Reed 2009)**

- Stakeholder surveys or interviews—Print, telephone, or online questioning that gathers advocacy stakeholder perspectives or feedback.
- Case studies—Detailed descriptions and analyses (often qualitative) of individual advocacy strategies and results.
- Focus groups—Facilitated discussions with advocacy stakeholders (usually about 8–10 per group) to obtain their reactions, opinions, or ideas.
- Media tracking—Counts of an issue's coverage in the print, broadcast, or electronic media.
- Media content or framing analysis—Qualitative analysis of how the media write about and frame issues of interest.
- Participant observation—Evaluator participation in advocacy meetings or events to gain firsthand experience and data.

- Policy tracking—Monitoring of an issue or bill's progress in the policy process.
- Public polling—Interviews (usually by telephone) with a random sample of advocacy stakeholders to gather data on their knowledge, attitudes, or behaviors.

Systems mapping can be a useful approach for advocacy aimed at systems change, through changing organizations, building relationships between policy actors, and affecting the policy environment (Coffman and Reed 2009). Systems maps emphasize the interconnections between entities in the system and how these are expected to change through an advocacy effort. Evaluation efforts can then be targeted to document evidence of these expected changes, using methods including network analysis to quantitatively measure new relationships that have been established. Social network analysis looks at the policy-making process as interactions among a network of policy actors, and allows for empirically measuring the position of a nonprofit within a network; for example, this method can be used to examine whether an organization plays a leading role within a coalition or a brokering role among various stakeholders (Varone et al. 2017).

Since an initiative cannot be measured simply by whether or not a desired initiative is turned into policy, gathering qualitative data from various stakeholders and actors can be used to assess long-term outcomes, as well as interim outcomes to find out if an issue is on people's radar and if there is will to do something about it. Qualitative approaches such as the use of focus groups, interviews, and in-depth surveys can be used to measure awareness, salience, attitudes/beliefs, public will, political will, and constituency or support base growth (Garnder and Brindis 2017). Bellwether methodology, developed by the Harvard Family Research Project, involves conducting structured interviews with a group identified as "bellwethers," or influential people in the public and private sectors whose jobs require that they track a broad range of policy issues. This method can be useful to assess the effectiveness of framing activities, whether an issue is tracking on agendas and changes political will (Coffman and Reed 2009). Policymaker ratings, also developed by the Harvard Family Research project, are assessments conducted by advocates using a standardized scale to rate policymakers' support for, and influence over, the issue of interest. Several advocates participate in completing the quantitative measure, then average their ratings or discuss together to arrive at consensus. The approach can be used to gauge whether a policymaker's interest in an issue shifts over time. The intense period debrief, developed by the Innovation Network, encourages advocates and stakeholders to reflect on what triggered a high-intensity activity period, how the organization responded, and insights for adjusting advocacy strategy in the future (Coffman and Reed 2009).

Contribution analysis and process tracing are methods focused on making causal inferences between activities and outcomes. Contribution analysis is a process to test assumptions underlying a theory of change against available evidence and alternative explanations. It was developed by John Mayne (2012), a Canadian public-sector evaluator, to answer the following question: "In light of the multiple factors influencing a result, has the [initiative] made a noticeable contribution to an observed result and in what way?" (Mayne 2012, p. 273). Over a series of steps, an evaluator assembles a "contribution story" with evidence on the causal claims being made, assessing weaknesses and other potential influences, and thus the strength of a contribution claim (Befani and Mayne 2014). Contribution analysis is particularly useful for evaluating advocacy because of its explicit examination of multiple actors and influences, to explore what works and why (Kane et al. 2017). Another related approach, process tracing is often used as part of case study designs to develop a narrative with a sequence of events and explore the causal ideas of how actions may lead to outcomes over time. The evaluator collects "diagnostic" evidence that may support or disprove the causal model and draws inferences in support of the proposed and alternative hypotheses (Collier 2011). The evaluation asks, "what do we expect to observe if the causal mechanism is realized?" and "what observations could only be made if the causal mechanism holds, and could not be made if it does not hold?" (Befani and Mayne 2014, p. 24). These two approaches can be used together to strengthen confidence in the conclusions drawn about the impact of an advocacy campaign on an outcome.

When deciding upon an evaluation approach, it is important to be aware of the potential for different forms of bias. Interviews with key informants and stakeholders are a primary source of data for evaluating advocacy campaigns, stressing the importance that data sources and reporting are independent, unbiased, and truthful. Participants' perceptions and self-reported feelings, attitudes, and beliefs are prone to social desirability and other forms of bias, suggesting the value of triangulating data sources and seeking viewpoints from neutral sources, as recommended in the bellwether methodology (Naeve et al. 2017).

# Conclusion

This book has presented and illustrated a set of strategies based on advocates' viewpoints of policy change. These strategies combine tactics that are expected to lead to certain outcomes, in the short and longer term. For practitioners, considering one's viewpoint on policy change can make explicit the tacit assumptions that often guide how an advocacy campaign is waged.

This book is one of the first systematic efforts to link policy advocates' viewpoints on policy change with theories relating activities to potential outcomes. The first step of the research reported in this book was to hypothesize a plausible conceptual framework for policy advocacy, based on practitioner literature and academic theories. This was tested through empirical data collected from nonprofits engaged in policy advocacy. What has emerged is a set of strategies, guided by perspectives about policy change, that runs along a spectrum from lobbying formal policymakers to grassroots organizing. Each strategy links tactics with their expected outcomes. The case studies have illustrated how similar tactics can be deployed creatively, for different issues and contexts. The integration of the conceptual framework with interview and case study data demonstrates how practitioner viewpoints can be enriched by policy theories, bridging the research-to-practice divide.

We argue that these strategies are fundamental to the American policymaking process and capture a broad array of policy advocacy, as demonstrated by the findings of the national survey. Future research will test the utility of these strategies in other political systems, particularly the Westminster system of the UK and its former colonial territories. Yet an important caveat to the book is that an empirically and theoretically supported strategy is no guarantee for policy advocacy success. Indeed, policy studies theory highlights that the conditions for change must be favorable and that the crowded political field makes it difficult to get an issue simultaneously on the political, policy, and public agendas. Use of any strategy is more likely to result in failure than success, especially when success is defined strictly as a favorable policy change.

But success in policy advocacy is *not* limited to policy change. As we saw in the opening cases of marriage equality, *progress* on an issue is also a success of advocacy. And as we saw in cases throughout the book, *public engagement* is a success, as are *public awareness and learning*. Indeed, in democratic societies—which are premised on an engaged citizenry—participation in policymaking processes is itself a sign that the democracy is healthy.

**Discussions**

9a. Reflect on the practices of policy advocacy of a nonprofit organization with which you are affiliated or familiar. Do any of the strategies in this book resonant with their current practices?

9b. Considering the policy advocacy strategy of this same nonprofit, can you identify any alternative strategies that might resonate based on the organization's apparent views on policy change?

9c. Develop a theory of change for a planned or existing advocacy campaign. The Advocacy Strategy Framework tool may be a useful starting place.

9d. For the theory of change that you have developed, which interim and long-term outcomes would your campaign hope to achieve? How would you measure these outcomes? Table 9.2 provides examples of interim outcomes and indicators for tracking them.

9e. How would you evaluate the efficacy of this current or planned advocacy campaign, drawing on the methods described in this chapter? For the methods you select, look for journal articles reporting on evaluation findings to learn more about how these methods can be used.

# References

Acosta, R. (2012). Advocacy networks through a multidisciplinary lens: Implications for research agendas. *VOLUNTAS: International Journal of Voluntary and Nonprofit Organizations, 23*(1), 156–181.

Alliance for Justice. (2005). *Build Your Advocacy Grant Making: Advocacy Evaluation Tool.* Washington, DC: Alliance for Justice.

Almog-Bar, M., & Schmid, H. (2014). Advocacy activities of nonprofit human service organizations: A critical review. *Nonprofit and Voluntary Sector Quarterly, 43*(1), 11–35.

Andrews, K., & Edwards, B. (2004). Advocacy organizations in the US political pro-cess. *Annual Review of Sociology, 30*(1), 479–506.

Arensman, B. (2019). Advocacy outcomes are not self-evident: The quest for outcome identification. *American Journal of Evaluation*, 1–18.

Befani, B., & Mayne, J. (2014). Process tracing and contribution analysis: A combined approach to generative causal inference for impact evaluation. *IDS Bulletin, 45*(6), 17–36.

Brousselle, A., & Champagne, F. (2011). Program theory evaluation: Logic analysis. *Evaluation and Program Planning, 34*(1), 69–78.

Carr, M., & Holley, M. (2013). A new approach to evaluating public policy advocacy: Creating evidence of cause and effect. In *38th Annual Meeting of the Association for Education Finance and Policy, New Orleans*.

Casey, J. (2011). *Understanding Advocacy: A Primer on the Policy-Making Role of Nonprofit Organizations*. New York: Center for Nonprofit Strategy, Baruch College, City University of New York.

Chapman, J., & Wameyo, A. (2001). *Monitoring and Evaluating Advocacy: A Scoping Study*. ActionAid. Retrieved from http://www.eldis.org/vle/upload/1/document/0708/DOC21800.pdf.

Coe, J., & Majot, J. (2013). *Monitoring, Evaluation and Learning in NGO Advocacy: Findings from Comparative Policy Advocacy MEL Review Project*. Washington, DC: Oxfam America. Retrieved from https://s3.amazonaws.com/oxfam-us/www/static/media/files/mel-in-ngo-advocacy-full-report.pdf.

Coffman, J., & Beer, T. (2015). *The Advocacy Strategy Framework: A Tool for Articulating an Advocacy Theory of Change*. Center for Evaluation Innovation. Retrieved from https://www.evaluationinnovation.org/wp-content/uploads/2015/03/Adocacy-Strategy-Framework.pdf.

Coffman, J., & Reed, E. (2009). *Unique Methods in Advocacy Evaluation*. Washington, DC: Center for Evaluation Innovation. Retrieved from http://www.pointk.org/resources/files/Unique_Methods_Brief.pdf.

Collier, D. (2011). Understanding process tracing. *PS: Political Science & Politics, 44*(4), 823–830.

DeVita, C. J., Montilla, M., Reid, B., & Fatiregun, O. (2004). *Organizational Factors Influencing Advocacy for Children*. Washington, DC: Center on Nonprofits and Philanthropy, The Urban Institute.

Devlin-Foltz, D., & Molinaro, L. (2010). *Champions and "Championness": Measuring Efforts to Create Champions for Policy Change*. Center for Evaluation Innovation. Retrieved from https://assets.aspeninstitute.org/content/uploads/files/content/docs/pubs/Champions_and_Championness_Aug2010.pdf.

Earl, S., Carden, F., & Smutylo, T. (2001). *Outcome Mapping: Building Learning and Reflection into Development Programs*. Ottawa, ON: International Development Research Centre.

Ebrahim, A. (2005). Accountability myopia: Losing sight of organizational learning. *Nonprofit and Voluntary Sector Quarterly, 34*(1), 56–87.

Ebrahim, A., & Rangan, V. K. (2010). *The Limits of Nonprofit Impact: A Contingency Framework for Measuring Social Performance* (No. 10-099). Harvard Business School.

Fagen, M. C., Reed, E., Kaye, J. W., & Jack, L., Jr. (2009). Advocacy evaluation: What it is and where to find out more about it. *Health Promotion Practice, 10*(4), 482–484.

Gardner, A., & Brindis, C. (2017). *Advocacy and Policy Change Evaluation: Theory and Practice*. Palo Alto: Stanford University Press.

Glasrud, B. (2001). The muddle of outcome measurement. *Nonprofit World, 19*(6), 35–37.

Guo, C., & Saxton, G. D. (2014). Tweeting social change: How social media are changing nonprofit advocacy. *Nonprofit and Voluntary Sector Quarterly, 43*(1), 57–79.

Guthrie, K., Louie, J., David, T., & Foster, C. C. (2005). *The Challenge of Assessing Policy and Advocacy Activities: Strategies for a Prospective Evaluation Approach*. Los Angeles: The California Endowment.

Harvard Family Research Project. (2007). Advocacy and policy change. *The Evaluation Exchange, XIII*(1), 2–4.

Holley, M. J., Carr, M. J., & King, M. H. (2014). Spring: Advocacy isn't "soft". *Stanford Social Innovation Review, 12*(2), 59–60.

Jun, K. N., & Shiau, E. (2012). How are we doing? A multiple constituency approach to civic association effectiveness. *Nonprofit and Voluntary Sector Quarterly, 41*(4), 632–655.

Kane, R., Levine, C., Orians, C., & Reinelt, C. (2017). *Contribution Analysis in Policy Work: Assessing Advocacy's Influence*. Center for Evaluation Innovation. Retrieved from http://www.evaluationinnovation.org/sites/default/files/Contribution.

Kingdon, J. W., & Thurber, J. A. (1984). *Agendas, Alternatives, and Public Policies* (Vol. 45, pp. 165–169). Boston: Little, Brown.

Knowlton, L. W., & Phillips, C. C. (2012). *The Logic Model Guidebook: Better Strategies for Great Results*. Los Angeles: Sage.

LeRoux, K., & Wright, N. S. (2010). Does performance measurement improve strategic decision making? Findings from a national survey of nonprofit social service agencies. *Nonprofit and Voluntary Sector Quarterly, 39*(4), 571–587.

Mandeville, J. (2007). Public policy grant making: Building organizational capacity among nonprofit grantees. *Nonprofit and Voluntary Sector Quarterly, 36*(2), 282–298.

Mayne, J. (2012). Contribution analysis: Coming of age? *Evaluation, 18*(3), 270–280.

Mintzberg, H., & Waters, J. A. (1985). Of strategies, deliberate and emergent. *Strategic Management Journal, 6*(3), 257–272.

Mosley, J. E. (2011). Institutionalization, privatization, and political opportunity: What tactical choices reveal about the policy advocacy of human service nonprofits. *Nonprofit and Voluntary Sector Quarterly, 40*(3), 435–457.

Naeve, K., Fischer-Mackey, J., Puri, J., Bhatia, R., & Yegbemey, R. (2017). *Evaluating Advocacy: An Exploration of Evidence and Tools to Understand What Works and Why* (3ie Working Paper 29). New Delhi: International Initiative for Impact Evaluation.

Patton, M. Q. (1994). Developmental evaluation. *Evaluation Practice, 15*(3), 311–319.

Patton, M. Q. (2010). *Developmental Evaluation: Applying Complexity Concepts to Enhance Innovation and Use*. New York: Guilford Press.

Patton, M. Q., McKegg, K., & Wehipeihana, N. (Eds.). (2015). *Developmental Evaluation Exemplars: Principles in Practice*. New York: Guilford Publications.

Reid, E. J. (2006). Advocacy and the challenges it presents for nonprofits. In E. T. Boris & C. E. Steuerle (Eds.), *Nonprofits and Government: Collaboration and Conflict* (2nd ed., pp. 343–371). Washington, DC: The Urban Institute Press.

Sabatier, P. A., & Jenkins-Smith, H. C. (1999). The advocacy coalition framework: An assessment. In P. Sabatier (Ed.), *Theories of the Policy Process* (pp. 117–166). Boulder, CO: Westview Press.

Salamon, L. M. (2002). *Explaining Nonprofit Advocacy: An Exploratory Analysis* (Center for Civil Society Studies Working Paper Series, 21).

Senge, P. M. (2006). *The Fifth Discipline: The Art and Practice of the Learning Organization*. New York City: Broadway Business.

Stanford Innovation Network. (2008). *Speaking for Themselves: Advocates' Perspectives on Evaluation*. Innovation Network. Retrieved from http://www.innonet.org/client_docs/File/advocacy/speaking_for_themselves_web_basic.pdf.

Teles, S., & Schmitt, M. (2016). *The Elusive Craft of Evaluating Advocacy*. Menlo Park: The William and Flora Hewlett Foundation. Retrieved from https://hewlett.org/wp-content/uploads/2016/08/Elusive_Craft.pdf.

Varone, F., Ingold, K., Jourdain, C., & Schneider, V. (2017). Studying policy advocacy through social network analysis. *European Political Science, 16*, 322–336.

Wilson-Grau, R., & Britt, H. (2012). *Outcome Harvesting*. Cairo: Ford Foundation. Retrieved from http://www.managingforimpact.org/sites/default/files/resource/outome_harvesting_brief_final_2012-05-2-1.pdf.

# Correction to: Nonprofits in Policy Advocacy

**Correction to:**
**S. Gen and A. C. Wright,** *Nonprofits in Policy Advocacy,*
**https://doi.org/10.1007/978-3-030-43696-4**

The original version of the book was inadvertently published with incorrect abstracts, which have now been corrected.

The updated version of the book can be found at
https://doi.org/10.1007/978-3-030-43696-4

# Appendix A: Derivation of the Composite Logic Model of Policy Advocacy

The development of the composite logic model of policy advocacy was guided by both practitioner and academic literatures. Initially, materials developed by sources such as foundations and nongovernmental organizations were identified from Internet searches using the terms "policy advocacy" plus "logic model." Logic models are visual depictions of social programs or change efforts (Knowlton and Phillips 2009). Some of the logic models led to the discovery of others, by checking their references. For inclusion in this study, logic models had to focus on policy advocacy and include at a minimum the categories of inputs, activities, and outcomes. Some logic models described this latter category as goals, indicators, short- and long-term outcomes, or outcomes and impacts. The elements of the logic model could be provided in a graphic, tabular, or narrative format. Reports that describe how to construct a logic model and use it for advocacy evaluation purposes, but did not identify concrete elements of a policy advocacy logic model (e.g., Guthrie et al. 2005) were excluded from the study.

As each qualifying logic model was retrieved, we listed the themes of its contents. By the time six logic models were examined, the themes identified in them became repetitive and we determined that a saturation of ideas had been reached (Glaser and Strauss 1967). The six source logic models were the following:

- Center for Community Health and Evaluation. (n.d.). *Measuring the Impact of Advocacy and Policy Efforts: Case Study Example.* Center for Community Health and Evaluation.
- Chapman, J., & Wameyo, A. (2001). *Monitoring and Evaluating Advocacy: A Scoping Study* (p. 55). ActionAid.

- Coffman, J. (2007). *Using the Advocacy and Policy Change Composite Logic Model to Articulate an Advocacy Strategy or Theory of Change.* Harvard Family Research Project.
- Grantmakers in Health. (2005). *Funding Health Advocacy* (Issue Brief No. 21). Grantmakers in Health.
- Morariu, J., Reed, E., Brennan, K., Stamp, A., Parrish, S., Pankaj, V., & Zandniapour, L. (2009). *Pathfinder: A Practical Guide to Advocacy Evaluation* (p. 10). Washington, DC: Innovation Network, Inc.
- Reisman, J., Gienapp, A., & Stachowiak, S. (2007). *A Guide to Measuring Advocacy and Policy* (p. 38). Baltimore, MD: The Annie E. Casey Foundation.

The scope of the logic models, in terms of focus on special advocacy topics and organizational authors, is broad. A number of the logic models identified were created by or at the behest of major foundations, including the Annie E. Casey Foundation, California Endowment, and Grantmakers for Health. Two of the organizational authors focus on evaluation: Center for Community Health and Evaluation and Innovation Network, Inc. One organization, ActionAid, is an international humanitarian aid organization. The saturation of ideas coming from a wide variety of sources gave us further confidence that an adequately representative sample (Cooper 1988) of policy advocacy logic models had been identified.

Next, these policy advocacy logic models were combined into a composite table through a process of coding each logic model for shared themes (see Table 2.1 in Chapter 2). This table is most akin to a theory of change, given its simplicity and purpose of explaining how social change is expected to occur. By contrast, a program logic model is intended to be comprehensive and outlines the connections needed to evaluate or monitor a social program. However, as the combined model was adapted from practitioner logic models, it includes elements more commonly found in program logic models than theory of change models (Knowlton and Phillips 2009). Its unit of analysis is the advocacy program or campaign that an organization engages, and it has three major categories of elements: inputs, activities, and outcomes. The breadth of activities we identified captured all those identified by Baumgartner and Leech's (1998, p. 152) comprehensive review of interest group activities, further confirming the adequate scope of our sample of logic models. The category of outcomes includes three levels: proximal (near-term and more direct), distal (long-term and more indirect), and impacts (intended change).

This task of combining logic models was guided by our expectation that there are common sets of inputs, activities, and expected outcomes for policy advocacy programs that transcend specific policy outcome goals. Still, the authors of the original logic models developed them under different contexts that required us to interpret some elements in the original logic models differently than the original authors had. For example, the logic model developed by ActionAid was intended for advocacy work in developing democracies. Thus, the activities they identified had goals of building democratic capacities and processes, rather than specific policy outcomes. Meanwhile, other logic models were developed in a US context that assumed that a stable level of democratic processes is in place. Thus, their logic models identified activities that aimed to change policies in specific fields (e.g., health, family welfare, etc.). We coded the logic models from a perspective of a functioning democracy characterized by "free elections for a popular mandate, with elected officials held responsible to the citizenry; the existence of an effective, independent judiciary; a depoliticized bureaucracy functioning according to written rules; legal guarantees (usually of a constitutional nature) of basic rights; and a free press" (Ramet 1992, p. 549). From this perspective, we independently coded the elements of the logic models, using inductive and deductive processes to identify key ideas. Codes were created and grouped until central themes emerged (Glaser and Strauss 1967), and complete coding agreement was achieved on the final round of coding.

Once the coded elements for the combined logic model had been identified, we turned to the academic literature to seek theoretical support for the elements in it, and connections between them. Specifically, we sought theoretical connections between advocacy activities and their expected outcomes. The combined logic model headings (and variations of the concepts) were used as search terms in major academic databases, including Academic Search Premier, Lexus/Nexis, and ProQuest. In addition, major policy theories were reviewed for their relevance, drawing on mainstream policy texts. On the basis of this review of literature, Table 2.2 in Chapter 2 was compiled with speculated connections between logic model elements.

# References

Baumgartner, F. R., & Leech, B. L. (1998). *Basic Interests: The Importance of Groups in Politics and in Political Science*. Princeton, NJ: Princeton University Press.

Cooper, H. M. (1988). Organizing knowledge synthesis: A taxonomy of literature reviews. *Knowledge in Society, 1*, 104–126.

Glaser, B., & Strauss, A. (1967). *The Discovery of Grounded Theory: Strategies for Qualitative Research*. New York, NY: Aldine Publishing Company.

Guthrie, K., Louise, J., David, T., & Foster, C. C. (2005, October). *The Challenge of Assessing Policy and Advocacy Activities: Strategies for a Prospective Evaluation*

*Approach*. Prepared by Blueprint Research & Design, Inc. for the California Endowment.

Knowlton, L. W., & Phillips, C. C. (2009). *The Logic Model Guidebook: Better Strategies for Great Results*. Los Angeles, CA: Sage.

Ramet, S. (1992). Balkan pluralism & its enemies. *Orbis, 36*(4)(Fall), 547–564.

# Appendix B: Methods

The original empirical data for the findings reported in this book came from two complementary sources. First, Q-methodology with a purposive sample of nonprofits was employed to identify distinct strategies of policy advocates and to develop case studies of typical advocacy campaigns. Second, a national sample of nonprofits was surveyed to characterize those that appear to use each advocacy strategy. This appendix details our implementation of these methods.

## Q-methodology

Q-methodology was employed with interviews of 31 individuals who manage their respective organizations' policy advocacy efforts. Q-methodology is a "systematic and rigorously quantitative means for examining human subjectivity" (McKeown and Thomas 1988, p. 7). Q-methodology identifies underlying viewpoints of its subjects, so Brown (1980) concluded that it is "pertinent to the study of public opinion and attitudes, groups, roles ... [and] virtually all areas of concern to the social and political sciences" (p. 58). Applied to this study, the statements are opinions about advocacy activities and their resulting outcomes, and respondents sorted them by their relative importance to their organizations. The resulting factors identify unique viewpoints of nonprofit organizations on the processes of policy change and how they seek to influence those processes. Our interpretation of these factors compares them to existing theories in policy studies.

Practitioners' professional discussions on policy advocacy, or their "concourse" in the language of Q-methodology (Watts and Stenner 2012, p. 34), are most formally represented by the logic models of policy change that have been

© The Editor(s) (if applicable) and The Author(s),
under exclusive license to Springer Nature Switzerland AG 2020
S. Gen and A. C. Wright, *Nonprofits in Policy Advocacy,*
https://doi.org/10.1007/978-3-030-43696-4

published by them (Center for Community Health and Evaluation, n.d.; Chapman and Wameyo 2001; Coffman 2007; Grantmakers in Health 2005; Morariu et al. 2009; Reisman et al. 2007). While these logic models identify the major categories of advocacy activities and outcomes, reflected in Table 2.1 in Chapter 2, most are not specific about the linkages between individual activities and outcomes. However, the policy studies literature suggests certain connections, as we report in Table 2.2 in Chapter 2. Drawing on these theoretical linkages between activities and outcomes, 24 statements about policy advocacy tactics were developed, constituting this study's Q-sample. These are individual statements of opinion on policy advocacy linkages, which respondents sorted onto a bell-shaped distribution ranging from −3 (least agree with organization's approach to policy advocacy) to +3 (most agree with organization's approach to advocacy). By analyzing how respondents sorted these statements of opinion on policy advocacy, distinct viewpoints on policy advocacy strategies were identified.

The sample of nonprofits recruited for the Q-method portion of this study was systematically and purposively selected. First, Guidestar was used to identify the population of nonprofits in San Francisco, Sacramento, and Washington, DC,[1] that self-identified themselves in their Internal Revenue Service (IRS) filings with National Taxonomy of Exempt Entities (NTEE) prefix code R (advocacy) or suffix code 01 (advocacy in a specific prefix area).[2] Of course, these filters would exclude many organizations that engage in policy advocacy, but they would certainly capture those that engage in advocacy as a primary activity, and would therefore be expected to provide relatively well-articulated approaches to policy advocacy in the interviews. Still, these NTEE codes do not distinguish between case advocates and cause advocates. Case advocates represent and assist clients to access resources and services, with the aim of improving the clients' welfare. Cause advocates, on the other hand, represent groups and their interests to affect policy processes and social

---

[1]The national capital, a state capital, and a major city were deliberately selected to capture organizations advocating at different levels of government. It was discovered, however, that organizations' locations did not reliably predict the levels of government in which they advocated, so the final sample focused primarily on San Francisco organizations for logistical reasons, while ensuring that all levels of government were represented by the respondents. Still, a few organizations from Sacramento and Washington, DC were included.

[2]The NTEE is a classification system for nonprofit organizations developed by the National Center for Charitable Statistics and used by the IRS. Nonprofits filing their revenues with the IRS self-identify their primary classification from a list of over 600 codes. Of these codes, 45 are related to advocacy. For a full explanation, see nccs.urban.org/classification/ntee.cfm.

**Table B.1** Sample of nonprofits in the Q-methodology portion of the study

| Organization number | Levels of government targeted in advocacy case | Policy issue area of advocacy case | Program expenses reported in Guidestar (year) |
|---|---|---|---|
| 1 | National, state, local | Environment | $133,418 (2009) |
| 2 | National | Public health | $13,267 (2007) |
| 3 | State, local | Residential care | $829,359 (2010) |
| 4 | Local | Child welfare | $1,147,295 (2012) |
| 5 | Local | Senior welfare | $304,979 (2012) |
| 6 | National, state | Criminal justice | $361,882 (2009) |
| 7 | National, local | Sustainability | $224,064 (2006) |
| 8 | Local | Land conservation | $1,955,370 (2010) |
| 9 | Local | Social equity | Not available |
| 10 | National, state, local | Civic engagement | $1,130,853 (2011) |
| 11 | National, local | Disabilities | $292,235 (2010) |
| 12 | Local | Parks | $233,686 (2009) |
| 13 | State, local | Arts | Not available |
| 14 | National, state, local | Land conservation | $119,592,234 (2012) |
| 15 | State | Energy, telecom | $3,497,658 (2010) |
| 16 | State, local | Juvenile justice | $1,397,100 (2009) |
| 17 | Local | Pedestrian | $60,163 (2011) |
| 18 | National, local | War, gun violence | $378,475 (2012) |
| 19 | National, state | Child welfare | $3,749,406 (2012) |
| 20 | National, state, local | Environment | $56,641,344 (2012) |
| 21 | National, state, local | Public health | $11,412,991 (2013) |
| 22 | State | Education | Not available |
| 23 | State, local | Education | Not available |
| 24 | Local | Education | $474,429 (2013) |
| 25 | National, state | Peace and justice | $31,211,428 (2011) |
| 26 | National, state | Criminal justice | $2,155,658 (2012) |
| 27 | State, local | Civil rights | $1,636,906 (2013) |
| 28 | State | Foster youth | $1,096,788 (2010) |
| 29 | Local | Environment | $3,390,216 (2012) |
| 30 | National, state | Civil rights | $5,594,924 (2011) |
| 31 | National, state | Environment | $2,539,617 (2012) |

**Table B.2** Factor loadings matrix from 6-factor extraction

| Organization number | Factor 1 | Factor 2 | Factor 3 | Factor 4 | Factor 5 | Factor 6 |
|---|---|---|---|---|---|---|
| 1 | 0.1618 | 0.0313 | 0.0538 | 0.3078 | 0.4323* | 0.5327** |
| 2 | −0.0740 | 0.3882 | 0.5807** | 0.0012 | 0.0056 | 0.1712 |
| 3 | −0.2266 | −0.2023 | −0.6820** | −0.2344 | −0.0002 | −0.2831 |
| 4 | 0.4558* | 0.2034 | 0.2061 | 0.1846 | 0.1989 | 0.2759 |
| 5 | 0.2818 | −0.4423* | −0.1680 | 0.1861 | 0.4588* | 0.0688 |
| 6 | 0.1584 | 0.0578 | 0.5176* | 0.3411 | 0.0621 | −0.2180 |
| 7 | −0.0647 | 0.1620 | 0.0400 | −0.5820** | −0.2605 | −0.4200* |
| 8 | 0.7361** | 0.0736 | 0.1988 | −0.3266 | 0.1596 | 0.0607 |
| 9 | −0.0473 | −0.6564** | 0.4689* | −0.0862 | 0.1020 | −0.2077 |
| 10 | −0.0597 | −0.0450 | 0.3397 | 0.6769** | 0.2956 | 0.2758 |
| 11 | −0.0781 | 0.0424 | −0.0792 | −0.0068 | 0.0807 | −0.4905* |
| 12 | −0.0420 | 0.3704 | 0.1135 | 0.1918 | 0.1901 | 0.5609** |
| 13 | 0.7104** | 0.0223 | −0.1457 | 0.1434 | −0.1060 | −0.1752 |
| 14 | 0.7634** | 0.1933 | 0.1751 | 0.0713 | 0.1980 | 0.1705 |
| 15 | 0.4491* | 0.2942 | −0.0403 | 0.3808 | 0.3695 | −0.0504 |
| 16 | 0.1031 | 0.1424 | 0.5070* | −0.0626 | 0.3280 | 0.5966** |
| 17 | 0.2873 | 0.6721** | 0.0980 | 0.1532 | 0.5496** | 0.1201 |
| 18 | 0.0662 | 0.0496 | −0.1202 | 0.8240** | −0.0390 | −0.1154 |
| 19 | 0.2319 | 0.6898** | −0.0260 | −0.1609 | 0.2721 | 0.2877 |
| 20 | 0.1579 | 0.1571 | 0.3026 | 0.7163** | −0.1715 | 0.3635 |
| 21 | 0.0208 | 0.6727** | 0.0715 | 0.0545 | −0.0956 | −0.0650 |
| 22 | 0.0704 | 0.5579** | 0.2832 | 0.2864 | −0.1431 | 0.3695 |
| 23 | 0.2940 | 0.2173 | −0.1153 | −0.1822 | 0.5971** | 0.0596 |
| 24 | 0.3200 | 0.1951 | −0.0794 | 0.4048* | 0.0902 | 0.0722 |
| 25 | −0.0757 | −0.0354 | 0.0316 | 0.0907 | 0.8151** | 0.0051 |
| 26 | 0.5693** | 0.0558 | 0.1160 | 0.2750 | 0.1823 | 0.3975 |
| 27 | −0.0343 | 0.0476 | 0.7948** | −0.2690 | −0.1494 | 0.1674 |
| 28 | 0.3396 | −0.1123 | 0.3728 | 0.1947 | 0.4520* | 0.1754 |
| 29 | 0.1419 | 0.7343** | 0.2869 | 0.0711 | 0.1277 | −0.1767 |

(continued)

**Table B.2** (continued)

| Organization number | Factor 1 | Factor 2 | Factor 3 | Factor 4 | Factor 5 | Factor 6 |
|---|---|---|---|---|---|---|
| 30 | −0.0304 | −0.2738 | 0.3953 | 0.1088 | −0.0065 | 0.2494 |
| 31 | −0.5206* | 0.2954 | 0.4104* | −0.1845 | 0.1093 | −0.0952 |
| Explained variance (61% total) | 11% | 12% | 11% | 10% | 9% | 8% |

*$p < 0.05$, **$p < 0.01$

systems and conditions (Kirst-Ashman and Hull 2008). While it is not unusual for an organization to do both kinds of advocacy, this study is interested in the latter because they more likely engage in policy advocacy. Therefore, as a final screen for the sample, Internet searches of the organizations were conducted to decipher whether they engage in policy advocacy, and if so, the levels of government they engage. From the resulting set, we purposively sampled organizations to capture wide variance among major issue areas (self-identified from their NTEE codes), levels of government, and reported expenditures.

We hypothesized at least five distinct advocacy strategies, based on an earlier analysis of advocacy organizations' logic models for policy advocacy (Gen and Wright 2013), so we targeted at least 20 organizations for our sample, to meet the recommended minimum for extracting five factors in Q-methodology (Watts and Stenner 2012, p. 197). Table B.1 summarizes key characteristics of the final 31 participating organizations. While 31 respondents would be inadequate in R-methodology's application of factor analysis, it is ample for Q-methodology. Five or six respondents significantly loading onto each factor usually produce "highly reliable factor scores" (Brown 1980, p. 67) that identify generalizable viewpoints.

For each organization, we identified the staff member who managed the organization's policy advocacy efforts. For smaller organizations, this was often the executive director. In larger organizations, it was often a policy director. A member of the research team met with each respondent and conducted a semi-structured interview followed by the Q-sort exercise. Each interview covered the organization's policy issues; its advocacy resources, activities, and outcomes; and a case of policy advocacy that represents the organization's approach. The researcher then facilitated the Q-sort, asking the respondent to review the 24 statements, then—in a sequence of structured steps—sort them onto the rating scale.

After the interviews, case studies were developed on the advocacy campaigns that the participants shared with us. Organizational documents and campaign

**Table B.3** Extracted factor arrays for 24 policy advocacy statements

| No. | Q-sample statements | Factor arrays | | | | | |
|---|---|---|---|---|---|---|---|
| | | 1 | 2 | 3 | 4 | 5 | 6 |
| 1 | Developing messages, framing issues, labeling, and other strategies of rhetoric can change policymakers' views | 1 | 3 | 0 | 0 | 2 | −1 |
| 2 | Lobbying and building relationships with policymakers can change their views | 3 | 2 | 0 | 0 | 2 | 1 |
| 3 | Monitoring and evaluating existing policy can change how it is implemented | −2 | −1 | 1 | −1 | 1 | 1 |
| 4 | Building coalitions and networks with like-minded organizations and individuals can change the public's views | −1 | 0 | 0 | 3 | 1 | −1 |
| 5 | Rebutting opposing views can change policymakers' views | −2 | 1 | 0 | −2 | −3 | −2 |
| 6 | Using the media to disseminate information can change policymakers' views | 1 | 3 | 2 | 1 | 0 | 2 |
| 7 | Monitoring and evaluating existing policy can set the policy agenda | −1 | −1 | 1 | −2 | −1 | 0 |
| 8 | Policies can change social and physical conditions | 3 | 1 | 3 | 2 | −2 | 3 |
| 9 | Using the media to disseminate information can change the public's views | −1 | 0 | 1 | 3 | 1 | 1 |
| 10 | Building coalitions and networks with like-minded organizations and individuals can change policymakers' views | 0 | 2 | −2 | 1 | 3 | 0 |
| 11 | Policy advocacy in general builds legitimacy in a democracy | 2 | −3 | −1 | 0 | −2 | −2 |
| 12 | Policy advocacy in general makes policymaking more people-centered | 0 | −2 | −3 | −1 | −1 | −3 |
| 13 | Pilot programs and demonstration projects can lead to policy change | −1 | −2 | −1 | −2 | 2 | 2 |
| 14 | Public mobilizations (e.g., protests, letter writing campaigns, rallies) can set the policy agenda | −2 | 0 | −3 | 1 | −1 | 0 |
| 15 | Research and analyses can change policymakers' views | 1 | 1 | −1 | −3 | 3 | 0 |
| 16 | Using the media to disseminate information can hasten policy change | 1 | 2 | 2 | 0 | 0 | 0 |

(continued)

**Table B.3** (continued)

| No. | Q-sample statements | Factor arrays | | | | | |
|---|---|---|---|---|---|---|---|
| 17 | Litigation can change policy | −3 | −3 | 3 | −1 | −2 | −1 |
| 18 | Rebutting opposing views can change the public's views | −3 | −1 | −2 | 0 | −3 | −2 |
| 19 | Changes in the public's views can change policymakers' views | 0 | 0 | 1 | 0 | 0 | 3 |
| 20 | Developing messages, framing issues, labeling, and other strategies of rhetoric can change the public's views | 0 | 1 | 2 | 2 | 0 | 1 |
| 21 | Public mobilizations (e.g., protests, letter writing campaigns, voter registration) can build democracy | 0 | −2 | −2 | 2 | 0 | −1 |
| 22 | Changes in policymakers' views can change policies | 2 | 0 | 0 | 1 | 1 | 2 |
| 23 | Research and analyses can change the public's views | 0 | 0 | −1 | −3 | 0 | 0 |
| 24 | Policy advocacy in general produces more effective policies | 2 | −1 | 0 | −1 | −1 | −3 |

materials were collected to bring more detail to the cases. Media audits were conducted to independently verify basic facts of the cases and to identify other perspectives on the events. It is important to note, however, that the focus of our research reported in this book is the viewpoints and strategies of policy advocates, not the events or merits of each campaign. Therefore, our case studies were limited to verifying and detailing their campaigns from their viewpoints.

The resulting Q-sort data were analyzed using PQMethod software, applying centroid factor analysis with varimax rotation, to identify distinct viewpoints on policy advocacy, and to identify the organizations that most significantly associate with each viewpoint. The resulting factors were each interpreted following the process prescribed by Watts and Stenner (2012, pp. 147–167) that converges both the statistical and interview data. The factors identified the organizations with common viewpoints, and those organizations' interview data pertaining to their advocacy activities and outcomes were incorporated to better understand the quantitative results.

The factor analysis was conducted four times, to extract four, five, six, and seven factors from the data. These extractions were compared by the cumulative variances they explained, the numbers of different organizations loading onto each factor, the numbers of confounding sorts (i.e., organizations that load onto more than one factor), and the numbers of nonsignificant sorts (i.e., organizations that do not load onto any factor). The six-factor extraction was the most efficient in that it loaded the most organizations onto the fewest factors. It explained 61% of the variance in the data while loading at least five organizations onto each factor, and accounting for all but one organization, at the 95% level of confidence. Table B.2 summarizes the organizations significantly loading onto each of the six factors. Note that a few of the significant loadings are negative, meaning that the organizations are negatively related to those factors. In practical terms, this means the organizations significantly disagree with the strategies represented by those factors. Positive loadings, on the other hand, mean the organizations are positively related to the factor and significantly agree with the strategies represented by those factors. These loadings can be interpreted like correlation coefficients, in that the closer the loading is to 1.0000, the stronger the relationship between the organization's strategy and the factor. A careful examination of Table B.2 reveals that few loadings are greater than 0.7, and only one reaches 0.8. Thus, no organization's strategy is perfectly represented by any of the factors. Instead, an organization's strategy might overlap with a factor or two. That is, the factors represent commonalities in the strategies among the organizations, but each organization might employ more than one strategy in their advocacy campaigns. For these reasons, the interview data were reviewed to find the parts of each organization's strategies that overlap with its factor, in order to describe and explain the factor.

Table B.3 summarizes the resulting Q-sort arrays for the six factors. Each array reports how the 24 Q-sample statements are sorted in the factor, on the same scale of −3 to +3. Interpretation of these arrays was guided by the "crib sheet" procedure prescribed by Watts and Stenner (2012). This process systematically focuses attention on not only the lowest and highest rated statements in each array, but also those statements with ratings that are lower or higher in one factor than in any other, no matter the absolute value of the rating. Doing so highlights the relative differences between the factors. The resulting factor descriptions constitute the six advocacy strategy viewpoints detailed in Chapters 3–8.

## Survey Method

The purpose of the survey component of our research was to measure the prevalence of advocacy activities and expected outcomes among nonprofits engaged in policy advocacy and to characterize those nonprofits who employ the different strategies described in this book. We developed an original survey instrument and used it to survey a representative sample of US nonprofits. Our process for this portion of the research was generally guided the practical advice prescribe by Berry et al. (2003).

## Instrument

Our original survey instrument sought to measure three major categories of variables. Most importantly, we measured the organizations' policy advocacy activities and expected outcomes to identify the advocacy strategies they appear to employ. The questions in this section of the survey were based upon the elements in the composite logic model (Table 2.2 in Chapter 2). Second, we measured the policy issues and targets (i.e., levels of government and branches of government) with which the organizations are engaged. The issue areas were defined by the twenty NTEE R—codes used by the IRS. Third, we measured common organizational characteristics, such as location, age, and income.

A draft survey was tested with 25 nonprofit professionals who provided feedback on wording, format, and other areas for improvement. It was also reviewed by Dr. Jennifer Shea, a public policy scholar with expertise in nonprofits. The resulting final instrument was programmed into Qualtrics for online implementation. The relevant passages of the survey instrument are reproduced at the end of this appendix.

## Sample

Our study population for this research is US nonprofits primarily engaged in policy advocacy. To capture this population, we developed a sampling frame from the Guidestar database. In July and August of 2013, we identified organizations in Guidestar that met three criteria. First, we included all US states, and all Metropolitan Statistical Areas, plus Washington, DC. US territories were excluded. Second, we included all 501c3 and 501c4 organizations. These nonprofits are most commonly associated with policy advocacy, so we excluded the other tax-exempt organizational categories. Lastly, we screened for organizations with National Taxonomy of Exempt Entities (NTEE) prefix code R—(advocacy) or suffix code—01 (advocacy in a specific prefix area). The rationale for this screening is the same for the sampling of organizations for the Q-method portion of the study. While many other nonprofits surely engage in policy advocacy, those who self-identify themselves by one of these codes see advocacy as their central purpose, and are more likely to have articulated views of their advocacy work. These three screens resulted in a 15,843 nonprofits, including duplicated organizations with the same names and addresses. We removed 256 duplicates, leaving 15,587 in the set.

The NTEE codes do not distinguish between case advocates and cause advocates, so, like the Q-method sampling, we needed to further screen these organizations for cause advocacy. Additionally, we needed to identify the person in each organization who manages their policy advocacy work. Such information is not captured in the Guidestar data. Doing so for over 15,000 organizations would be unnecessarily laborious, given that we aimed to sample about 2000 organizations, with the hope of yielding 800–1000 respondents. So we screened organizations in random batches of 500 at a time, until we yielded a sample of over 2000.

We developed a screening protocol that involved an Internet search of each organization, followed by a phone call in some cases. First, we searched for the organization's website using common search engines. If no website was found for an organization, that organization was not further pursued. At each organizational website, we checked the organization's physical address to confirm a match with the organization in our dataset. With each match, we verified whether the organization engages in cause advocacy, based upon the descriptions on their website. If so, we recorded the name and contact information of the person in charge of the organization's policy advocacy. In larger organizations, they often had titles such as "policy director," "policy manager," "advocacy coordinator," and "vice president for policy strategy." In smaller organizations, it was often the executive director. If the website did not clearly identify a person in charge of the organization's policy advocacy work, then we called that organization to get that information. We repeated this process in batches of 500 organizations, until we achieved our final sample of 2206 nonprofits in policy advocacy.

## Respondents

A link to the online survey was embedded in an email that was sent to the sample between April 14 and June 17, 2014. A drawing for five $100 gift certificates to Amazon.com was used as a small incentive to participate. Reminder emails for those who had not yet responded were sent after one, two, and four weeks from the original invitation. Representatives from 811 organizations responded, resulting in a response rate of at least 37%.[3]

We analyzed the characteristics of the respondents, to ensure that our resulting sample represented the broad ranges of nonprofits in the country. Figures B.1,

---

[3]We do not know how many of the email invitations did not reach the intended recipient due to personnel turnover, emails sent to junk folders, or other reasons. It is therefore possible that the response rate is slightly higher.

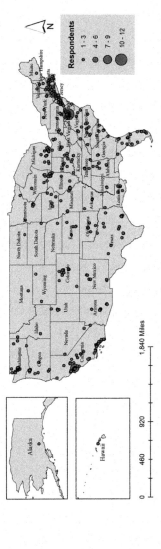

**Fig. B.1** Locations of organizations surveyed

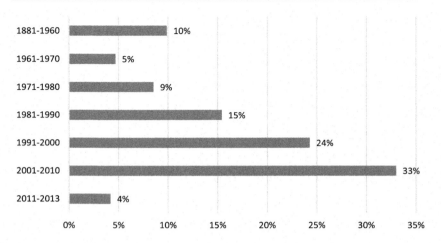

**Fig. B.2**  Founding years of organizations surveyed

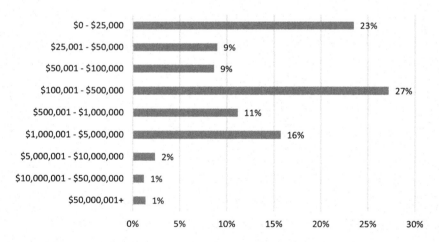

**Fig. B.3**  2013 Incomes of organizations surveyed

B.2, and B.3 display the geographic dispersion of our respondents, and their organizational age and income distribution. These distributions confirm the wide range of organizations who participated in our study.

# References

Berry, J. M., Arons, D. F., Bass, G. D., Carter, M. F., & Portney, K. E. (2003). *Surveying Nonprofits: A Methods Handbook*. Washington, DC: The Aspen Institute.

Brown, S. R. (1980). *Political Subjectivity: Applications of Q Methodology in Political Science*. New Haven, CT: Yale University Press.

Center for Community Health and Evaluation. (n.d.). *Measuring the Impact of Advocacy and Policy Efforts: Case Study Example*. Center for Community Health and Evaluation.

Chapman, J., & Wameyo, A. (2001). *Monitoring and Evaluating Advocacy: A Scoping Study*. ActionAid.

Coffman, J. (2007). *Using the Advocacy and Policy Change Composite Logic Model to Articulate an Advocacy Strategy or Theory of Change*. Harvard Family Research Project.

Gen, S., & Wright, A. C. (2013). Policy advocacy organizations: A framework linking theory and practice. *Journal of Policy Practice, 12*(3), 163–193.

Grantmakers in Health. (2005). *Funding Health Advocacy* (Issue Brief No. 21). Grantmakers in Health.

McKeown, B., & Thomas, D. (1988). *Q Methodology* (Sage University Paper Series on Quantitative Applications in the Social Sciences, Series Number 07-066). Beverly Hills: Sage.

Morariu, J., Reed, E., Brennan, K., Stamp, A., Parrish, S., Pankaj, V., & Zandniapour, L. (2009). *Pathfinder: A Practical Guide to Advocacy Evaluation*. Washington, DC: Innovation Network, Inc.

Reisman, J., Gienapp, A., & Stachowiak, S. (2007). *A Guide to Measuring Advocacy and Policy*. Baltimore, MD: The Annie E. Casey Foundation.

Watts, S., & Stenner, P. (2012). *Doing Q Methodological Research: Theory, Method & Interpretation*. Thousand Oaks, CA: Sage.

---

# Relevant Passages of the Survey Instrument

## Advocacy Activities

In this survey, "advocacy" refers to your organization's intentional activities to influence public programs, services, decisions, rules, laws, or policymaking processes.

1. Below are example advocacy **activities** that nonprofits engage. How often is each of the following activities a part of your organization's advocacy efforts? Please mark your response on a scale from 0 to 4, where 0 is never, and 4 is always.

| | Never 0 | Rarely 1 | Some-times 2 | Often 3 | Always 4 |
|---|---|---|---|---|---|
| Coalition building (e.g., networking with other organizations, forming coalitions) | 0 | 1 | 2 | 3 | 4 |
| Engaging and mobilizing the public (e.g., community organizing, voter registration, letter writing campaigns, protests) | 0 | 1 | 2 | 3 | 4 |
| Engaging policy decision makers (e.g., building relationships with officials, lobbying legislators) | 0 | 1 | 2 | 3 | 4 |
| Producing research (e.g., policy analyses, white papers) | 0 | 1 | 2 | 3 | 4 |
| Framing issues and messages | 0 | 1 | 2 | 3 | 4 |
| Educating stakeholders (e.g., presentations, brochures, field trips) | 0 | 1 | 2 | 3 | 4 |
| Media work (e.g., press releases, earned media) | 0 | 1 | 2 | 3 | 4 |
| Pilot studies, demonstration projects | 0 | 1 | 2 | 3 | 4 |
| Litigation, legal services | 0 | 1 | 2 | 3 | 4 |
| Defensive activities (e.g., responding to opponents, reading and reacting to the political climate) | 0 | 1 | 2 | 3 | 4 |
| Monitoring policy implementation (e.g., program evaluations, monitoring implementation agencies) | 0 | 1 | 2 | 3 | 4 |
| Other (describe) | 0 | 1 | 2 | 3 | 4 |
| Other (describe) | 0 | 1 | 2 | 3 | 4 |

Expected outcomes of advocacy

2. How important are each of the following **outcomes** to your advocacy campaigns? Please mark your response on a scale from 0 to 4, where 0 is not at all important, and 4 is extremely important.

| | Not at all important 0 | Slightly important 1 | Moderately important 2 | Very important 3 | Extremely important 4 |
|---|---|---|---|---|---|
| Improved government transparency/account-ability | 0 | 1 | 2 | 3 | 4 |
| Enhanced power/ capacity of public stakeholders | 0 | 1 | 2 | 3 | 4 |
| Changes in public's views, or strengthened base of support | 0 | 1 | 2 | 3 | 4 |
| Changes in decision makers' views, or strengthened political will to act | 0 | 1 | 2 | 3 | 4 |
| Getting your issue on the political agenda | 0 | 1 | 2 | 3 | 4 |
| Adoption of favored policy, or blocking of opposed policy | 0 | 1 | 2 | 3 | 4 |
| Improved policy implementation or enforcement | 0 | 1 | 2 | 3 | 4 |
| Improved conditions of constituents/people | 0 | 1 | 2 | 3 | 4 |
| Improved services or systems | 0 | 1 | 2 | 3 | 4 |
| People-centered policymaking | 0 | 1 | 2 | 3 | 4 |
| Other (describe) | 0 | 1 | 2 | 3 | 4 |
| Other (describe) | 0 | 1 | 2 | 3 | 4 |

## Advocacy scope and scale

7. How important are your organization's advocacy activities to achieve your organization's mission? Please check the most appropriate box.

| not at all important | slightly important | moderately important | very important | extremely important |
|---|---|---|---|---|
| ☐ | ☐ | ☐ | ☐ | ☐ |

8. Overall, what percentages of your organization's staff time and resources would you say is devoted to advocacy?

    a. Percent of **staff time** devoted to advocacy:    \_\_\_\_\_%

    b. Percent of **financial resources** devoted to advocacy:    \_\_\_\_\_%

9. In which of the following **public issues** does your organization engage? Check all that apply.

☐ education

☐ youth development

☐ recreation, sports, leisure

☐ community development

☐ public safety, emergency preparedness

☐ crime, criminal justice

☐ social welfare, poverty

☐ housing, shelter

☐ transportation

☐ economy, jobs, business

☐ taxes, monetary policy

☐ health, mental health

☐ agriculture, food, nutrition

☐ environment, natural resources, energy

☐ science, technology, research

☐ arts, culture, religion

☐ civil rights

☐ immigration, immigrants

☐ foreign relations, trade

☐ defense, national security

☐ other (describe):

☐ other (describe):

☐ other (describe):

☐ other (describe):

10. Which **levels of government** does your organization's advocacy primarily target? Check all that apply.

☐ international governments and international policy making bodies
   ☐ national government
   ☐ state government
   ☐ local government (e.g., county, city, district)
   ☐ none

11. Which **branches of government** does your organization's advocacy primarily target? Check all that apply.

☐ executive (e.g., president, governors, mayors)
   ☐ legislative (e.g., councils, boards, state legislatures, Congress)
   ☐ judicial (e.g., courts)
   ☐ bureaucratic (e.g., government agencies and programs)
   ☐ none

## Organizational characteristics

12. In which year was your organization founded? _____    ☐ Don't know

13. What is the zip code of your office (where you work)? _____

14 . What was your organization's approximate income in 2013?
   ☐ $0 - $25,000
   ☐ $25,001 - $50,000
   ☐ $50,001 - $100,000
   ☐ $100,001 - $500,000
   ☐ $500,001 - $1,000,000
   ☐ $1,000,001 - $5,000,000
   ☐ $5,000,001 - $10,000,000
   ☐ $10,000,001 - $50,000,000
   ☐ $50,000,001 +

15. How many full-time equivalent (FTE) staff members does your organization have? (For example, 2 half-time employees equals 1 full-time equivalent employee.)

_____ FTE paid employees

_____ FTE volunteers

16. Does your organization have members? Check all that apply.
   □ No membership
   □ Individual members.
   Approximately how many individual members? _____
   □ Organizational members (public, nonprofit, private, etc.)
   Approximately how many organizational members? _____

# Index

**A**
Adversarial legalism, 27, 33, 126
Advocacy Coalition Framework, 27, 28, 35, 175
Advocacy evaluation, 197, 204, 213
Advocacy examples by issue
    arts and culture, 16, 45–46, 53, 107, 219
    children and youth, vii–x, 73, 57–64, 98
    child welfare (including foster care), vii–x, 49, 89–94
    civil rights, 17, 53, 106, 121–123, 161, 177, 193
    consumer rights, 8, 64–68
    criminal justice system reform, 53, 57–64, 83, 84–89, 106, 161
    defense/national security, 181–185
    economy/jobs, 106, 107
    education, 1, 16, 53, 73–75, 97–99, 105, 111–113, 151, 153, 160, 177, 185–189, 193, 219
    environment, 16, 23, 28, 33, 108–111, 133, 140–147, 151–155, 164–168, 194, 219
    health, 53, 74, 97, 105, 114–117, 133–140, 177
    housing, 17, 53, 106
    human rights, 1, 151, 181–185
    immigration, 53, 106, 177, 193
    LGBTQI rights, xi–xiii, 1–5, 92
    mental health, 17, 53, 74, 106, 177
    public safety, 17, 53, 80, 106
    religion, 17, 53, 107
    social welfare/poverty, 106
    taxes/monetary policy, 107, 114–117
    transportation, 28, 53, 80, 106
Advocacy organizations
    American Cancer Society, 115
    American Civil Liberties Union (ACLU), xii, 1
    American Friends Service Committee (AFSC), 85, 86
    American Heart Association, 133
    American Lung Association (ALA), 108, 114
    Asian Pacific American Legal Center, xii
    Ban Trans Fats, 132
    Californians for the Cure, 115
    California Youth Connection (CYC), 93
    Children's Defense Fund, vii
    Children Now, 97, 98, 100
    Codepink, 178, 181–183
    Coleman Advocates for Children and Youth, vii, ix
    Ella Baker Center for Human Rights, 57
    Environmental Integrity Project (EIP), 133, 156
    Gay and Lesbian Alliance Against Defamation, xii
    Lamda Legal, xii
    Lawyers' Committee for Civil Rights (LCCR), 121

National Association for the Advancement of Colored People (NAACP), 33
National Center for Lesbian Rights (NCLR), xii, 3, 5, 6, 17
National Rifle Association, 29
Neighborhood Parks Council (NPC), 164, 168
Our Children's Earth Foundation (OCE), 152, 153, 156
Parents for Public Schools (PPS), 179, 189
Partnership for Children & Youth (PCY), 73–75
Planned Parenthood, 29
San Francisco Parks Alliance, 168
Save the Bay, 110
Sierra Club, 16, 133, 145–147
StudentsFirst, 108, 111, 113
Theatre Bay Area, 45
The Utility Reform Network (TURN), 65
Amicus curiae brief, 83

**B**
Bellwether methodology, 204–206
Branches of government
    bureaucratic, 7, 81, 107, 123, 192
    executive, 54, 81, 107, 123, 163, 193
    judiciary, 192
    legislative, 54, 81, 107, 123, 129, 162, 177, 193
Briefings and presentations, 100

**C**
Case advocates, 218, 224, 226, 228
Cause advocates, 218, 226
Civic or citizen engagement (public engagement), 6–8, 28, 50, 64, 78, 87, 126, 171, 174, 183, 199, 215, 219
Class action lawsuit, 8, 14, 87, 124, 126, 134

Coalition building, 25–28, 39, 77, 78, 83, 103, 104, 115, 171, 175, 191, 194, 230
Contribution analysis, 204, 206
Conveying public opinion, 156

**D**
Defensive activities, 25, 27, 34, 35, 175, 230
Demonstration programs (pilot programs), 25, 39, 48, 75, 76, 102, 125, 156, 157, 173, 222
Developmental evaluation, 203, 204
Devolution, 9, 10
Domino theory, 137

**E**
Educating stakeholders, 104, 230
Elite theory, 27, 30

**F**
Federalism, 9, 10
    cooperative, 10
    dual, 9
Framing, 10, 13, 25, 27, 31, 39, 47, 48, 50, 66, 67, 75, 76, 78, 100, 101, 104, 125, 127, 157, 171, 172, 175, 176, 192, 201, 204, 205, 222, 223, 230

**G**
Guidestar, 16, 17, 218, 219, 225, 226

**I**
Impacts, 27, 73, 151, 152, 197, 198, 203, 213, 214
Incrementalism, 27, 31, 34, 126
Information campaigning, 25, 27, 28, 30, 31, 36
Inputs, 24, 27, 197, 198, 213, 214
Institutionalism, 27, 29, 30, 49

Intense period debriefs, 204
Interest group (pressure group), 6, 9, 12–15, 24, 28, 29, 102, 103, 111, 142, 214
Interest group studies, 27

**L**
Labeling issues, 125
Litigation, 1, 5, 25, 27, 32–34, 39, 48, 75, 77, 102, 121–127, 132, 133, 140, 152, 153, 156, 157, 164, 172, 175, 177, 192, 194, 223, 230
Lobbying, 14, 16, 25, 29, 36, 46–51, 53–57, 62–64, 66, 74–78, 83, 85, 98, 100–103, 113, 125, 126, 146, 155, 157, 158, 171–173, 191, 192, 207, 222, 230
Logic model, 24, 26, 35, 36, 197, 198, 213–215, 217, 218, 221, 225

**M**
Media work, 27, 39, 50, 66, 75, 100, 102, 104, 116, 127, 140, 146, 152, 156, 166, 175, 176, 192, 230
Membership organizations, 16, 55, 107, 130, 191
Messaging, 16, 39, 48, 66, 67, 75, 116, 124, 173, 175, 192
Monitoring policy implementation, 156, 175, 192, 230
Multiple streams theory (Kingdon), 36, 103

**N**
National Taxonomy of Exempt Entities (NTEE), 16, 17, 38, 105, 129, 218, 221, 225, 226
Nonprofit, 1, 5–10, 13–17, 23, 24, 37, 38, 45, 46, 48, 56, 57, 65, 73–75, 90, 97, 108, 110, 111, 113, 114, 130, 131, 141, 152, 158, 159, 163, 165, 166, 175–178, 181, 182, 187,

191, 193–196, 199, 203, 205, 207, 217–219, 224–226, 230
definition, 6
scale (in the United States), 15

**O**
Outcomes, 5, 23, 24, 26, 27, 31, 32, 34, 36, 37, 48, 50, 51, 59, 61, 63, 67, 68, 77, 78, 111, 126, 147, 159, 176, 192, 194–201, 203–207, 213–215, 217, 218, 221, 223–225
Outputs, 30, 49, 123, 197–199

**P**
*Pluralism*, 9
Policy advocacy, definition, 6
Policy analysis, 25, 30, 98, 142
Policy cycle
   policy evaluation and change, 13
   policy formulation, 13
   policy implementation, 13, 14
   policy legitimation, 13, 14
   problem recognition and definition, 13
Policy development, 10, 114
Policy maker ratings, 204
Policy monitoring, 25, 27, 127, 133, 194
Policy subsystem, 28, 35
Process tracing, 204, 206
Public debate, 13, 35, 68, 75, 115
Public mobilizations, 39, 47, 48, 76, 77, 101, 102, 126, 156, 157, 172, 173, 175, 222, 223
Public opinion, 7, 12, 102, 167, 192, 193, 217
   polls, 12
Public participation, 26, 27, 36, 77, 78, 174

**Q**
Q-methodology, 23, 37, 38, 117, 217, 219, 221

**R**
Rationality, 31
Referendum, 12, 114
Research dissemination, 100, 124
Rhetoric, 27, 31, 32, 47, 76, 101, 125, 157,
      172, 222, 223

**S**
Separation of powers, 9, 10
      executive branch, 10
      judicial branch, 10
      legislative branch, 10
Systems mapping, 205

**T**
Theory of change, 24, 193, 197, 200, 206,
      214

**W**
Walker's insider and outsider approaches,
      102, 156

Printed by Printforce, United Kingdom